TOWER OF TRUTH
A Study of the Book of Revelation

Glenn H. Bourne

Kissimmee, Florida

:

Wipf and Stock Publishers
150 West Broadway • Eugene OR 97401
2001

Tower of Truth
A Study of the Book of Revelation
By Bourne, Glenn H.
Copyright©1988 by Bourne, Glenn H.

ISBN: 1-57910-572-6

Reprinted by *Wipf and Stock Publishers*
150 West Broadway • Eugene OR 97401

Previously published by Bourne, Glenn H., 1988.

A WORD ABOUT THE AUTHOR

It was after having taught the Book of Revelation fifty times that Glenn Bourne completed this commentary. He taught this Book as a part of the curriculum of St. Louis Christian College and Central Florida Bible College. On numerous other occasions he taught it in the local congregations as a part of the outreach program of these two colleges. This commentary was written in response to the many requests of students who studied this Book under his teaching.

Glenn H. Bourne, son of Mr. and Mrs. H. A. Bourne, was born in Alma, Nebraska where his father served as a preacher. He received his Bachelor of Arts degree from Johnson Bible College and his Master of Divinity degree from the School of Religion, Butler University.

He served student ministries in Virginia, Indiana and Ohio. Upon completion of college work he served the Traders Point Christian Church in Indianapolis, Indiana before moving to Bridgeport, Illinois where he served eight years.

On December 1, 1963 he became the vice-president and professor of St. Louis Christian College. On the same date he led in the planting of a new congregation, the Halls Ferry Christian Church. On June 1, 1966 he became president of St. Louis Christian College and served in this position for twelve years.

On June 1, 1978 he and his family moved to Orlando, Florida where he presently serves as professor of Christian ministries with the Florida Christian College.

He preaches nearly every Sunday, holds many evangelistic meetings and has participated in more than 300 faith promise missionary rallies. He served as chairman of the National Missionary Convention in 1970. He has served as a member of the continuation committee for the Christian Educator's Conference and the North American Christian Convention. He has served on two mission boards. He is a member of Theta Phi.

Mr. and Mrs. Glenn (Carolyn) Bourne have four children.

Their two oldest children, David and Miriam, are graduates of St. Louis Christian College. Their two youngest children, Sarah and Mark, are graduates of Central Florida Bible College. All four children are married and actively involved with their spouses in Christian ministries. Glenn has one brother, Richard, who also is a Christian minister. 1982

CONTENTS

TOWER OF TRUTH

VICTORY IN CHRIST
Chapters 21, 22
"but thanks be to God, who giveth us the victory through our Lord Jesus Christ" 1 Corinthians 15:57.

THE DEFEAT OF SATAN
Chapters 19, 20
"I beheld Satan, Fallen as lightning from heaven" Luke 10:18

THE CONSEQUENCES OF SIN
Chapters 17, 18
"The wages of sin is death" Romans 6:23a.

JUDGMENT - Chapters 15, 16
"He that believeth on him is not judged: he that believeth not hath been judged already, because he hath not believed on the name of the only begotten Son of God" John 3:18.

BLESSED ASSURANCE - Chapter 14
"He that heareth my word, and believeth him that sent me, hath eternal life, and cometh not into judgment, but hath passed out of death into life" John 5:24

THE ENEMY - Chapter 13
"For our wrestling is not against flesh and blood, but against principalities, against the powers, against the world-rulers of this darkness, against the spiritual hosts of wickedness in the heavenly places" Ephesians 6:12.

OVERCOMERS IN CONFLICT - Chapter 12
"Be strong in the Lord, and in the strength of his might" Ephesians 6:10.

TRUTH TRIUMPHS - Chapters 10, 11
"Ye shall know the truth, and the truth shall make you free" John 8:32

TRUMPETS WARN - Chapters 8, 9
"Whosoever heareth the sound of the trumpet, and taketh not warning,....his blood shall be upon his own head" Ezekiel 33:4.

A WORD OF ENCOURAGEMENT - Chapter 7
"In this world ye have tribulation: but be of good cheer: I have overcome the world" John 16:33b.

JOURNEY TO JUDGMENT Chapter 6
"It is appointed unto men once to die, and after this cometh judgment" Hebrews 9:27.

GOD IS IN CONTROL Chapters 4, 5
"I have spoken, I will also bring it to pass; I have purposed, I will also do it;" Isaiah 46:11b.

CHURCHES OF CHRIST - Chapters 2, 3
"Upon this rock I will build my church" Matthew 16:18b.

A FIRM FOUNDATION Chapter 1
"For other foundation can no man lay than that which is laid, which is Jesus Christ" I Corinthians 3:11.

INTRODUCTION

This study views the Book of Revelation as God's TOWER OF TRUTH. Truth is the vehicle God uses to lift man from the depths of sin to the heights of eternal life. God's tower enables man to see the events of history from heaven's perspective. The tower concept is illustrated on page vi. Each tier of the tower is used to describe the progression of the message in this Book. The idea of a tower is intended to challenge the student to consider a fresh approach to the study of the Book of Revelation. An alternative to chronology is suggested by dividing the Book into a series of building blocks which rest upon each other in the construction of God's TOWER OF TRUTH. As such, this stands in sharp contrast to the tower of Babel, man's vain effort to reach heaven.

Frequently the Book of Revelation is presented as a divine drama, and for good reason. The various scenes combine in two acts and portray vividly the sovereignty of God. To imagine being in an auditorium and witnessing a dramatic presentation has proved helpful in understanding the contents of this Book. A different approach has been taken in this study for the purpose of providing a distinct challenge to the student.

The scripture text has been included with the commentary and many of the scripture references have been recorded to save time in looking them up. The 1901 American Revised Bible (Standard Edition) has been used throughout.

It is obvious that John had an excellent knowledge of the Old Testament and cited it frequently in his Book. The student of the Book of Revelation will appreciate the Old and New Testaments as the best commentary ever written for the Book of Revelation. This Book does not contain new truths so much as it illustrates and reinforces existing truths. It is God's picture book. Conclusions reached in the study of the Book of Revelation that cannot be established elsewhere in the Bible should be evaluated carefully.

This book provides a verse-by-verse commentary. There is a

danger in this method of study: attention to detail may cause the student to fail in seeing the larger picture. Commentary on each verse is needed and helpful in understanding the message, but it must not become a substitute for seeing the total picture. All pictures have detail. Sometimes the detail fills in the scenery and sometimes it is important to the understanding of the picture. The verse by verse method of study is a beneficial way to study this Book but should not be regarded the only way or the best way. Many books have been written on the Book of Revelation employing a variety of methods, each making a significant contribution.

The author of the Book of Revelation is identified as John. John was a common name in Bible days. Scholars are not agreed on which John is the author. The traditional view, and probably most popular, is John the apostle.

Several dates have been suggested for the time of writing. The time of Nero, about 68 A.D., and the time of Domitian, 95 or 96 A.D., are the two most likely choices. Persecution was more widespread during the time of Domitian. Other factors favor the late date for the time of writing. It is not the purpose of this work to discuss introductory material in detail.

It is helpful for the student to know the characteristics of apocalyptic literature before reading the Book of Revelation. This Book is apocalyptic. The apocalyptic style was used as an appropriate way to offer encouragement during difficult and trying times. Truth is presented in figurative language employing symbols, visions and drama. A strong emphasis is given to the future to strengthen faith and hope for the present. Apocalyptic literature should always be studied in light of the background of the times that produced it. Throughout the study of the Book of Revelation it is important for the student to know the history of John's period in an effort to answer this very important question: what message was conveyed through this Book to the Christians of the first and second centuries?

The correct interpretation of the symbols used presents a serious challenge to the twentieth century student. This is not to suggest that the symbols cannot be understood, but it is wise to exercise delicate caution in reaching a conclusion.

Sometimes impossible pictures are drawn to stimulate the imagination to look beyond the picture, beyond the symbol, and see the truth. Much misunderstanding of this Book results from confusing the sign with that which is signified.

There is good reason why two people may be honest in their study of this Book and reach two different conclusions. Some study this Book with the idea that it is a history book. They look to the history of John's day for their understanding. Others believe this Book is an outline of history beginning at the time of Christ's first coming and continuing until His return. Still others think this Book is primarily prophetic and are looking to the future for the fulfillment of its message. Those who regard this as a book of philosophy or principles will reach different conclusions in their study. Which is the proper method? The answer depends upon the person answering the question. It is safe to approach the study of the Book of Revelation by asking, *what did this mean to those who first read it, who lived in the day it was written?* It is wise to seek understanding in light of the historical background. In fact, all scripture should be studied in light of its setting for full appreciation and understanding. Once the truth is understood it must be applied. The Book of Revelation is just as relevant in the twentieth century as it was in the first and second centuries.

The story of this Book is about a war between God and Satan in which all people are involved. God equips His soldiers with truth and Satan supplies his warriors with lies. It is a spiritual war. So much of the time the story makes it appear that the war is almost over and Satan will be victorious. The primary purpose of the story, however, is to make clear that appearances can and do deceive. Deception is Satan's instrument. Though the church may seem to be defeated, God leads His army of Christians to victory in Christ! No book offers a clearer warning or a greater hope than the Book of Revelation. It is a book of blessed assurance. It should be studied prayerfully and carefully.

The Book of Revelation is God's TOWER OF TRUTH for men to reach heaven and see the unfolding of His eternal purpose throughout history from the divine vantage point.

A FIRM FOUNDATION

CHAPTER ONE

1:1　THE REVELATION OF JESUS CHRIST, WHICH GOD
GAVE HIM TO SHOW UNTO HIS SERVANTS, EVEN
THE THINGS WHICH MUST SHORTLY COME TO
PASS: AND HE SENT AND SIGNIFIED IT BY HIS
ANGEL UNTO HIS SERVANT JOHN;

The word REVELATION comes from the Latin word
revelare meaning "to draw back the veil." REVELATION is a
translation of the Greek word *apokalupto* meaning "to uncover."
The transliteration of this Greek word gives us the English word
"apocalypse." The word *apokalupto* is used elsewhere in scripture. See 2 Thessalonians 1:7; 1 Peter 1:7; Ephesians 1:17; Galatians 1:12; 2:1; Romans 16:25. The word REVELATION conveys
the thought of God making known to man what man could not
know any other way. God's revelation is referred to in scripture
with the word "mystery."

THE REVELATION OF JESUS CHRIST may be under-
stood in two ways. It may mean that Jesus Christ is being revealed or it may mean that Jesus Christ is the source. The grammar
of the Greek text permits both meanings. Thus, it is necessary to
study the entire book to reach a conclusion regarding the preferred meaning. It is not necessary to take just one position.
Jesus Christ is revealed in this book and He is the Revealer. This
must be understood, however, in light of the following phrase in
verse one.

WHICH GOD GAVE HIM indicates God as the ultimate
source of the REVELATION. It is a significant truth that all
truth originates with God. Apart from God there is no knowledge
and understanding. The role of Jesus in revelation is explained in
several scriptures. Consider John 7:16 and 12:49 for clear state-
ments regarding the relationship between the Father and the

1

Son in the unveiling of truth. Jesus is truth personified.

The tense of the verb GAVE is aorist. This means that this giving can be pinpointed in history as a single act of God. At a specific time in history God made known to man that which He willed for man to know according to His eternal purpose and plan. See Ephesians 3:8-12 for the fact that God does have an eternal purpose.

TO SHOW makes plain the design of God in giving the revelation. This book enables us to see truth as well as read and hear it. Word pictures are a valuable aid in understanding. It is important to keep the symbolic and dramatic characteristics of this book in mind while reading and studying it. A good imagination is a helpful tool for the study of this book. Visualize a dramatic presentation as you read the contents.

UNTO HIS SERVANTS refers to Christians. The biblical use of SERVANT is better understood with the word slave. A slave is entirely the property of another. The Christian is rightly understood as one who is completely subjected to God. It is an interesting paradox that every man is both slave and free. To be a slave of God is to be free from sin and sin's domination. To be a slave of sin, however, is to be separated from God and His power. When you consider the fact that a slave has no rights, don't forget that a slave also has no need for worry concerning food, shelter, care, etc. It is an honor to be a slave of God. It is not correct to make SERVANTS refer only to church officials. All Christians are included in this term. Christians are the only ones who have need of this revelation and are in a position to understand and appreciate it.

EVEN THE THINGS WHICH MUST SHORTLY COME TO PASS: A moral necessity is implied in the word MUST. SHORTLY must be understood in light of 2 Peter 3:8 "But forget not this one thing, beloved, that one day is with the Lord as a thousand years, and a thousand years as one day." Revelation was written to meet an immediate need. It should be understood in light of the historical setting of that time. That which came to pass soon after the writing of Revelation should be examined carefully. Revelation was meaningful to those who first received it. The certain fulfillment of the plan of God is stated in the phrase MUST

2

SHORTLY COME TO PASS.

AND HE SENT AND SIGNIFIED IT BY HIS ANGEL. SIGNIFIED means that the message was made known with signs. Signs and symbols are the nature of this book. This also explains the difficulty in understanding the contents. We must be careful in determining the correct meaning of the signs and symbols. In some instances we may have to settle for the fact that we do not know for certain what the meaning is. The messenger was an ANGEL. This may refer to an earthly harbinger or to a supernatural being. Angels play an important part in the plan of God throughout Revelation.

UNTO HIS SERVANT JOHN. JOHN was absolutely surrendered to the will of God. The apostle John was living at the right time and in the right place to be the person indicated both here and in verses four and nine.

1:2　WHO BARE WITNESS OF THE WORD OF GOD, AND OF THE TESTIMONY OF JESUS CHRIST, EVEN OF ALL THINGS THAT HE SAW.

WHO refers to John. WITNESS is a translation of the Greek *maturia* which transliterated into English gives us the word "martyr." John was a faithful witness of everything he saw—THE WORD OF GOD AND THE TESTIMONY OF JESUS CHRIST. Though the primary reference is to the contents of this book we must not totally divorce this from his total ministry as an apostle. Observe that the word EVEN is in italics. This means that the word is supplied for easier reading but it is not in the Greek text. This is true with all italicized words in the Bible.

1:3　BLESSED IS HE THAT READETH, AND THEY THAT HEAR THE WORDS OF THE PROPHECY, AND KEEP THE THINGS WHICH ARE WRITTEN THEREIN: FOR THE TIME IS AT HAND.

This is the first of seven beatitudes in the book of Revelation. The other six are recorded in 14:13; 16:15; 19:9; 20:6; 22:7 and 22:14. Many groups of seven appear in this book. This is evidently by design.

BLESSED speaks of a condition based upon relationship, not upon events or circumstances. The Christian's joy is the result of being a child of God and is not due to what may or may not hap-

3

pen. This explains an admirable character difference in the life of a Christian when compared to the non-Christian during an experience of adversity and trial. In each beatitude in scripture God explains how this inner joy can be a part of your life. In this instance it results from reading, hearing and obeying THE THINGS WHICH ARE WRITTEN THEREIN.

HE THAT READETH may refer to the public reader of scripture, though it has equal application to each individual who reads. It has been customary through church history for the scriptures to be read publicly in the worship service. This follows the Jewish custom of reading the scriptures aloud in the synagogues. Read Luke 4:16 and Acts 13:15. From a reference in the writings of Tertullian we assume that there was a person designated as a reader in the early church. With regard to the public reading of scripture let it be said that those who read aloud in the service ought to prepare carefully and read well to make this a meaningful experience for the hearers.

THEY THAT HEAR THE WORDS OF THE PROPHECY should be understood as meaning those who continue in their listening. Hearing God's Word must be without ceasing. Paul admonished the saints in Thessalonica to "pray without ceasing." Prayer is conversation with God. Many Christians would find prayer a more rewarding experience if they would let God do more of the talking. Hearing God's Word as well as reading God's Word is letting God talk with you in prayer. "Take heed...how ye hear" Luke 8:18. PROPHECY is that which is spoken forth. That the primary function of a prophet was not to foretell the future is illustrated in every prophetic book of the Old Testament. The admonitions and warnings were underscored as being both serious and essential by an accurate announcement of future events. The prophet was basically a spokesman. THE WORDS OF THE PROPHECY refer to the contents of this book — words spoken as inspired of God.

AND KEEP THE THINGS WHICH ARE WRITTEN THEREIN: means a constant obedience of the will of God. A proper recognition of the authority of God necessitates ceaseless obedience. He is your lord whom you obey. Where there is no obedience there is no lord. Jesus said, "Why do you call me Lord,

4

Lord, and do not the things I tell you?" Obedience of God's word is participation in God's blessings. Apart from submission and involvement one cannot please God. "Be ye doers of the word, and not hearers only, deluding your own selves" James 1:22. The Psalmist informs us of the great reward associated with obedience (19:11). ARE WRITTEN speaks of the fact that the revelation is complete. No further revelation is needed. The adequacy of divine revelation is established in 2 Timothy 3:16-17. See 2 Peter 3:15,16.

FOR THE TIME IS AT HAND. This phrase gives emphasis to the first part of the verse. TIME refers to a specific period. AT HAND means near. The message of Revelation will begin to have an immediate fulfillment. Revelation assures the Christian both of ultimate victory and present comfort.

1:4   JOHN TO THE SEVEN CHURCHES THAT ARE IN ASIA: GRACE TO YOU AND PEACE, FROM HIM WHO IS AND WHO WAS AND WHO IS TO COME; AND FROM THE SEVEN SPIRITS THAT ARE BEFORE HIS THRONE;

There were more than SEVEN CHURCHES at that time IN ASIA. The churches in Troas, Miletus, Colossae and Hierapolis are not mentioned. The fact that SEVEN CHURCHES are listed is by design and is another evidence of divine authorship. Throughout the book of Revelation the number SEVEN symbolizes sacredness and completeness. The churches not named were close enough to the SEVEN CHURCHES to assure the availability of this message for their reading. ASIA is not to be understood as the large continent as we know it today but rather the Roman province of Asia where Turkey is presently located. The letters to the SEVEN CHURCHES in chapters two and three supply important historical data for a proper appreciation and understanding of the message of Revelation. The number SEVEN indicates that this message is for the entire church throughout the Christian era. There is no hint that these churches are representative of seven periods in church history. Characteristics of these churches prevail throughout history and are not confined within certain periods.

GRACE is an expressive salutation. It speaks of God's goodness and beauty. It is unmerited favor. It is God doing for man what man does not and will never deserve. It is love that stoops. It is that quality of God that makes Him winsome and attractive and explains why men are drawn unto Him.

PEACE is the fruit of GRACE. PEACE speaks of the harmony between man and God that results from the awareness of the forgiveness of sin. "There is no peace, saith my God, to the wicked" Isaiah 57:21.

FROM HIM WHO IS AND WHO WAS AND WHO IS TO COME. This is an expression of the eternality of God. Within and beyond the limit of time God is.

FROM THE SEVEN SPIRITS THAT ARE BEFORE THIS THRONE. The SEVEN SPIRITS is an apocalyptic expression of the Holy Spirit. This conclusion is reached upon the basis of the symbolic meaning of the number seven. The fact that the SEVEN SPIRITS are mentioned between references to the Father and to the Son lends credence to this conclusion.

1:5   AND FROM JESUS CHRIST, WHO IS THE FAITHFUL
       WITNESS, THE FIRSTBORN OF THE DEAD, AND THE
       RULER OF THE KINGS OF THE EARTH. UNTO HIM
       THAT LOVETH US, AND LOOSED US FROM OUR SINS
       BY HIS BLOOD;

Jesus Christ is THE FAITHFUL WITNESS upon whom we can rely. Jesus said to Pilate, "To this end have I been born, and to this end am I come into the world, that I should bear witness unto the truth. Every one that is of the truth heareth my voice" John 18:37. Jesus gives us first-hand knowledge of God. Jesus said, "My teaching is not mine, but his that sent me" John 7:16.

Jesus is THE FIRSTBORN OF THE DEAD. Jesus "was declared to be the Son of God with power, according to the spirit of holiness, by the resurrection from the dead" Romans 1:4. "But now hath Christ been raised from the dead, the firstfruits of them that are asleep" 1 Corinthians 15:20. Jesus arose to die no more. He is the first to have done so. Others who were raised, such as Lazarus, again experienced physical death. This title of Jesus speaks of His authority and victorious power. The resurrection of Jesus is the basis of our hope in Christ.

Jesus is THE RULER OF THE KINGS OF THE EARTH. "I

6

will make him my first-born, The highest of the kings of the earth" Psalm 89:27. Jesus said, "In the world ye have tribulation: but be of good cheer; I have overcome the world" John 16:33. "All authority hath been given unto me in heaven and on earth" Matthew 28:18.

Jesus never ceases loving us. The verb tense of LOVETH implies continued action. In contrast with this and the verb tense of LOOSED speaks of past, completed action. Jesus set us free from our sins in the shedding of His blood on the cross. The one time act of our Lord has continuing blessings. "Apart from shedding of blood there is no remission" Hebrews 9:22.

1:6   AND HE MADE US TO BE A KINGDOM, TO BE PRIESTS UNTO HIS GOD AND FATHER: TO HIM BE THE GLORY AND THE DOMINION FOR EVER AND EVER. AMEN. *Being your best in public*

underscores how great it is →

→ Acknowledge His dominion He is in control

This verse states the results of our redemption in Christ. HE MADE US TO BE A KINGDOM. "And ye shall be unto me a kingdom of priests" Exodus 19:6. Jesus is the King. Christians are His subjects and in this sense are regarded a kingdom. As a kingdom we reign with Christ. "For if, by the trespass of the one, death reigned through the one; much more shall they that receive the abundance of grace and the gift of righteousness reign in life through the one, even Jesus Christ" Romans 5:17. "Faithful is the saying: For if we die with him, we shall also live with him: if we endure, we shall also reign with him" 2 Timothy 2:11,12. "Jesus answered, My kingdom is not of this world: if my kingdom were of this world, then would my servants fight, that I should not be delivered to the Jews: but now is my kingdom not from hence" John 18:36. It is significant that the subject of the kingdom is not brought up until redemption has been realized as noted in verse five.

Christians are made TO BE PRIESTS UNTO HIS GOD AND FATHER. "Ye also, as living stones, are built up a spiritual house, to be a holy priesthood, to offer up spiritual sacrifices, acceptable to God through Jesus Christ...But ye are an elect race, a royal priesthood, a holy nation, a people for God's own possession, that ye may show forth the excellencies of him who called you out of darkness into his marvellous light" 1 Peter 2:5,9. It is

7

because we are priests and Christ is our High Priest that we can "draw near with boldness unto the throne of grace, that we may receive mercy, and may find grace to help us in time of need; Hebrews 4:16. All Christians are clergymen. We are engaged in the "ministry of reconciliation." "We are ambassadors therefore on behalf of Christ, as though God were entreating by us: we beseech you on behalf of Christ, be ye reconciled to God" 2 Corinthians 5:20.

TO HIM BE THE GLORY AND THE DOMINION FOR EVER AND EVER. GLORY magnifies God by honoring and praising Him. We praise God when we do His will and make known His goodness. DOMINION speaks of the sovereignty of God. This is a recognition that God is the Ruler of the universe and that all things are under His control. EVER AND EVER is an expression of eternity, time without end.

1:7 BEHOLD, HE COMETH WITH THE CLOUDS; AND EVERY EYE SHALL SEE HIM, AND THEY THAT PIERCED HIM; AND ALL THE TRIBES OF THE EARTH SHALL MOURN OVER HIM. EVEN SO, AMEN.

Jesus is coming again! There will be nothing secret about it. EVERY EYE SHALL SEE HIM. His coming will be just as was said at the time of His ascension. "He was taken up; and a cloud received him out of their sight. And while they were looking stedfastly into heaven as he went, behold, two men stood by them in white apparel; who also said, Ye men of Galilee, why stand ye looking into heaven? this Jesus, who was received up from you into heaven, shall so come in like manner as ye beheld him going into heaven" Acts 1:9-11. The Christian must never lose sight of this promised fact. The church must continually expect the return of Jesus.

THEY THAT PIERCED HIM must be understood in light of the fact that it is possible to crucify Christ afresh. See Hebrews 6:4-6. This expression is borrowed from Zechariah 12:10.

ALL THE TRIBES OF THE EARTH SHALL MOURN OVER HIM. Mourning is occasioned by a failure to receive Jesus as Lord and Saviour. All will face God in judgment. Christ's coming precedes the final judgment. To be unprepared for the judgment gives rise to intense mourning. MOURN means "wail." The

8

cause of the mourning is within the life of each individual. The only one who can forgive sins has been rejected. THE TRIBES OF THE EARTH are not Christians. The hostile world will be impressed by the sovereignty of God at the time of Christ's coming.

EVEN SO, AMEN. These words underscore the certainty of the Lord's return. The assurance of the Lord's return sustains the Christian during the days when "mockers shall come with mockery, walking after their own lusts, and saying, Where is the promise of his coming? for from the day that the fathers fell asleep, all things continue as they were from the beginning of the creation" 2 Peter 3:3,4. EVEN SO is a strong yes. AMEN means so let it be.

1:8   I AM THE ALPHA AND THE OMEGA, SAITH THE LORD GOD, WHO IS AND WHO WAS AND WHO IS TO COME, THE ALMIGHTY.

ALPHA AND OMEGA are the first and last letters of the Greek alphabet. This is another way of expressing the eternality of God. There is nothing that precedes or follows God. To know God in this light is to be assured that what He says can be depended upon as being true. This is God's way of expressing eternity, which exceeds time limitations, to man whose thinking is time oriented. This same thought is further amplified with the expression WHO IS AND WHO WAS AND WHO IS TO COME.

God is ALMIGHTY. This means He has complete control of things. This is especially comforting during a time of persecution and trial. At a time when it seemed as if Rome was almighty, it was reassuring to be reminded that only God is ALMIGHTY. No power even comes close to the power of God. God's strength and complete control of history assures us of His ultimate victory in the conflict of the ages. ALMIGHTY is a particularly meaningful word in the book of Revelation. Keep in mind that this book was written to encourage and strengthen the church at a time when this was needed. ALMIGHTY is a clear expression of God's sovereignty.

1:9   JOHN, YOUR BROTHER AND PARTAKER WITH YOU IN THE TRIBULATION AND KINGDOM AND PATIENCE WHICH ARE IN JESUS, WAS IN THE ISLE THAT IS CALLED PATMOS, FOR THE WORD OF GOD

9

AND THE TESTIMONY OF JESUS.

John identifies himself with the Christians as a BROTHER AND PARTAKER in Christ. We are more prone to listen to comforting words when we know the comforter has shared our experience and therefore is understanding. The Indian prayer contains a similar thought: "Grant that I may not criticize my neighbor until I have walked a mile in his moccasins." John was sympathetic and appreciative of the Christian's experience in difficult times. Revelation has always been particularly precious and comforting to those who suffer hardships.

TRIBULATION is understood in light of being IN JESUS. "Because Christ also suffered for you, leaving you an example, that ye should follow his steps" 1 Peter 2:21. Many pressures are placed upon Christians in time of persecution. "Through many tribulations we must enter into the kingdom of God" Acts 14:22. Tribulations must not be considered unusual for those in the KINGDOM. "Beloved, think it not strange concerning the fiery trial among you, which cometh upon you to prove you, as though a strange thing happened unto you: but insomuch as ye are partakers of Christ's sufferings, rejoice; that at the revelation of his glory also ye may rejoice with exceeding joy. If ye are reproached for the name of Christ, blessed are ye; because the Spirit of glory and the Spirit of God resteth upon you" 1 Peter 4:12-14. PATIENCE is to be understood as steadfast endurance. Our oneness with Jesus explains our patience and tribulation as well as our being a part of His kingdom.

John was probably on the isle of PATMOS between 94 and 96 A.D. PATMOS is a small isle about five miles wide and ten miles long, located forty miles southwest of Miletus.

John explains his presence on the isle as FOR THE WORD OF GOD AND THE TESTIMONY OF JESUS. This could mean that he went to Patmos to preach THE WORD OF GOD. It could also mean that he went to the isle to receive THE WORD OF GOD. The probable meaning is that he was banished to the isle of PATMOS because of his faithful Christian witness. Banishment to an isle was one means of persecution. Death was another as we shall note in the letter to the church in Pergamum (2:13).

1:10 I WAS IN THE SPIRIT ON THE LORD'S DAY, AND I

HEARD BEHIND ME A GREAT VOICE, AS OF A
TRUMPET

This is the earliest known usage of the expression THE
LORD'S DAY. It has been a frequently used designation for the
first day of the week since that time. It is not to be confused with
the expression, "the day of the Lord" 2 Thessalonians 2:2. There
are many reasons why this designation is particularly appropriate for the first day of the week. Pentecost, the day of the
resurrection of Christ, the day when the early church assembled
to observe the Lord's Supper and to bring their offerings to God
combine to make the first day of the week THE LORD'S DAY in a
special way, but not in a way that would suggest the other days of
the week do not belong to the Lord.

IN THE SPIRIT describes the nature of John's experience.
It was his spiritual state that enabled him to receive the revelation and communicate it to others. This trance-like experience
may be compared with Peter's experience at Joppa (Acts 10:10;
11:5) and Paul's experience (Acts 22:17; 2 Corinthians 12:2-4).

BEHIND ME may suggest both suddenness and unexpectedness. AS OF A TRUMPET makes it clear that the GREAT
VOICE was not a trumpet but was loud and clear. (See Matthew
24:31 and 1 Thessalonians 4:16.)

1:11 SAYING, WHAT THOU SEEST, WRITE IN A BOOK
AND SEND IT TO THE SEVEN CHURCHES: UNTO
EPHESUS, AND UNTO SMYRNA, AND UNTO PERGA-
MUM, AND UNTO THYATIRA, AND UNTO SARDIS,
AND UNTO PHILADELPHIA, AND UNTO LAODICEA.

WHAT THOU SEEST indicates that John sees a series of visions. We do well in our study to try to visualize what John has
written as if a drama were being presented before us.

WRITE IN A BOOK. This is a command. It means that John
is to do this immediately. We must understand that in John's day
they did not have books as we know them, thus John was commanded to record what he saw on a scroll.

SEND IT TO THE SEVEN CHURCHES. This, also, is to be
regarded as a command. In locating these seven churches on a
map there is logic in the order. Ephesus was located closest to
Patmos. The other churches follow in order making a circuit from

11

which additional churches could also have access to the revelation. Though the number seven speaks of the total church we
must not fail to see the letters were written and the revelation
was sent to seven historic churches.

1:12   AND I TURNED TO SEE THE VOICE THAT SPAKE
      WITH ME. AND HAVING TURNED I SAW SEVEN
      GOLDEN CANDLESTICKS;

The VOICE is identified with the speaker. John turned to see
the speaker. The last verse of this chapter informs us that the
SEVEN CANDLESTICKS ARE SEVEN CHURCHES. Through-
out the book it will be observed that much of the imagery John
uses is borrowed from the Old Testament. In Exodus 25:31 we
read "And thou shalt make a candlestick of pure gold." GOLDEN
suggests the idea of precious. Every saint and congregation is
precious in the sight of the Lord.

1:13   AND IN THE MIDST OF THE CANDLESTICKS ONE
      LIKE UNTO A SON OF MAN, CLOTHED WITH A GAR-
      MENT DOWN TO THE FOOT, GIRT AT THE BREASTS
      WITH A GOLDEN GIRDLE.

LIKE UNTO A SON OF MAN is recorded also in Daniel 7:13.
"I saw in the night-visions, and, behold, there came with the
clouds of heaven one like unto a son of man, and he came even to
the ancient of days, and they brought him near before him." SON
OF MAN pictures the humanity of Him who was both God and
man. Jesus said, "For where two or three are gathered together
in my name, there am I in the midst of them" Matthew 20:20.
Jesus is always present with His people and is therefore knowl-
edgeable and understanding of them.

CLOTHED WITH A GARMENT DOWN TO THE FOOT
ascribes to the Lord the same kind of garment worn by the high
priests. See Exodus 28:4. The garment speaks of His life and work
as our High Priest. Dignity is symbolized by high girding. The
girdle served both to hold the robe in place and also as an adornment. GOLDEN GIRDLE suggests something unusual. Ordinarily the girdle was made of linen. Royalty may be suggested in
the material of this girdle. The Christian is admonished to "stand
therefore, having girded your loins with truth" Ephesians 6:14.

1:14   AND HIS HEAD AND HIS HAIR WERE WHITE AS

WHITE WOOL, WHITE AS SNOW: AND HIS EYES
WERE AS A FLAME OF FIRE;

WHITE symbolizes purity. WHITE HAIR symbolizes old
age. The omniscience and the penetration of the Lord's vision is
pictured with the phrase HIS EYES WERE AS A FLAME OF
FIRE. "Come now, and let us reason together, saith Jehovah:
though your sins be as scarlet, they shall be as white as snow;
though they be red like crimson, they shall be as wool" Isaiah
1:18.

1:15 AND HIS FEET LIKE UNTO BURNISHED BRASS, AS
IF IT HAD BEEN REFINED IN A FURNACE: AND HIS
VOICE AS THE VOICE OF MANY WATERS.

BURNISHED BRASS symbolizes firmness. The imagery for
the VOICE is borrowed from Ezekiel 43:2 "and, behold, the glory
of the God of Israel came from the way of the east: and his voice
was like the sound of many waters; and the earth shined with his
glory." The VOICE speaks with power and authority.

1:16 AND HE HAD IN HIS RIGHT HAND SEVEN STARS: *Angels of the churches*
AND OUT OF HIS MOUTH PROCEEDED A SHARP
TWO-EDGED SWORD: AND HIS COUNTENANCE WAS
AS THE SUN SHINETH IN HIS STRENGTH.

The twentieth verse of this chapter informs us that the
SEVEN STARS ARE THE ANGELS OF THE SEVEN CHUR-
CHES. The special care the Lord gives His own is indicated by
the fact that He has them IN HIS RIGHT HAND. Concerning the
loving care of Jesus we read in John 10:28 "And I give unto them
eternal life; and they shall never perish, and no one shall snatch
them out of my hand."

The word of God proceeds from HIS MOUTH. Paul informs
us that the word of God is the sword of the Spirit (Ephesians 6:17).
"For the word of God is living, and active, and sharper than any
two-edged sword, and piercing even to the dividing of soul and
spirit, of both joints and marrow, and quick to discern the
thoughts and intents of the heart" Hebrews 4:12. "In the beginning was the Word, and the Word was with God, and the Word was
God...And the Word became flesh, and dwelt among us" John
1:1,14.

John may have recalled the Mount of Transfiguration ex-

13

perience when he wrote HIS COUNTENANCE WAS AS THE
SUN SHINETH IN HIS STRENGTH. This portrays the glory of
the Lord's presence. Paul similarly speaks of the Lord's presence
to the young evangelist Timothy. "...the appearing of our Lord
Jesus Christ; which in its own times he shall show, who is the
blessed and only Potentate, the King of kings, and Lord of lords;
who only hath immortality, dwelling in light unapproachable;
whom no man hath seen, nor can see: to whom be honor and
power eternal. Amen" 1 Timothy 6:14-16.

1:17　AND WHEN I SAW HIM, I FELL AT HIS FEET AS ONE
　　　DEAD. AND HE LAID HIS RIGHT HAND UPON ME,
　　　SAYING, FEAR NOT; I AM THE FIRST AND THE
　　　LAST,

Ezekiel had a similar experience to that of John. "As the appearance of the bow that is in the cloud in the day of rain, so was
the appearance of the brightness round about. This was the appearance of the likeness of the glory of Jehovah. And when I saw
it, I fell upon my face, and I heard a voice of one that spake (1:28).
At the time of Isaiah's call to the prophetic ministry he said,
"Woe is me! for I am undone; because I am a man of unclean lips,
and I dwell in the midst of a people of unclean lips: for mine eyes
have seen the King, Jehovah of hosts" Isaiah 6:5. The light of
God's presence is that which reveals to man his own sinfulness
most adequately. This presence filled John with fear. But the
Lord does not want His people to be filled with fear. FEAR NOT
is both a word of comfort and a command. Implied in this command is the ability to obey. The literal meaning is "stop being
afraid." Phobia is the transliteration of the Greek word
translated FEAR. Fear is dispelled through knowing Christ. To
be afraid is to indicate a lack of trust in Christ and thus weakens a
Christian's witness. I AM THE FIRST AND THE LAST. After
commissioning His disciples to evangelize the world Jesus gave
this reassuring word to those who obey — "and Lo, I am with you
always, even unto the end of the world" Matthew 28:20. Jesus is
always present. He knows the end from the beginning. His omni-
presence, omniscience and omnipotence is our basis for not being
afraid.

1:18　AND THE LIVING ONE; AND I WAS DEAD, AND

BEHOLD, I AM ALIVE EVERMORE, AND I HAVE THE
KEYS OF DEATH AND OF HADES.

The Greek grammar makes it clear that Jesus became dead
of His own free will. "And being found in fashion as a man, he
humbled himself, becoming obedient even unto death, yea, the
death of the cross" Philippians 2:8. Christ asserts His life, power
and authority. KEYS symbolize authority. HADES is the abode
of the dead. It is because Jesus is THE LIVING ONE that death
has no dominion over Him and the grave could not keep Him.
"The sting of death is sin; and the power of sin is the law: but
thanks be to God, who giveth us the victory through our Lord
Jesus Christ" 1 Corinthians 15:56, 57.

1:19   WRITE THEREFORE THE THINGS WHICH THOU
        SAWEST, AND THE THINGS WHICH ARE, AND THE
        THINGS WHICH SHALL COME TO PASS
        HEREAFTER;

John is commanded to WRITE instantly. Perhaps one reason
for this urgency was to prevent forgetting any of those things
which were seen. Another reason would be the urgency of getting
this message to those who needed comfort.

Things past, present and future are contained in this book.
This is not to suggest an order for the contents but rather a description of the various aspects of the message. Revelation is not
to be understood as a chronological record of events. The span of
the Christian era is covered several times within this book.
Though it is not technically accurate to say history repeats itself
we can say that history has many parallels. This becomes evident
in our understanding of Revelation. With these parallels there is
progress as history moves toward consummation. The spiritual
truths and eternal principles recorded by John are timeless.

1:20   THE MYSTERY OF THE SEVEN STARS WHICH THOU
        SAWEST IN MY RIGHT HAND, AND THE SEVEN
        GOLDEN CANDLESTICKS. THE SEVEN STARS ARE
        THE ANGELS OF THE SEVEN CHURCHES: AND THE
        SEVEN CANDLESTICKS ARE SEVEN CHURCHES.

The word MYSTERY in its biblical usage speaks of that
information which is available to man only by means of God's
revelation. In this instance it is the explanation God gives to the

symbols of the STARS and CANDLESTICKS.

ANGELS may be messengers or heavenly beings. It has been suggested that the ANGELS in this verse refer to guardian angels, to the evangelists of the churches, to the elders of the churches, or to those who were designated representatives of the churches. Because of the plurality of elders in each congregation that suggestion may be ruled out.

It is appropriate that CHURCHES are symbolized with CANDLESTICKS in that Christians always shine with borrowed light. That is, Christians simply reflect the glory of God in their lives. The light within the church is the light of Christ. Churches are the reflectors of the true Light. Consider Matthew 5:14 and Philippians 2:15 in this manner.

CHURCHES OF CHRIST

CHAPTERS TWO AND THREE

2:1 TO THE ANGEL OF THE CHURCH IN EPHESUS
WRITE: THESE THINGS SAITH HE THAT HOLDETH
THE SEVEN STARS IN HIS RIGHT HAND, HE THAT
WALKETH IN THE MIDST OF THE SEVEN GOLDEN
CANDLESTICKS:

Paul visited the CHURCH IN EPHESUS three times. On his second missionary journey he stayed in Ephesus nearly three years. It was to the Ephesian Christians that Paul said, "I testify unto you this day, that I am pure from the blood of all men. For I shrank not from declaring unto you the whole counsel of God. Take heed unto yourselves, and to all the flock, in which the Holy Spirit hath made you bishops, to feed the church of the Lord which he purchased with his own blood. I know that after my departing grievous wolves shall enter in among you, not sparing the flock; and from among your own selves shall men arise, speaking perverse things, to draw away the disciples after them. Wherefore watch ye, remembering that by the space of three years I ceased not to admonish every one night and day with tears. And now I commend you to God and to the word of his grace, which is able to build you up, and to give you the inheritance among all them that are sanctified. I coveted no man's silver, or gold, or apparel. Ye yourselves know that these hands ministered unto my necessities, and to them that were with me. In all things I gave you an example, that so laboring ye ought to help the weak, and to remember the words of the Lord Jesus, that he himself said, It is more blessed to give than to receive" Acts 20:26-35. John and Timothy also labored with the Christians in Ephesus.

Ephesus was located in the center of the Christian population both numerically and geographically. It was also about the center of the Roman empire and about halfway between Rome

17

and Jerusalem. The location contributed to the greatness and wealth of Ephesus in the first century.

The Ephesians were permitted to govern themselves. The Panionian games (similar to the Olympics) were played here each May. Pagan immorality was encouraged through such influences as the temple of Artemis (Diana).

The Lord identified Himself differently to each of the seven churches. Each identification is particularly meaningful to the situation in the church. HE THAT HOLDETH THE SEVEN STARS IN HIS RIGHT HAND speaks of the protecting care the Lord gives to His messengers. The word HOLDETH suggests a complete grasp. It is holding in the sense of having a dime in the clutch of your hand and not in the sense of holding a bucket. HE THAT WALKETH IN THE MIDST OF THE SEVEN GOLDEN CANDLESTICKS suggests His firsthand knowledge. "For where two or three are gathered together in my name, there am I in the midst of them" Matthew 20:20. Christ is presented as one having an intimate concern and care for the church.

2:2   I KNOW THY WORKS, AND THY TOIL AND PA-
       TIENCE, AND THAT THOU CANST NOT BEAR EVIL
       MEN, AND DIDST TRY THEM THAT CALL THEM-
       SELVES APOSTLES, AND DIDST FIND THEM FALSE;

Sound doctrine

I KNOW (*oida*) means that His knowledge is complete. TOIL is to be understood in light of weariness and trouble that accompany labour. The Ephesian Christians worked hard. PATIENCE is steadfast endurance. EVIL MEN were regarded as an encumbrance and rightly so. Paul's warning for them to watch for those who speak perverse things was not in vain (Acts 20:29-31). The Ephesian Christians were commended for their disciplinary action in determining the difference between the true and false apostles.

At the end of the first century there were different kinds of false prophets. Some used Christianity as a means of becoming professional beggars. The Judaizers sought to entangle Christians with the Law. Gnostics claimed to have superior knowledge which became their basis for living contrary to the teachings of Christ. The first letter of John is best understood in light of the Gnostic problem. John warned, "Beloved, believe not every

18

spirit, but prove the spirits, whether they are of God; because many false prophets are gone out into the world" 1 John 4:1. Jesus said, "Beware of false prophets, who come to you in sheep's clothing, but inwardly are ravening wolves. By their fruits ye shall know them" Matthew 7:15,16. Paul cautioned the Corinthians, "For such men are false apostles, deceitful workers, fashioning themselves into apostles of Christ. And no marvel; for even Satan fashioneth himself into an angel of light. It is no great thing therefore if his ministers also fashion themselves as ministers of righteousness; whose end shall be according to their works" 2 Corinthians 11:13-15. Jesus said, "Therefore by their fruits ye shall know them" Matthew 7:20.

2:3 AND THOU HAST PATIENCE AND DIDST BEAR FOR MY NAME'S SAKE, AND HAST NOT GROWN WEARY.

They did not become "weary in well-doing" Galatians 6:9. "If a man suffer as a Christian, let him not be ashamed; but let him glorify God in this name" 1 Peter 4:16. FOR MY NAME'S SAKE denotes loyalty to Christ.

2:4 BUT I HAVE THIS AGAINST THEE, THAT THOU DIDST LEAVE THY FIRST LOVE.

In each of the seven letters the words of commendation always precede the rebuke. LOVE was the missing ingredient in this church. The importance of love is made clear in 1 John 3:14, "We know that we have passed out of death into life, because we love the brethren." Love is absolutely essential to the Christian life. Without love everything else is meaningless. Paul made this clear in 1 Corinthians 13:1-3. FIRST is a significant word. It points to that love that characterized their lives when they first received Jesus as their Saviour. They were not in the process of losing their first love, they had already lost it. There is a warmth, tenderness and freshness in love that the Lord intends shall always characterize the Christian. The fervency of spirit was lacking. Having said all of this we must not make the mistake in thinking of love in purely emotional terms. LOVE is both emotional and volitional. There is an ever present danger of losing love while engaged in the battle for sound doctrine.

2:5 REMEMBER THEREFORE WHENCE THOU ART FALLEN, AND REPENT AND DO THE FIRST WORKS:

OR ELSE I COME TO THEE, AND WILL MOVE THY CANDLESTICK OUT OF ITS PLACE, EXCEPT THOU REPENT.

One of the greatest blessings the Christian has is his ability to REMEMBER. After beautifully enumerating the ingredients of fruitful Christian living Peter adds, "Wherefore I shall be ready always to put you in remembrance of these things, though ye know them, and are established in the truth which is with you" 2 Peter 1:12. Memory took the prodigal son out of the pig pen and led him back home. To remember what Christ has done for us will prove most helpful in sustaining us through trials and temptations. The benefits derived through memory caused Jesus to institute the Lord's Supper. "This do in remembrance of me" 1 Corinthians 11:24.

THEREFORE looks back to the preceding verse. The fact that their FIRST LOVE was missing is the occasion for encouraging them to remember what life was like when they were experiencing FIRST LOVE. ART FALLEN is completed action. It is as if they are already in the valley as a result of falling from the top of the cliff. Now they are admonished to look back up to the top where they were before the fall.

REPENT means to change your mind for the better with the implication that when the mind is changed the behavior will also be changed. This is to be understood as a command. Repentance is a personal matter. This cannot be done by proxy.

DO THE FIRST WORKS. Christianity is a matter of doing as well as being and believing. "Faith, if it have not works, is dead in itself" James 2:17. FIRST WORKS gives evidence of repentance. OR ELSE is a threat. To remove the CANDLESTICK OUT OF ITS PLACE is to bring the church into extinction. Revival is both possible and necessary for the church in Ephesus.

2:6   BUT THIS THOU HAST, THAT THOU HATEST THE WORKS OF THE NICOLAITANS, WHICH I ALSO HATE.

There is a definite place for HATE in the Christian life. "Abhor that which is evil" Romans 12:9. Abhor means hate. WHICH I ALSO HATE identifies their feelings with those of the Lord.

The word NICOLAITANS is derived from two Greek words (*nikao* and *laos*) meaning "to conquer people." The word "Balaam" is derived from two Hebrew words (*bela* and *ha'am*) meaning "to conquer people." This gives us a hint as to the possible explanation of the Nicolaitans. The Old Testament records the story of Balaam. This will be noted in the comments on verse fourteen in this chapter. The NICOLAITANS were enemies of the faith, perhaps as compromisers or abusers of the Christian freedom.

2:7   HE THAT HATH AN EAR, LET HIM HEAR WHAT THE SPIRIT SAITH TO THE CHURCHES. TO HIM THAT OVERCOMETH, TO HIM WILL I GIVE TO EAT OF THE TREE OF LIFE, WHICH IS IN THE PARADISE OF GOD.

The individual is commanded to HEAR. This hearing is for the purpose of heeding. Is everyone capable of hearing? Jesus spoke of those hearing who "hear not" Matthew 13:13. Paul said, "if our gospel is veiled, it is veiled in them that perish: in whom the god of this world hath blinded the minds of the unbelieving, that the light of the gospel of the glory of Christ, who is the image of God, should not dawn upon them" 2 Corinthians 4:3,4. Those capable of hearing are expected to do so at once.

The SPIRIT speaks through the word. "For no prophecy ever came by the will of man: but men spake from God, being moved by the Holy Spirit" 2 Peter 1:21.

OVERCOMETH is a word used more by John than any of the other New Testament writers. This same Greek word (*nikao*) is also translated "conquer." "In all these things we are more than conquerors through him that loved us" Romans 8:37. OVERCOMETH suggests conflict. Indeed the Christian is in conflict with sin, but in Christ victory is assured. "For whatsoever is begotten of God overcometh the world: and this is the victory that hath overcome the world, even our faith" 1 John 5:4. Jesus said, "In the world ye have tribulation: but be of good cheer; I have overcome the world" John 16:33. "Thanks be to God, who giveth us the victory through our Lord Jesus Christ" 1 Corinthians 15:57. The Christian may appear to be defeated in the eyes of the world but steadfastness in the Christian faith assures us of victory even now.

21

This is the first time we read of THE TREE OF LIFE since the record of Genesis. THE TREE OF LIFE and THE PARADISE OF GOD both convey the thought of God's choice and eternal blessings which are available only to the Christian who remains faithful unto death. The scene of man prior to his fall aids us in appreciating our future in Christ once the conflict of the ages has come to an end. Eternal life with God is to be understood both quantitatively and qualitatively.

2:8   AND TO THE ANGEL OF THE CHURCH IN SMYRNA WRITE: THESE THINGS SAITH THE FIRST AND THE LAST, WHO WAS DEAD, AND LIVED AGAIN:

SMYRNA was located about thirty-five miles north of Ephesus. It, too, was located on the shores of the Aegean Sea. This was the home of Polycarp, friend of John, who was martyred at the age of eighty-six years because of his powerful Christian witness.

THE FIRST AND THE LAST is borrowed from Isaiah 44:6. See comments on 1:17. WHO WAS DEAD AND LIVED AGAIN is a reference to the resurrection of Christ. This phrase would have had particular meaning to those living in SMYRNA. SMYRNA was a city that had been destroyed and builded again. The rebuilding of the city helps to account for its beauty. The resurrection is the basis of the Christian faith. "If the Spirit of him that raised up Jesus from the dead dwelleth in you, he that raised up Christ Jesus from the dead shall give life also to your mortal bodies through his Spirit that dwelleth in you" Romans 8:11.

2:9   I KNOW THY TRIBULATION, AND THY POVERTY (BUT THOU ART RICH), AND THE BLASPHEMY OF THEM THAT SAY THEY ARE JEWS, AND THEY ARE NOT, BUT ARE A SYNAGOGUE OF SATAN.

TRIBULATION is pressure. There are many kinds of pressure that can crush down upon the Christian. The contents of this letter help us to understand the persecutions of Smyrna. It is comforting to know that God knows when His people suffer, for He cares.

Their POVERTY was destitution. This word describes not those who have little but rather those who have nothing. The parenthetical reference to their riches presents a contrast be-

22

tween spiritual riches and material poverty. "Hearken, my beloved brethren; did not God choose them that are poor as to the world to be rich in faith, and heirs of the kingdom which he promised to them that love him" James 2:5?

THEM THAT SAY THEY ARE JEWS is to be understood religiously, not nationally. The Lord speaks of those who call themselves JEWS and means by this that they are God's people. "For he is not a Jew who is one outwardly; neither is that circumcision which is outward in the flesh: but he is a Jew who is one inwardly; and circumcision is that of the heart, in the spirit not in the letter; whose praise is not of men, but of God" Romans 2:28,29. This hypocrisy of those who make a false claim to be the people of God is considered BLASPHEMY. BLASPHEMY comes from two Greek words (*blapto* and *pheme*) meaning, "to hurt with speech." SYNAGOGUE is the combination of two Greek words (*sun* and *ago*) and literally means "A bringing together." When hypocrites assemble together it is properly designated as a gathering of Satan's people. Jesus said, "why call ye me, Lord, Lord, and do not the things which I say" Luke 6:46? "Many will say to me in that day, Lord, Lord, did we not prophesy by thy name, and by thy name cast out demons, and by thy name do many mighty works? And then will I profess unto them, I never knew you: depart from me, ye that work iniquity" Matthew 7:22,23.

2:10 FEAR NOT THE THINGS WHICH THOU ART ABOUT TO SUFFER: BEHOLD, THE DEVIL IS ABOUT TO CAST SOME OF YOU INTO PRISON, THAT YE MAY BE TRIED: AND YE SHALL HAVE TRIBULATION TEN DAYS. BE THOU FAITHFUL UNTO DEATH, AND I WILL GIVE THEE THE CROWN OF LIFE.

Jesus said, "Remember the word that I said unto you, A servant is not greater than his lord. If they persecuted me, they will also persecute you" John 15:20. Peter wrote, "Beloved, think it not strange concerning the fiery trial among you, which cometh upon you to prove you, as though a strange thing happened unto you: but insomuch as ye are partakers of Christ's sufferings, rejoice; that at the revelation of his glory also ye may rejoice with exceeding joy" 1 Peter 4:12,13. THOU ART ABOUT TO SUFFER is an example of the foreknowledge of the Lord. It also speaks of His honesty. Jesus never tried to get followers by leading men to believe life as His disciple would always be easy. In fact, Jesus was very specific in announcing the suffering that would take place. THE DEVIL IS ABOUT TO CAST SOME OF YOU INTO PRISON, THAT YE MAY BE TRIED. Satan means this persecution for evil but God allows Satan to work in this way to give strength to the Christian witness. This statement might be illustrated with the words of Joseph to his brothers after their reunion. "Joseph said unto them, Fear not: for am I in the place of God? And as for you, ye meant evil against me; but God meant it for good, to bring to pass, as it is this day, to save much people alive" Genesis 50:19,20. "The proving of your faith worketh patience" James 1:3.

TEN DAYS does not have to be understood literally. It does suggest a limitation. Even with a limitation cruel persecution may seem like an eternity while it continues. The number TEN is a symbol for completeness. DAYS suggests a short time.

BE THOU FAITHFUL UNTO DEATH. "It is required in stewards, that a man be found faithful" 1 Corinthians 4:2. In a success-oriented society it is well to remember that the Lord placed the emphasis upon faithfulness. The text means to keep on being faithful, grow in your faithfulness. Be willing to pay the price of death, if need be, to remain faithful. This is exactly what being faithful has cost many Christians throughout church history beginning with Stephen.

THE CROWN OF LIFE is the reward for faithfulness. "For I reckon that the sufferings of this present time are not worthy to be compared with the glory which shall be revealed to us-ward" Romans 8:18. Two Greek words are translated "crown." One is a royal crown and the other is a victor's crown. It is the victor's crown that is here mentioned. This is in keeping with the truth that the CROWN awaits the overcomer. LIFE is not a meaningless existence in our present state. It is the abundant life which flows from God and triumphs over the second death. THE CROWN OF LIFE is God's reward for His faithful servants. God's rewards should not be confused with God's gift of salvation lest we think we can merit salvation. See Ephesians 2:8-10. It is difficult to comprehend God's rewards in light of our present surroundings. Suffice it to say God takes note of all we do and rewards us accordingly. Might the reward be in the form of a greater capacity to enjoy heaven?

2:11 HE THAT HATH AN EAR, LET HIM HEAR WHAT THE SPIRIT SAITH TO THE CHURCHES. HE THAT OVERCOMETH SHALL NOT BE HURT OF THE SECOND DEATH.

See comments on 2:7.

The SECOND DEATH is clearly identified in 20:14. "And death and Hades were cast into the lake of fire. This is the SECOND DEATH, even the lake of fire." This is the ultimate condemnation of those not in Christ. Once the SECOND DEATH is realized there remains no more a possibility of eternal life.

2:12 AND TO THE ANGEL OF THE CHURCH IN PERGAMUM WRITE: THESE THINGS SAITH HE THAT HATH THE SHARP TWO-EDGED SWORD:

Pergamum was located in Mysia about fifty-five miles from Smyrna. Paganism had a strong influence in this place as will be noted in the study of this letter and as is verified in history.

THE SHARP TWO-EDGED SWORD refers to the word of God. See Hebrews 4:12 and Ephesians 6:17. The discerning quality of the word is particularly important here. In this identification the Lord is telling the people that He knows those who are faithful and those who are not. Close proximity to a faithful Christian does not become a substitute for your own faithfulness. Jesus illustrated this in His prophetic message. "Then shall two men be in the field; one is taken, and one is left: two women shall be grinding at the mill; one is taken, and one is left" Matthew 24:40,41. Consider further the importance of the word of the Lord. Jesus said, "if any man hear my sayings, and keep them not, I judge him not: for I came not to judge the world, but to save the world. He that rejecteth me, and receiveth not my sayings, hath one that judgeth him: the word that I spake, the same shall judge him in the last day" John 12:47,48. "Heaven and earth shall pass away, but my words shall not pass away" Matthew 24:35.

2:13 I KNOW WHERE THOU DWELLEST, EVEN WHERE SATAN'S THRONE IS: AND THOU HOLDEST FAST

25

MY NAME, AND DIDST NOT DENY MY FAITH, EVEN IN THE DAYS OF ANTIPAS MY WITNESS, MY FAITHFUL ONE, WHO WAS KILLED AMONG YOU, WHERE SATAN DWELLETH.

I KNOW WHERE THOU DWELLEST. The thought being expressed is I know where you live and I intend that you shall continue living there. Because of the strong Satanic influence in this place it would have been tempting for the Christian to move away, but this is the very place where the Christian witness is most needed. Where the darkness of sin is greatest the light of the Christian must shine forth in all its beauty.

The intensity of evil presence is expressed in two phrases — WHERE SATAN'S THRONE IS and WHERE SATAN DWELLETH. Satan is pictured as having made his permanent dwelling in Pergamum. Here he also established his dominion. Various evils, prevalent in Pergamum, have been offered as possible explanations. Temples were erected to several pagan deities. The location of the temple of Zeus has suggested the imagery of a throne to some. The popularity of the god, Aesculapius, must be considered as a strong pagan influence. Aesculapius was considered a saviour both from the effects of disease and from the results of sin. Aesculapius was symbolized by a serpent. The Christian knows this to be the symbol of Satan. In the early part of the first century a temple was dedicated to Rome and the Caesar. No doubt Caesar worship is a glaring aspect of Satanic power in this place. The combination of all pagan and evil forces at work may best explain SATAN'S THRONE.

THOU HOLDEST FAST MY NAME. In addition to the temptation to move out of Pergamum because of the extreme wickedness that prevailed there would be a tendency to deny any relationship to the Lord Jesus Christ in order to avoid persecution. They are commended, however, for their spiritual strength in making their identity as Christians obvious. This strong Christian witness is noteworthy in light of the fact that ANTIPAS was killed as a FAITHFUL WITNESS. The title ascribed to Jesus (1:5) is given to ANTIPAS.

MY FAITH is to be understood as faith in Christ, steadfastness in the Christian faith. There was no wavering in the faith

26

of Christians in Pergamum. "Beloved, while I was giving all diligence to write unto you of our common salvation, I was constrained to write unto you exhorting you to contend earnestly for
the faith which was once for all delivered unto the saints" Jude 3.

2:14 BUT I HAVE A FEW THINGS AGAINST THEE, BE-
      CAUSE THOU HAST THERE SOME THAT HOLD THE
      TEACHING OF BALAAM, WHO TAUGHT BALAK TO
      CAST A STUMBLINGBLOCK BEFORE THE CHILD-
      REN OF ISRAEL, TO EAT THINGS SACRIFICED TO
      IDOLS, AND TO COMMIT FORNICATION.

THOU HAST THERE SOME THAT HOLD THE TEACH-
ING OF BALAAM. Not all Christians in the church were faithful.
The Lord indicated in His own designation at the beginning of
this letter that He possessed the discerning quality to distinguish
between those faithful and unfaithful.

THE TEACHING OF BALAAM is understood in light of the
record contained in Numbers 22:25. "Behold, these caused the
children of Israel, through the counsel of Balaam, to commit trespass against Jehovah in the matter of Peor, and so the plague was
among the congregation of Jehovah" Numbers 31:16. As a result
of Balaam's word the Moabite women enticed the Israelites into
fornication and idolatry. God responded to the wickedness with a
disciplinary action resulting in 24,000 deaths (Numbers 25:9).
Balaam's advice was to destroy the identity of the Israelites by
intermarriage with the Moabites. In this way the Moabites would
escape the wrath of God. It didn't work that way. It has always
been God's will that His people be clearly identified as belonging
to Him. Any effort to destroy this distinction is dangerous and
wrong.

Encouragement TO EAT THINGS SACRIFICED TO
IDOLS, AND TO COMMIT FORNICATION were two aspects of
the doctrine of Balaam. There was no question on the position of
the church in these matters. It had been established at the Jerusalem conference "that ye abstain from things sacrificed to idols,
and from blood, and from things strangled, and from fornication"
Acts 15:29. That which is spoken of here should not be confused
with Paul's statement regarding meat in his first letter to the
Corinthians (8:13). The Lord rebukes the practice of eating meat

27

as a part of pagan worship. 1 Corinthians 6:12-20 is one of several passages in the New Testament that speaks clearly of God's will in these areas.

2:15 SO HAST THOU ALSO SOME THAT HOLD THE TEACHING OF THE NICOLAITANS IN LIKE MANNER. See comments on 2:6.

2:16 REPENT THEREFORE; OR ELSE I COME TO THEE QUICKLY, AND I WILL MAKE WAR AGAINST THEM WITH THE SWORD OF MY MOUTH.

REPENT is a call for action to those guilty of wrong practices and to those who permit such practices without administering any discipline. The urgency of their repentance is noted in the words I COME TO THEE QUICKLY. The purpose of this coming in judgment is to MAKE WAR AGAINST THEM WITH THE SWORD OF MY MOUTH. The Lord wages war with the word of truth. Through this word men are made aware of truth and are convicted of sin. Contained in the word of the Lord is both authority and power. Read Ephesians 6:10-20.

2:17 HE THAT HATH AN EAR, LET HIM HEAR WHAT THE SPIRIT SAITH TO THE CHURCHES. TO HIM THAT OVERCOMETH, TO HIM WILL I GIVE OF THE HIDDEN MANNA, AND I WILL GIVE HIM A WHITE STONE, AND UPON THE STONE A NEW NAME WRITTEN, WHICH NO ONE KNOWETH BUT HE THAT RECEIVETH IT.

Jesus said, "Your fathers ate the manna in the wilderness, and they died. This is the bread which cometh down out of heaven, that a man may eat thereof, and not die. I am the living bread which came down out of heaven: if any man eat of this bread, he shall live forever: yea and the bread which I will give is my flesh, for the life of the world" John 6:49-51. The HIDDEN aspect of the manna may be understood in light of 2 Corinthians 4:3,4 "And even if our gospel is veiled, it is veiled in them that perish: in whom the god of this world hath blinded the minds of the unbelieving, that the light of the gospel of the glory of Christ, who is the image of God, should not dawn upon them." The HIDDEN MANNA should be understood in contrast to the eating of THINGS SACRIFICED TO IDOLS. Another contrast of food is

28

made in the ministry of Jesus. "...the disciples prayed him, saying, Rabbi, eat. But he said unto them, I have meat to eat that ye know not. The disciples therefore said one to another, Hath any man brought him aught to eat? Jesus saith unto them, My meat is to do the will of him that sent me, and to accomplish his work" John 4:30-34.

I WILL GIVE HIM A WHITE STONE. Many explanations have been offered for the meaning of this statement. One is a possible reference to the white stone that was used in casting a vote in favor of innocence. In contrast a black stone would be placed in the urn if the person regarded the one on trial as guilty. If this is a proper understanding of the imagery here used the stone would speak of our freedom in Christ. The stone may also symbolize the favor with which God looks upon His people. There is not sufficient data to be dogmatic regarding the meaning of the WHITE STONE. There was a NEW NAME WRITTEN on this stone WHICH NO ONE KNOWETH BUT HE THAT RECEIVETH IT. A name was more than just a word. The person's character was involved in his name. We use the word in this manner when speaking of a person having a good name, meaning a good reputation. The new nature we have in Christ for eternity cannot be fully comprehended while we are yet in the flesh.

2:18   AND TO THE ANGEL OF THE CHURCH IN THYATIRA WRITE: THESE THINGS SAITH THE SON OF GOD, WHO HATH HIS EYES LIKE A FLAME OF FIRE, AND HIS FEET ARE LIKE UNTO BURNISHED BRASS:

THYATIRA was the home of Lydia, a seller of purple (Acts 16:14). The location of this city was about forty miles southeast of Pergamum. The fact that several trade guilds were located here aids us in our understanding of part of this letter. It was not uncommon for immorality and pagan practices to characterize guild meetings. This presented a serious conflict for the working Christian.

Caiaphas said to Jesus, "I adjure thee by the living God, that thou tell us whether thou art the Christ, THE SON OF GOD. Jesus said unto him, Thou hast said" Matthew 26:63,64. THE SON OF GOD is identified by HIS EYES and HIS FEET. EYES speak of vision and knowledge. That they are LIKE A FLAME OF

FIRE suggests the penetration of His vision and the completeness of His knowledge. Nothing can be hidden from the Lord. It has also been suggested by some that this pictures the blazing anger of God against sin. HIS FEET may speak of judgment inasmuch as "trodden under foot" is an expression of judgment. The judgment of God is both true and righteous (Romans 2:2,5). Certainly the judgment of God will come upon all those who fail to measure up to His will.

2:19   I KNOW THY WORKS, AND THY LOVE AND FAITH AND MINISTRY AND PATIENCE, AND THAT THY LAST WORKS ARE MORE THAN THE FIRST.

The Lord is always careful to offer praise when praise is due. The mention of LOVE before FAITH is typical of John in his writings. Paul would have reversed the order. MINISTRY speaks of service that benefits others. The significant fact is that there was a noticeable growth in the area of their WORKS. This is as it should be in every church. It is commendable THAT THY LAST WORKS ARE MORE THAN THE FIRST.

2:20   BUT I HAVE THIS AGAINST THEE, THAT THOU SUFFEREST THE WOMAN JEZEBEL, WHO CALLETH HERSELF A PROPHETESS: AND SHE TEACHETH AND SEDUCETH MY SERVANTS TO COMMIT FORNICATION, AND TO EAT THINGS SACRIFICED TO IDOLS.

The name JEZEBEL is evidently used to identify that one in the church whose character and life is so much like the Jezebel of the Old Testament. The Jezebel of the Old Testament was a wicked woman who tried to turn the people against God and involve them in pagan worship of Baal. 2 Kings 9:22 informs us further of her character: "What peace, so long as the whoredoms of thy mother Jezebel and her witchcrafts are so many?"

Clearly the JEZEBEL in Thyatira was a false PROPHETESS. Her influence was strong enough to affect the saints, MY SERVANTS. Both FORNICATION and heathen sacrificial feasts were condemned by God. This woman would weaken the Christian witness through the introduction of these sinful practices in the lives of the Christians. Read Acts 15:29. It is possible that she was suggesting that if working conditions made it necessary to engage in these sinful activities it would be alright in view of the fact that work was necessary for the support of the individual and his family. The philosophy that the end justifies the means is false. Under no condition is the Christian permitted to live immorally or engage in pagan practices. "Beware of the false prophets, who come to you in sheep's clothing, but inwardly are ravening wolves" Matthew 7:15.

2:21 AND I GAVE HER TIME THAT SHE SHOULD REPENT; AND SHE WILLETH NOT TO REPENT OF HER FORNICATION.

FORNICATION may be understood in the Bible both literally and figuratively. Unfaithfulness to God and unfaithfulness in the marriage relationship are both sinful. FORNICATION is the translation of the Greek *porneia* from which we get the word "pornography."

It wasn't easy for the church in the first century to maintain the standard of moral purity because there was no strong voice against immorality outside of the church. Furthermore, immorality was a part of pagan worship. Tragically, there were even those who claimed to be Christians who tolerated immorality. No wonder that such sin is so frequently mentioned in the New Testament. In an immoral world Christianity holds high the standard of purity.

The Lord is patient, "not wishing that any should perish, but that all should come to repentance" 2 Peter 3:9. But, Jezebel refused to repent. She had been warned. Judgment, therefore, was inevitable.

2:22 BEHOLD, I CAST HER INTO A BED, AND THEM THAT COMMIT ADULTERY WITH HER INTO GREAT TRIBULATION, EXCEPT THEY REPENT OF HER WORKS.

BEHOLD means "look here." The Lord is calling attention to His disciplinary action. Evil workers are to be exposed for what they really are. I CAST HER INTO A BED. Since the Lord would not cast her into a bed of prostitution as she had done on her own accord, this bed is probably a reference to the diseases that are associated with adultery and here is to be regarded as a bed of sickness which serves as a punishment of her sin.

Those who participated with her in sin will suffer GREAT

31

TRIBULATION, EXCEPT THEY REPENT OF HER WORKS.
Time yet remains for these to repent, but the time for repentance
is past for the woman. The severe suffering that awaits those who
refused to repent of their adulterous activities would probably be
in line with the nature of the evil committed.

2:23   AND I WILL KILL HER CHILDREN WITH DEATH;
       AND ALL THE CHURCHES SHALL KNOW THAT I AM
       HE THAT SEARCHETH THE REINS AND HEARTS:
       AND I WILL GIVE UNTO EACH ONE OF YOU ACCOR-
       DING TO YOUR WORKS.

It is not clear whether the word CHILDREN is to be understood literally or figuratively. If these are literally her CHILD-
REN death may be viewed as a blessing in light of the hideous
and sinful life of the mother. These may be regarded the offspring
of adultery. It is more likely, however, that the word CHILDREN
describes those who share the traits and temperament of Jezebel
as children do of their mother. Though people may suffer the consequences of others' sins, comdemnation and guilt comes only as a
result of one's own sin. Long ago Jeremiah prophesied "In those
days they shall say no more, The fathers have eaten sour grapes,
and the children's teeth are set on edge. But every one shall die
for his own iniquity: every man that eateth the sour grapes, his
teeth shall be set on edge" Jeremiah 31:29,30.

The purpose of this punishment is that ALL THE CHUR-
CHES may KNOW THAT I AM HE THAT SEARCHETH THE
REINS AND HEARTS. THE CHURCHES SHALL KNOW by
observation the work of God. The word REINS (kidneys) is used
to designate the seat of man's emotions. HEARTS, in this instance, speaks of man's will and intellect. This is a typical Jewish
use of these terms. The Greeks, on the other hand, spoke of the
heart as the seat of man's emotions and the mind as the seat of
the will and thought. When mind and heart or HEART and
REINS are used together they speak of the total person — man's
thoughts, feelings and will.

I WILL GIVE UNTO EACH ONE OF YOU ACCORDING TO
YOUR WORKS. "Be not deceived; God is not mocked: for whatsoever a man soweth, that shall he also reap. For he that soweth
unto his own flesh shall of the flesh reap corruption; but he that

soweth unto the Spirit shall of the Spirit reap eternal life" Galatians 6:7,8.

2:24   BUT TO YOU I SAY, TO THE REST THAT ARE IN THYATIRA, AS MANY AS HAVE NOT THIS TEACHING, WHO KNOW NOT THE DEEP THINGS OF SATAN, AS THEY ARE WONT TO SAY: I CAST UPON YOU NONE OTHER BURDEN.

There is no indication as to the number of people included in THE REST, except that they are referred to as MANY. To KNOW NOT THE DEEP THINGS OF SATAN means there is not the knowledge that comes through experience. There was no awareness of Satan's works that lay beneath the surface. DEEP THINGS refer to that which is mysterious or hidden from those not properly trained or educated. It is also an expression that explains the fulness of God's revelation. "But unto us God revealed them through the Spirit: for the Spirit searcheth all things, yea, the deep things of God" 1 Corinthians 2:10.

The Lord assures the faithful in Thyatira that they will not be further burdened. Sometimes the burdened live in fear of additional burdens but there was no need for such a fear in this case.

2:25   NEVERTHELESS THAT WHICH YE HAVE, HOLD FAST TILL I COME.

The coming of the Lord is always the Christian's blessed hope. "For our light affliction, which is for the moment, worketh for us more and more exceedingly an eternal weight of glory; while we look not at the things which are seen, but at the things which are not seen: for the things which are seen are temporal; but the things which are not seen are eternal" 2 Corinthians 4:17,18.

THAT WHICH YE HAVE refers to their faith and to their purity from the defilement of Jezebel's teaching.

2:26   AND HE THAT OVERCOMETH, AND HE THAT KEEPETH MY WORKS UNTO THE END, TO HIM WILL I GIVE AUTHORITY OVER THE NATIONS:

"Let the saints exult in glory: Let them sing for joy upon their beds. Let the high praises of God be in their mouth, And a two-edged sword in their hand; To execute vengeance upon the nations, And their nobles with fetters of iron; To execute upon

33

them the judgment written: This honor have all his saints. Praise ye Jehovah" Psalm 149:5-9. "If we endure, we shall also reign with him" 2 Timothy 2:12.

OVERCOMETH and KEEPETH both speak of continuing action. AUTHORITY means the right to exercise power. The saints of God will share with Christ in the ultimate victory over Satan.

2:27   AND HE SHALL RULE THEM WITH A ROD OF IRON, AS THE VESSELS OF THE POTTER ARE BROKEN TO SHIVERS: AS I ALSO HAVE RECEIVED OF MY FATHER:

The Messianic rule is pictured as both firm and loving with the reference to the shepherd's iron-tipped staff: RULE THEM WITH A ROD OF IRON. RULE is the translation of the Greek *poimanei*, meaning "shepherd." A ROD may also be understood as a staff or a sceptre. The language of this verse is taken from the second Psalm. "I will tell of the decree: Jehovah said unto me, Thou art my son; This day have I begotten thee. Ask of me, and I will give thee the nations for thine inheritance, And the uttermost parts of the earth for thy possession. Thou shalt break them with a rod of iron; Thou shalt dash them in pieces like a potter's vessel" Psalm 2:7-9. The total destruction of world powers is illustrated in the second chapter of Daniel. The ROD OF IRON may be understood as an iron-tipped staff. BROKEN TO SHIVERS suggests complete victory. Christians share in this victory.

2:28   AND I WILL GIVE HIM THE MORNING STAR.

In Revelation 22:16 we are informed that Jesus is THE MORNING STAR. The glory and splendor of heavenly royalty will be the Christian's to enjoy. This is a further indication of victory. THE MORNING STAR is a sign of dawn. In Christ the Christian begins a new day at the time of his conversion and at the time when the history of this world is consummated and eternity begins.

2:29   HE THAT HATH AN EAR, LET HIM HEAR WHAT THE SPIRIT SAITH TO THE CHURCHES. See comments on 2:7.

3:1   AND TO THE ANGEL OF THE CHURCH IN SARDIS WRITE: THESE THINGS SAITH HE THAT HATH THE

SEVEN SPIRITS OF GOD, AND THE SEVEN STARS: I
KNOW THY WORKS, THAT THOU HAST A NAME
THAT THOU LIVEST, AND THOU ART DEAD.

SARDIS was located thirty miles southeast of Thyatira. The
city was known for its wealth. To a people of possessions the Lord
speaks of His own possessions: HE THAT HATH THE SEVEN
SPIRITS OF GOD, AND THE SEVEN STARS. Wealth tends to
give one a feeling of independence. Man, however, is always
dependent upon God. It is also important that the Christian never
fails to appreciate the lordship of Christ in his life.

Apparently the CHURCH IN SARDIS had "a form of godliness" but "denied the power thereof" 2 Timothy 3:5. They were
nominally Christians but failed to function as such. The paradox
of being alive and dead at the same time is illustrated in 1
Timothy 5:6 "But she that giveth herself to pleasure is dead while
she liveth." DEAD describes life outside the will of God. "We
were dead through our trespasses" Ephesians 2:5. Death is
separation. Physical death is the separation of the spirit and soul
from the body. Spiritual death is man's separation from God.

SEVEN SPIRITS symbolically represent the Holy Spirit.
THE SEVEN STARS were explained in the first chapter (vs. 20)
to be the angels of the churches. I KNOW is the fullness of knowledge (oida). Regardless of her appearance the Lord knew the
DEAD condition of this church.

3:2   BE THOU WATCHFUL, AND ESTABLISH THE
      THINGS THAT REMAIN, WHICH WERE READY TO
      DIE: FOR I HAVE FOUND NO WORKS OF THINE PER-
      FECTED BEFORE MY GOD.

BE THOU WATCHFUL should have had special meaning to
those living in Sardis if they were aware of their own history.
Twice there had been an effort to attack the city that proved
successful because one side of the city was left unguarded. That
side was at the top of a cliff and thus seemed to need no guard.
Nevertheless, during the time of Cyrus of Persia and later in 214
B.C. the city suffered the consequences from an enemy attack for
not being watchful all around the city. "Wherefore let him that
thinketh he standeth take heed lest he fall" 1 Corinthians 10:12.
"Watch ye, stand fast in the faith, quit you like men, be strong" 1

Corinthians 16:13. "Be sober, be watchful: your adversary the devil, as a roaring lion, walketh about, seeking whom he may devour" 1 Peter 5:8.

ESTABLISH THE THINGS THAT REMAIN. They were to make strong all signs of life that remained. PERFECTED is to be understood as accomplished and fulfilled. This suggests a falling short of God's ideal and a failure to complete what they started in their Christian living and service. BEFORE MY GOD indicates that God is the one who determines the value of our WORKS. The church in Sardis was content with mediocrity.

3:3 REMEMBER THEREFORE HOW THOU HAST RE-CEIVED AND DIDST HEAR; AND KEEP IT AND RE-PENT. IF THEREFORE THOU SHALT NOT WATCH, I WILL COME AS A THIEF, AND THOU SHALT NOT KNOW WHAT HOUR I WILL COME UPON THEE.

Remembering what we have heard and know in Christ is vital to Christian life and growth. Memory must be fed by continual use. It has been correctly stated that what you use you keep and what you fail to use you lose. The Christian needs both to hear and tell the good news over and over again. REMEMBER literally means to keep on remembering. Perseverance is a necessity in the Christian life. Obedience and application of Christian truth is to be regarded as a continuing experience. REPENT calls for positive action. It means making a right decision. A Christian does not really live in the state of indecision, for a failure to make a right decision is to have already made a wrong decision. "No man can serve two masters" Matthew 6:24.

The fact that the Lord WILL COME AS A THIEF to those who do NOT WATCH suggests surprise and perhaps a failure to even realize that He came. This may speak of the Lord coming in judgment upon those who have not repented. Such a coming will occur without any awareness. Understanding this meaning of the text should not be confused with the second coming of Christ when all men will certainly be aware of what has happened though many will be surprised. AS A THIEF is an expression used frequently to denote unexpectedness. See Matthew 24:43; 1 Thessalonians 5:2 and 2 Peter 3:10.

WHAT HOUR I WILL COME UPON THEE in judgment is

the thought expressed. The Lord visits judgment upon the church in many different ways. Sardis is warned that this time of judgment may come soon and certainly unexpectedly.

3:4 BUT THOU HAST A FEW NAMES IN SARDIS THAT DID NOT DEFILE THEIR GARMENTS: AND THEY SHALL WALK WITH ME IN WHITE; FOR THEY ARE WORTHY.

A FEW NAMES refers to those who remained faithful to God. Since the woolen trade was strong in this place it is likely that these people were conscious of clothes, thus the reference to GARMENTS. The garment of the Christian would be a reference to his character and deeds. The pagan society at that time would not think of entering a temple if their clothes were soiled. The emphasis of Christianity is not so much upon the cleanliness of the clothes as it is upon the cleanliness of the life. "Pure religion and undefiled before our God and Father is this, to visit the fatherless and widows in their affliction, and to keep oneself unspotted from the world" James 1:27.

WHITE speaks of robes of righteousness and purity. While others engage in sinful practices there were those faithful few who remained "pure in heart" Matthew 5:8. THEY ARE WORTHY not because of their own righteousness but because of their faith in God. "As it is written, There is none righteous, no, not one" Romans 3:10. "For by grace have ye been saved through faith; and that not of yourselves, it is the gift of God; not of works, that no man should glory" Ephesians 2:8,9.

THEY SHALL WALK WITH ME. This means that their activities and life shall be in harmony with the will of God.

3:5 HE THAT OVERCOMETH SHALL THUS BE ARRAYED IN WHITE GARMENTS; AND I WILL IN NO WISE BLOT HIS NAME OUT OF THE BOOK OF LIFE, AND I WILL CONFESS HIS NAME BEFORE MY FATHER, AND BEFORE HIS ANGELS.

The promise and assurance of the Lord as stated in this verse provides a strong encouragement for the overcomers to continue to live a victorious, conquering life in Christ.

WHITE GARMENTS speak of purity, holiness and righteousness. THE BOOK OF LIFE is God's record book in which there are no mistakes. The fact that the Lord says I WILL IN NO WISE BLOT HIS NAME OUT does not mean that a person once saved can never be lost. This promise is given only to the over-comer who continues as an overcomer. Faithfulness unto death is a continual challenge to the Christian. The Christian's relation-ship with God can never be taken for granted. "Wherefore let him that thinketh he standeth take heed lest he fall" 1 Corinthians 10:12. I WILL CONFESS HIS NAME BEFORE MY FATHER should be understood in light of Matthew 10:32,33 "Every one therefore who shall confess me before men, him will I also confess before my Father who is in heaven. But whosoever shall deny me before men, him will I also deny before my Father who is in heaven."

The threefold promise made to the overcomers offers hope to this church and provides assurance for the life to come.

3:6   HE THAT HATH AN EAR, LET HIM HEAR WHAT THE SPIRIT SAITH TO THE CHURCHES.

See comments on 2:7.

3:7   AND TO THE ANGEL OF THE CHURCH IN PHILA-DELPHIA WRITE: THESE THINGS SAITH HE THAT IS HOLY, HE THAT IS TRUE, HE THAT HATH THE KEY OF DAVID, HE THAT OPENETH AND NONE SHALL SHUT, AND THAT SHUTTETH AND NONE OPENETH:

THE CHURCH IN PHILADELPHIA received no rebuke. In this regard there is a similarity of this letter and the letter sent to the church in Smyrna. Philadelphia was located in a fertile area where three countries met—Phrygia, Mysia and Lycia. Earth-quakes and tremors were a frequent occurrence in this location which may help in understanding verse twelve.

HOLY means that the Lord is different in a good sense. The Lord is different in that He is without sin and that in Him the will : of God is perfected. When Christians are called upon to be HOLY they are called upon to separate themselves from sin and be con-secrated unto God.

TRUE is to be understood as real and genuine. Jesus is who He claims to be. His word is absolutely to be trusted. He correctly said, "he that hath seen me hath seen the Father" John 14:9.

THE KEY OF DAVID is an expression taken from Isaiah 22:22. It conveys the thought of authority. Jesus said, "All authority hath been given unto me in heaven and on earth"- Matthew 28:18. With this authority the Lord can open and shut doors. "Jesus saith...I am the way, and the truth, and the life: no one cometh unto the Father, but by me" John 14:6. While it is true that the Lord has the authority to open and close the door to the kingdom of God it is also true that the Lord opens doors of opportunity for service. The next verse supplies an example of a door of opportunity.

3:8   I KNOW THY WORKS (BEHOLD, I HAVE SET BEFORE THEE A DOOR OPENED, WHICH NONE CAN SHUT), THAT THOU HAST A LITTLE POWER, AND DIDST KEEP MY WORD, AND DIDST NOT DENY MY NAME.

In light of the identification the Lord gives Himself in the previous verse it is particularly significant for Him to speak of having the fullness of knowledge of their WORKS. The DOOR OPENED is most likely a door of opportunity to witness for Christ. This understanding is in harmony with the use given this expression in 1 Corinthians 16:9, 2 Corinthians 2:12, Colossians 4:3 and Acts 14:27. The Lord honors service with opportunities for additional service. It was His knowledge of their WORKS that resulted in His opening A DOOR. Furthermore, it is significant that what God opens NONE CAN SHUT. An example of an attempt to close a door which God opened is the inability of the Sanhedrin to stop the witness of Peter and John. Read Acts 4:13-22.

The honesty of the Lord shows through such a statement as THOU HAST A LITTLE POWER. There was no superficial flattery in suggesting they had great power, when in reality it was not great. LITTLE may refer to quantity meaning that there were only a few Christians in the congregation. This is more in keeping with the parenthetical expression than to suggest that it means weakness in the area of faith.

Keeping the Lord's WORD is an indication of obedience. The conclusion of the Sermon on the Mount illustrates the wisdom of obedience. The Psalmist wrote, "Thy word have I laid up in my heart, That I might not sin against thee" Psalm 119:11. Read

James 1:22. When the WORD is in the heart the NAME is on the tongue. Confessing Christ is the meaning of DIDST NOT DENY MY NAME. The name of Christ can be denied by cowardly silence or by word. "If a man suffer as a Christian, let him not be ashamed; but let him glorify God in this name" 1 Peter 4:16.

3:9   BEHOLD, I GIVE OF THE SYNAGOGUE OF SATAN, OF THEM THAT SAY THEY ARE JEWS, AND THEY ARE NOT, BUT DO LIE; BEHOLD, I WILL MAKE THEM TO COME AND WORSHIP BEFORE THY FEET, AND TO KNOW THAT I HAVE LOVED THEE.

See comments on 2:9.

Those who were Jews nationally claimed to be Jews religiously. Jesus was speaking to Jews when He said, "Ye are of your father the devil, and the lusts of your father it is your will to do. He was a murderer from the beginning, and standeth not in the truth, because there is no truth in him. When he speaketh a lie, he speaketh of his own: for he is a liar, and the father thereof" John 8:44. "For they are not all Israel that are of Israel: neither, because they are Abraham's seed, are they all children: but, In Isaac shall thy seed be called. That is, it is not the children of the flesh that are children of God; but the children of the promise are reckoned for a seed" Romans 9:6-8. "And if ye are Christ's then are ye Abraham's seed, heirs according to the promise" Galatians 3:29. Recall the encounter John the Baptist had with the Jewish leaders. "But when he saw many of the Pharisees and Sadducees coming to his baptism, he said unto them, Ye offspring of vipers, who warned you to flee from the wrath to come? Bring forth therefore fruit worthy of repentance: and think not to say within yourselves, We have Abraham to our father: for I say unto you, that God is able of these stones to raise up children unto Abraham" Matthew 3:7-9. Be aware that God's Jew in the twentieth century is the Christian. Do not confuse the Old Covenant Jew with the New Covenant Jew. Under the New Covenant it is spiritual birth, not physical birth, that brings you into the family of God.

Those who DO LIE will be made to see their own lie and the love relationship the Lord enjoys with His people. "Wherefore also God highly exalted him, and gave unto him the name which is above every name; that in the name of Jesus every knee should bow, of things in heaven and things on earth and things under the earth, and that every tongue should confess that Jesus Christ is Lord, to the glory of God the Father" Philippians 2:9-11. "Wherefore, my beloved brethren, be ye stedfast, unmovable, always abounding in the work of the Lord, forasmuch as ye know that your labor is not vain in the Lord" 1 Corinthians 15:58.

3:10   BECAUSE THOU DIDST KEEP THE WORD OF MY PA-
TIENCE, I ALSO WILL KEEP THEE FROM THE HOUR
OF TRIAL, THAT HOUR WHICH IS TO COME UPON
THE WHOLE WORLD, TO TRY THEM THAT DWELL
UPON THE EARTH.

There is reward for faithfulness. MY PATIENCE refers to the PATIENCE of Christ. THE WORD OF MY PATIENCE is the WORD that is understood and appreciated in light of the Lord's PATIENCE. That Jesus was patient is clear in the WORD. "Let us run with patience the race that is set before us, looking unto Jesus the author and perfector of our faith, who for the joy that was set before him endured the cross, despising the shame, and hath sat down at the right hand of the throne of God" Hebrews 12:1,2. Endurance is patience. Christ is our example in stedfast endurance.

I ALSO WILL KEEP THEE FROM THE HOUR OF TRIAL does not necessarily mean that they would face no trial but that the grace of God would supply the needed strength to assure conquest. God's grace did not prevent Daniel from being cast into the den of lions, but it did prevent the lions from harming him. Christians will not escape temptation. "There hath no temptation taken you but such as man can bear: but God is faithful, who will not suffer you to be tempted above that ye are able; but will with the temptation make also the way of escape, that ye may be able to endure it" 1 Corinthians 10:13.

THE HOUR WHICH IS TO COME UPON THE WHOLE WORLD is a reference to persecution and temptation that knows no geographic boundaries. This means that in every period of history the church may expect opposition. Jesus said, "If they persecuted me, they will also persecute you" John 15:20. "And ye shall be hated of all men for my name's sake: but he that endureth to the end, the same shall be saved" Matthew 10:22.

God uses the very efforts of Satan to work toward His own purpose as is illustrated in the phrase TO TRY THEM THAT DWELL UPON THE EARTH. "Count it all joy, my brethren, when ye fall into manifold temptations; knowing that the proving of your faith worketh patience" James 1:2,3. The testing that proves the faith of the saints will manifest the sinfulness of the heathen.

3:11   I COME QUICKLY: HOLD FAST THAT WHICH THOU HAST, THAT NO ONE TAKE THY CROWN.

The assurance of the Lord's coming is comforting to the Christian, particularly in the hour of trial. It is an encouragement to HOLD FAST THAT WHICH THOU HAST, THAT NO ONE TAKE THY CROWN. This is not a crown of royalty but one of victory. Thus, the holding FAST is not to prevent loss from theft but rather loss from failure to continue steadfast in the faith. When one wins a race the only way he can continue to enjoy the honor of being a winner is to win again and again, as often as a race is scheduled. In the sense of continuous obedience and allegiance to Christ the Christian is to HOLD FAST. CROWN symbolizes the Lord's reward for faithfulness.

3:12   HE THAT OVERCOMETH, I WILL MAKE HIM A PILLAR IN THE TEMPLE OF MY GOD, AND HE SHALL GO OUT THENCE NO MORE: AND I WILL WRITE UPON HIM THE NAME OF MY GOD, AND THE NAME OF THE CITY OF MY GOD, THE NEW JERUSALEM, WHICH COMETH DOWN OUT OF HEAVEN FROM MY GOD, AND MINE OWN NEW NAME.

PILLAR symbolizes strength. James, Cephas and John were called pillars in the church. This means that they were strong members of the church. To be made A PILLAR IN THE TEMPLE suggests a place of importance in God's will. The security the overcomer enjoys in the Lord is further illustrated with the phrase HE SHALL GO OUT THENCE NO MORE. Because of the earthquakes and tremors in Philadelphia it was often necessary to evacuate buildings and the city for safety. No such evacuation will ever be necessary for those in God's TEMPLE.

NAME speaks of identification. The Christian is clearly identified as belonging to the Lord and as a part of the community of the saved. NAME also speaks of character and thus THE NAME OF MY GOD suggests godliness and holiness. Read Revelation 19:11,13,16.

3:13 HE THAT HATH AN EAR, LET HIM HEAR WHAT THE SPIRIT SAITH TO THE CHURCHES.

See comments on 2:7.

3:14 AND TO THE ANGEL OF THE CHURCH IN LAODICEA WRITE: THESE THINGS SAITH THE AMEN, THE FAITHFUL AND TRUE WITNESS, THE BEGINNING OF THE CREATION OF GOD:

LAODICEA was located near Colossae and thus explains the reference in Colossians 2:1 "For I would have you know how greatly I strive for you, and for them at Laodicea." LAODICEA was located about forty miles east of Ephesus and nearly the same distance southeast of Philadelphia. Money, manufacturing and medicine characterized this community and are factors to consider in examining the contents of this letter.

For the Lord to identify Himself as the AMEN is to affirm with special emphasis the verity of His words. This is a guarantee of accuracy and reliability. THE FAITHFUL AND TRUE WITNESS is to be listened to carefully because of the genuineness and trustworthiness of the witness. In every sense of the term Jesus qualified as a WITNESS for He was one with God. THE BEGINNING OF THE CREATION OF GOD does not mean Jesus was the first creature. Jesus is the image of the invisible God, the firstborn of all creation; for in him were all things created, in the heavens and upon the earth, things visible and things invisible, whether thrones or dominions or principalities or powers; all things have been created through him, and unto him; and he is before all things, and in him all things consist. And he is the head of the body, the church: who is the beginning, the firstborn from the dead; that in all things he might have the pre-eminence" Colossians 1:15-18. "All things were made through him; and without him was not anything made that hath been made" John 1:3. Jesus is the source of all that exists.

3:15 I KNOW THY WORKS, THAT THOU ART NEITHER COLD NOT HOT: I WOULD THOU WERT COLD OR

HOT.

3:16 SO BECAUSE THOU ART LUKEWARM, AND NEITHER HOT NOR COLD, I WILL SPEW THEE OUT OF MY MOUTH.

The Lord describes a condition in the church that makes Him sick. The emphasis is upon LUKEWARM, likened unto nausea which results from swallowing that which upsets the stomach. SPEW means "vomit." I WOULD THOU WERT COLD OR HOT does not suggest that the Lord actually prefers one to be spiritually dead (COLD) so much as it adds weight to His strong distaste of the LUKEWARM state. In these two verses we should apply the principle that is important in understanding the meaning of a parable. To try to make every detail mean something in a parable sometimes confuses the primary lesson. Likewise, too much emphasis upon the COLD or inactive and the HOT or zealous as more desirable may result in lessening the impact the Lord intends to leave with the word LUKEWARM. Lukewarmness is an attempt at the impossible. "No man can serve two masters: for either he will hate the one, and love the other; or else he will hold to one, and despise the other. Ye cannot serve God and mammon" Matthew 6:24. The warm mineral water that flowed from the springs nearby aided the Laodiceans in their understanding of this portion of the letter. Hypocrisy and insincerity describe the Laodiceans.

3:17 BECAUSE THOU SAYEST, I AM RICH, AND HAVE GOTTEN RICHES, AND HAVE NEED OF NOTHING; AND KNOWEST NOT THAT THOU ART THE WRETCHED ONE AND MISERABLE AND POOR AND BLIND AND NAKED:

This verse explains the meaning of lukewarmness as it applied to the church in Laodicea. Their words were a meaningless boast. They were so totally wrong in their own self-assessment that the very opposite of what they said was the true picture. They were like the Pharisee who "prayed thus with himself, God, I thank thee, that I am not as the rest of men" Luke 18:11. Of such men Jesus said, "Ye are they that justify yourselves in the sight of men; but God knoweth your hearts: for that which is exalted among men is an abomination in the sight of God" Luke 16:15.

Material riches are deceitful. See Mark 4:19. "Every one that is proud in heart is an abomination to Jehovah" Proverbs 16:5.

AND KNOWEST NOT THAT THOU ART THE WRETCH-ED ONE AND MISERABLE AND POOR AND BLIND AND NAKED. Man only knows himself when he sees himself in God's light. "There is a way which seemeth right unto a man, But the end thereof are the ways of death" Proverbs 16:25. It was the result of seeing the Lord that prompted Isaiah to say, "Woe is me! for I am undone; because I am a man of unclean lips, and I dwell in the midst of a people of unclean lips: for mine eyes have seen the King, Jehovah of hosts" Isaiah 6:5. Five words describe the same situation as if it said that they had one problem that can be explained five different ways. WRETCHED is the same word Paul used to describe himself while in the clutches of the body of death. See Romans 7:24. It was their nauseating sin that con-demned them and placed them in the category of the WRETCH-ED. MISERABLE means "to be pitied." It describes a condition that calls for mercy. POOR suggests a beggarly situation. BLIND is used here metaphorically to describe a person who is ignorant because he does not see the true picture. They were NAKED in that there was nothing to cover their shame and sin. Five words combine to paint a tragic picture of sin.

3:18   I COUNSEL THEE TO BUY OF ME GOLD REFINED BY FIRE, THAT THOU MAYEST BECOME RICH; AND WHITE GARMENTS, THAT THOU MAYEST CLOTHE THYSELF, AND THAT THE SHAME OF THY NAKED-NESS BE NOT MADE MANIFEST; AND EYESALVE TO ANOINT THINE EYES, THAT THOU MAYEST SEE.

I COUNSEL THEE is the Lord's approach as a friend advis-ing those whom he loves. Only God has the commodity they need, thus the advise TO BUY OF ME. There will be no purchasing, however, until the need for the purchase is realized. "Ho, every one that thirsteth, come ye to the waters, and he that hath no money; come ye, buy, and eat; yea, come, buy wine and milk with-out money and without price" Isaiah 55:1.

Three items are needed: GOLD, WHITE GARMENTS, and EYESALVE. Just as the five words describing their condition are to be understood as depicting one state so these three words portray three aspects of their one basic need. GOLD is symbolic of true riches, spiritual values. Peter illustrates this by speaking of "faith being more precious than gold that perisheth" 1 Peter 1:7. WHITE GARMENTS symbolize purity and righteousness. "I will greatly rejoice in Jehovah, my soul shall be joyful in my God; for he hath clothed me with garments of salvation, he hath covered me with the robe of righteousness, as a bridegroom decketh himself with a garland, and as a bride adorneth herself with her jewels" Isaiah 61:10. EYESALVE may be seen as the Holy Spirit working through the word to illuminate our understanding. "Thy word is a lamp unto my feet, And light unto my path" Psalm 119:105.

3:19   AS MANY AS I LOVE, I REPROVE AND CHASTEN: BE ZEALOUS THEREFORE, AND REPENT.

True LOVE expresses itself in discipline. "For whom the Lord loveth he chasteneth, And scourgeth every son whom he receiveth" Hebrews 12:6. REPROVE means to expose the wrong in such a way that the one being disciplined will understand why. A good example of this is the manner in which Nathan exposed the sin of David. It is bringing a person to an awareness of his own sin for the purpose of evoking repentance. CHASTEN involves teaching such as the instruction a parent gives to the child. Discipline may involve punishment but it always includes instruction, otherwise it is not discipline.

BE ZEALOUS means to be enthusiastic. The Christian witness is to be alive and fervent. REPENT is in a verb tense that means to do it now. Stop being lukewarm. Start being ZEALOUS. THEREFORE is a word that is always understood in light of that which has previously been said or done. In this case the Lord expected a change to take place as a result of His discipline.

3:20   BEHOLD, I STAND AT THE DOOR AND KNOCK: IF ANY MAN HEAR MY VOICE AND OPEN THE DOOR, I WILL COME IN TO HIM, AND WILL SUP WITH HIM, AND HE WITH ME.

BEHOLD is a word intended to get attention, as if to say, look here! Throughout scripture God is presented as the one who takes the initiative. It is a privilege for man to be able to come to God, but it is grace that causes God to search for man. I STAND

AT THE DOOR AND KNOCK. It is almost beyond comprehension to appreciate fully the King of kings continually knocking at the door of the wretched sinner, seeking entrance into his life, yet this is the picture of these words. He not only knocks once, but again and again, and then waits for a response. This is patience. This is grace.

IF ANY MAN HEAR MY VOICE AND OPEN THE DOOR indicates the responsibility of man to respond and the fact that God does not force Himself upon man against his own will. Among some people it is a custom to call out for the person at the same time you are knocking at their door. The voice identifies the knocker before the door is opened.

The Greek word translated SUP refers to the evening meal which was the principal meal of the day. Involved in the dining together is the idea of fellowship which was more apt to take place in the evening when the family ate together without any pressures to cause them to hurry through the meal as work might do in the morning and at noon. To receive Christ into our lives is to be in fellowship with Him. This fellowship is intended to last forever.

3:21   HE THAT OVERCOMETH, I WILL GIVE TO HIM TO SIT DOWN WITH ME IN MY THRONE, AS I ALSO OVERCAME, AND SAT DOWN WITH MY FATHER IN HIS THRONE.

"The Spirit himself beareth witness with our spirit, that we are children of God: and if children, then heirs; heirs of God, and jointheirs with Christ; if so be that we suffer with him, that we may be also glorified with him" Romans 8:16, 17.

The highest position of honor is promised to the overcomer. The overcomer is the one who has shared in the conflict against sin with Christ and will also share in His exaltation and triumphant reign. "If we endure, we shall also reign with him:..." 2 Timothy 2:12.

3:22   HE THAT HATH AN EAR, LET HIM HEAR WHAT THE SPIRIT SAITH TO THE CHURCHES.

See comments on 2:7.

Every member of every congregation throughout church history needs to consider each of the seven letters carefully as if it were personally addressed to each Christian. The letter is understood by each Christian in so far as he understands each letter historically. The conclusion of each letter in chapters two and three makes it clear that the Lord intended the individuals as well as the congregations in Asia Minor to hear and heed. The Lord intends that all Christendom continue to hear and heed.

Chapter three concludes the important historical background material so vital in the understanding of the apocalyptic section which follows in chapter four. It will be very important to keep in mind the characteristics of apocalyptic literature in the study of the remainder of Revelation.

GOD IS IN CONTROL

CHAPTERS FOUR AND FIVE

4:1   AFTER THESE THINGS I SAW, AND BEHOLD, A
DOOR OPENED IN HEAVEN, AND THE FIRST VOICE
THAT I HEARD, A VOICE AS OF A TRUMPET SPEAK-
ING WITH ME, ONE SAYING, COME UP HITHER, AND
I WILL SHOW THEE THE THINGS WHICH MUST
COME TO PASS HEREAFTER.

AFTER THESE THINGS designates the sequence in which
John received the visions. It is not necessary to think in terms of
time lapse. THESE THINGS are understood in light of the contents of the first three chapters.

I SAW speaks of the vision recorded in this chapter.
BEHOLD suggests that he would like for the reader to see what
he saw, thus he presents this word picture.

We must be very careful to understand that the words of this
book are presented in the form of a drama. Visions and symbols
are used repeatedly. The contents of Revelation should be
studied in light of the historical background. Do not expect that
what is recorded is written in chronological order or that it is an
announcement of future events. It is a portrayal of the continuing
conflict of the ages between God and Satan in which all men are
involved. The visions of this book portray scenes that may occur
over and over throughout history. An effort to understand each
vision through the eyes of those who lived at the end of the first
century will be the best aid for our proper application of these
truths in the twentieth century. The conflict of the ages is portrayed with the final outcome being assured as defeat for Satan
and victory for God.

Heaven does not have a door like the door to a building. A
DOOR OPENED conveys the thought of access and availability.
HEAVEN is seen because the entrance way is open for view.
When John saw the open door he heard A VOICE AS OF A

TRUMPET SPEAKING. The voice was strong, clear and distinct like a trumpet. The VOICE gave John an invitation to COME UP HITHER. For John to be translated into heaven in this vision will give him a different perspective. It is important that man view history and understand events as God views and understands them. This is particularly important when the events of history are distressing to man. How differently the friends of Job might have advised him if they had seen the situation as God saw it. Habakkuk did not understand why God was permitting certain things to happen in his day. John's heavenly perspective would be especially important to the persecuted Christians of his day. This same perspective is important for us all.

I WILL SHOW THEE speaks of the vision John is about to receive. THE THINGS WHICH MUST COME TO PASS HERE-AFTER are the things that definitely will take place in history. HEREAFTER does not tell us anything about the timing except that it will happen sometime after that point in history when John received this vision. The way HEREAFTER has been inter-preted accounts for some of the various explanations given on the contents of this book. MUST makes the coming TO PASS of these THINGS a certainty. It would be natural for those living in John's day to look for the fulfillment of these things. That which happens in history must be viewed in light of God's eternal plan and His control over all things.

4:2   STRAIGHTWAY I WAS IN THE SPIRIT: AND BEHOLD, THERE WAS A THRONE SET IN HEAVEN, AND ONE SITTING UPON THE THRONE;

STRAIGHTWAY indicates immediately, at once. The spiritual nature of John's experience in seeing this vision is ex-plained with the phrase I WAS IN THE SPIRIT. Paul once had a spiritual experience that he described to the Corinthians. "I will come to visions and revelations of the Lord. I know a man in Christ, fourteen years ago (whether in the body, I know not; or whether out of the body, I know not; God knoweth), such a one caught up even to the third heaven. And I know such a man (whether in the body, or apart from the body, I know not; God knoweth), how that he was caught up into Paradise, and heard unspeakable words, which it is not lawful for a man to utter" 2

Corinthians 12:1-4. God is Spirit. Truth, though spiritual, is here portrayed in symbolic language for our understanding. THRONE is a symbol for omnipotence, rule and dominion. God is the ONE SITTING UPON THE THRONE.

4:3 AND HE THAT SAT WAS TO LOOK UPON LIKE A JASPER STONE AND A SARDIUS: AND THERE WAS A RAINBOW ROUND ABOUT THE THRONE, LIKE AN EMERALD TO LOOK UPON.

The beauty of God's character and the loveliness of His attributes are symbolically described with precious gems. It has been suggested that the JASPER STONE symbolizes His holiness, glory and purity. The SARDIUS symbolizes His righteousness in judgment. The RAINBOW which was LIKE AN EMERALD TO LOOK UPON symbolizes hope and mercy. No form is given to God in this description which is appropriate when we remember God is Spirit. This verse pictures God's majesty and grace. This picture is intended to be awe-inspiring.

4:4 AND ROUND ABOUT THE THRONE WERE FOUR AND TWENTY THRONES: AND UPON THE THRONES I SAW FOUR AND TWENTY ELDERS SITTING, ARRAYED IN WHITE GARMENTS: AND ON THEIR HEADS CROWNS OF GOLD.

A variety of answers has been given to explain the FOUR AND TWENTY ELDERS. ELDERS is a translation of the Greek word meaning "older men." This word may be used with or without any reference to position. It is a term applied to people. The number twelve and multiples of this number are symbolic of the people of God. The significance of doubling the number twelve in this verse is explained by the intention of including both the people of God in the Old Testament era and the people of God in the Christian era. Twenty-four elders may be understood as a numerical way of including both Jew and Gentile in the picture of God's people. There are twenty-four courses of priests (1 Chronicles 24:1-10) but there does not appear to be any similarity here beyond the number and the fact of worship.

The FOUR AND TWENTY ELDERS are ARRAYED IN WHITE GARMENTS and are wearing CROWNS OF GOLD. The WHITE GARMENTS symbolize purity made possible by the blood of Jesus Christ. The CROWNS OF GOLD are crowns worn by victors. They are not royal crowns. GOLD symbolizes the value of victory in Christ. The WHITE GARMENTS worn by the twenty-four elders speak of being overcomers in the conflict of the ages. Following their earthly struggle they enjoy the blessings of triumph. "Thanks be to God, who giveth us the victory through our Lord Jesus Christ" 1 Corinthians 15:57.

At a time in the ministry of Jesus when the disciples were perplexed at His sayings and concluded that salvation was outside the realm of possibility Jesus said, "With men this is impossible; but with God all things are possible. Then answered Peter and said unto him, Lo, we have left all, and followed thee; what then shall we have? And Jesus said unto them, Verily I say unto you, that ye who have followed me, in the regeneration when the Son of man shall sit on the throne of his glory, ye also shall sit upon twelve thrones, judging the twelve tribes of Israel" Matthew 19:26-28. There may be a relationship of the thrones mentioned here and those in this verse.

4:5 AND OUT OF THE THRONE PROCEED LIGHTNINGS AND VOICES AND THUNDERS, AND THERE WERE SEVEN LAMPS OF FIRE BURNING BEFORE THE THRONE, WHICH ARE THE SEVEN SPIRITS OF GOD;

LIGHTNINGS AND VOICES AND THUNDERS symbolize Divine power, strength and judgment. God's presence is pictured in this language. When Moses was at Mt. Sinai to receive the Law "there were thunders and lightnings, and a thick cloud upon the mount, and the voice of a trumpet exceeding loud" Exodus 19:16. The Psalmist described God's majestic presence in similar language. "The voice of thy thunder was in the whirlwind; The lightnings lightened the world: The earth trembled and shook" Psalm 77:18.

THE SEVEN SPIRITS OF GOD symbolize the Holy Spirit. LAMPS give light. SEVEN is the perfect, sacred and complete number. The FIRE BURNING BEFORE THE THRONE symbolizes the revealing and illuminating aspect of the Spirit's work.

4:6 AND BEFORE THE THRONE, AS IT WERE A SEA OF GLASS LIKE UNTO CRYSTAL; AND IN THE MIDST OF THE THRONE, AND ROUND ABOUT THE THRONE,

FOUR LIVING CREATURES FULL OF EYES BEFORE AND BEHIND.

John sees something that resembles A SEA OF GLASS. It is not a sea. The GLASS and CRYSTAL suggest transparency. Thus, this may picture the holiness and righteousness of God in which is nothing to be hid for sin is totally absent. SEA may suggest the great expanse of holiness. It may also portray the separateness of God from His creatures.

Two explanations suggested for the FOUR LIVING CREATURES are that they represent nature or that they are cherubs. These two explanations may be harmonized. Angelic beings may be used here to represent nature. The imagery of the FOUR LIVING CREATURES is borrowed from Ezekiel. Read Ezekiel 1 and 10. The material world created by God is symbolized with the number FOUR. CREATURES may also be understood as beings or ones, but they are not beasts.

The many EYES speak of omniscience and vigilance.

The importance of the FOUR LIVING CREATURES is shown in their close proximity to THE THRONE and the nature of their service and praise.

4:7   AND THE FIRST CREATURE WAS LIKE A LION, AND THE SECOND CREATURE LIKE A CALF, AND THE THIRD CREATURE HAD A FACE AS OF A MAN, AND THE FOURTH CREATURE WAS LIKE A FLYING EAGLE.

Each creature is probably intended to symbolize a specific aspect of nature. The number four symbolizes the earth or nature. It is suggested that nature is pictured as including that which is strong, brave, intelligent and swift. Other words may describe nature as the characteristics of the LION, the CALF, A MAN, and A FLYING EAGLE are pondered.

In church history these four creatures have been used symbolically of Christ and His ministry; also of the four gospel records as depicting various aspects of Christ's life and work.

Nature is portrayed in God's presence as sharing in the fulfillment of the Divine will.

4:8   AND THE FOUR LIVING CREATURES, HAVING EACH ONE OF THEM SIX WINGS, ARE FULL OF

53

EYES ROUND ABOUT AND WITHIN: AND THEY HAVE NO REST DAY AND NIGHT, SAYING, HOLY, HOLY, HOLY, IS THE LORD GOD, THE ALMIGHTY, WHO WAS AND WHO IS AND WHO IS TO COME.

These words are borrowed from Isaiah 6. Isaiah "saw the Lord sitting upon a throne, high and lifted up; and his train filled the temple. Above him stood the seraphim: each one had six wings; with twain he covered his face, and with twain he covered his feet, and with twain he did fly. And one cried unto another, and said, Holy, holy, holy, is Jehovah of hosts: the whole earth is full of his glory" Isaiah 6:1-3. Nature is pictured as bringing continuous praise to God. This is observable at all times. There is never a time that God's creation is not speaking clearly to His glory. "The heavens declare the glory of God; And the firmament showeth his handiwork. Day unto day uttereth speech, And night unto night showeth knowledge" Psalm 19:1,2.

God is praised for His holiness, His great power and His eternality. HOLY speaks of the difference made when sin is absent. ALMIGHTY is an encouraging word to a people frustrated by the apparent power of wickedness. The omnipotence of God assures God's people of victory in the conflict against sin. ALMIGHTY is a very important word in the book of Revelation. Because God is ALMIGHTY His people can be overcomers and are. Overcoming is explained by God's omnipotence.

Three is God's number and may explain the triple use of the word HOLY. Rules of Greek grammar are broken to emphasize God's eternality with the expression WHO WAS AND WHO IS AND WHO IS TO COME.

4:9   AND WHEN THE LIVING CREATURES SHALL GIVE GLORY AND HONOR AND THANKS TO HIM THAT SITTETH ON THE THRONE, TO HIM THAT LIVETH FOR EVER AND EVER,

WHEN does not suggest any idea of infrequency, rather it conveys the idea of repetition. It also prepares us for the result in verse ten of the worship of the living creatures. God occupies the throne. Praise is expressed in the giving of GLORY AND HONOR AND THANKS.

4:10   THE FOUR AND TWENTY ELDERS SHALL FALL

DOWN BEFORE HIM THAT SITTETH ON THE THRONE, AND SHALL WORSHIP HIM THAT LIVETH FOR EVER AND EVER, AND SHALL CAST THEIR CROWNS BEFORE THE THRONE, SAYING,

It is only natural that the people of God should be prompted to give praise to God when they observe nature praising God. FALL DOWN BEFORE HIM is an expression of humility. CAST THEIR CROWNS BEFORE THE THRONE is an expression of submission. Both humility and submission are essential in true worship of God. In the past is has been a custom for a conquered king to surrender his crown to the conquering king. True Christian discipleship demands total surrender and devotion to the Lord. John sees a representation of God's people joining with all creation in praise and adoration of the eternal God.

4:11 WORTHY ART THOU, OUR LORD AND OUR GOD, TO RECEIVE THE GLORY AND THE HONOR AND THE POWER: FOR THOU DIDST CREATE ALL THINGS, AND BECAUSE OF THY WILL THEY WERE, AND WERE CREATED.

When Jesus cleansed the temple the Jews were disturbed and questioned His authority in doing so. They asked, "What sign showest thou unto us, seeing that thou doest these things? Jesus answered and said unto them, Destroy this temple, and in three days I will raise it up" John 2:18,19. The resurrection of Christ was His sign of authority. The reason given here for God's worthiness to RECEIVE GLORY AND THE HONOR AND THE POWER is the fact of creation and the fact that He is the Creator. Man will always be creature. God alone is Creator. Man may rebel against his being creature and strive to be God, as he has often done. This is sin. Truth is recognition that God alone is deserving of our praise and obedience by virtue of His creative power and will. BECAUSE OF THY WILL THEY WERE indicates purpose and plan. Rightly understood history is the record of God's purpose and plan being executed. The book of Revelation helps us to understand and appreciate this important truth.

God is on His throne. This is recognized and appreciated by nature and by His people. Only in this light are we in a position to evaluate properly our present state on earth.

5:1 AND I SAW IN THE RIGHT HAND OF HIM THAT SAT ON THE THRONE A BOOK WRITTEN WITHIN AND ON THE BACK, CLOSE SEALED WITH SEVEN SEALS.

In chapter four we were presented with a picture of God our Creator. In this chapter we will see Christ our Redeemer at the right hand of God. Chapters four and five should be studied and viewed together as an important unit in the entire book. Both chapters prepare the reader for the action which begins in chapter six.

AND I, John, SAW A BOOK, a scroll. There were no books, as we know them now, in John's day. The word BOOK is an anachronism. At that time writing was contained and preserved on scrolls made of papyrus. The scroll containing the book of Revelation would have been about fifteen feet in length.

WRITTEN WITHIN AND ON THE BACK may indicate that there was much to be written. Writing on both sides was sometimes a necessity because of the shortage of papyrus. The front side upon which writing was usually done was the *recto* side. The back side was the *verso* side. It was easier to write on the *recto* side because the strips used in making this writing material ran horizontally on this side.

The fact that the book was SEALED indicates secrecy of the contents and the preservation of this secrecy. There have always been certain facts God has kept secret. One well-known secret of God is the time of the Lord's return. "Of that day and hour knoweth no one, not even the angels of heaven, neither the Son, but the Father only" Matthew 24:36. Other secrets of God have been made known when the time was right. Paul wrote, "Unto me, who am less than the least of all saints, was this grace given, to preach unto the Gentiles the unsearchable riches of Christ; and to make all men see what is the dispensation of the mystery which for ages hath been hid in God who created all things" Ephesians 3:8,9. The breaking of these SEVEN SEALS reveals what prior to this time was a secret in the mind of God. SEVEN SEALS indicates that God is the One who has preserved this secret of the future. SEVEN is the divine and complete number.

The contents of the BOOK should be understood in light of the fact that John was called to heaven in order that he might see those things "which must come to pass hereafter" Revelation 4:1. The BOOK not only contains information but is itself a symbol of the execution of the events of history under the sovereignty of God. As the SEALS are broken John sees these events and records them at the direction of God for the benefit of all who will read and hear.

The BOOK is the possession of HIM THAT SAT ON THE THRONE. It was shown to John clearly as God held it in His RIGHT HAND. This BOOK has been given various designations by men, such as "the book of destiny" and "the decrees of God."

5:2   AND I SAW A STRONG ANGEL PROCLAIMING WITH A GREAT VOICE, WHO IS WORTHY TO OPEN THE BOOK, AND TO LOOSE THE SEALS THEREOF?

No identity is given to the ANGEL apart from that of strength. This limited identification enables us to recognize the STRONG ANGEL in 10:1 and 18:21. We accept the fact of the angel's strength without any reason given for this. Apparently, however, the strength enabled the angel to make the proclamation heard far and wide.

WHO IS WORTHY TO OPEN THE BOOK? The question is not a challenge for men to try. The question asks for one who is qualified. Who possesses the qualities and character that would enable him to stand before God and open the BOOK? There was a time in the ministry of Jesus when worthiness was a condition for action. Some scribes and Pharisees had brought a woman taken in adultery to Jesus for the purpose of testing Jesus. When they had stated the Mosaic penalty of stoning as the proper punishment Jesus replied, "He that is without sin among you, let him cast a stone at her" John 8:7. No one lifted up a stone. It was not because they were physically unable to lift and throw a stone. It was because they were not qualified. So they all left. The result of the challenge WHO IS WORTHY TO OPEN THE BOOK brings a similar response, for no man is without sin.

5:3   AND NO ONE IN THE HEAVEN, OR ON THE EARTH, OR UNDER THE EARTH, WAS ABLE TO OPEN THE BOOK, OR TO LOOK THEREON.

There was no angel, no man and no demon able to respond to the challenge. The entire universe is represented as failing to

57

qualify. Men who think themselves capable of living without God need to consider the truth of this chapter very carefully. Throughout the Old Testament era God gave man ample opportunity to solve his own problems either through the Jews with the Law of God or through the pagan Gentiles with their multiplicity of gods. Man without God is in a dilemma of sin into which he sinks deeper and deeper.

The inability TO OPEN THE BOOK, OR TO LOOK THEREON is the result of sin. In vain do men seek God apart from the Lord Jesus Christ. Read John 14:6. Only through revelation can man learn God's plan.

5:4   AND I WEPT MUCH, BECAUSE NO ONE WAS FOUND WORTHY TO OPEN THE BOOK, OR TO LOOK THEREON:

John expected to learn what was going to take place. With the challenge declined by all it appeared that his hopes had vanished and he began to cry. John WEPT MUCH. He was exceedingly disappointed. John's weeping is explained not merely by the lack of information but by the lack of execution of God's plan indicated in the closed book.

Tears are often unnecessary and are explained by our lack of patience and knowledge. John has not seen the challenge accepted yet. He jumped to a false conclusion. When he was made aware of the truth he then had no reason to continue weeping.

5:5   AND ONE OF THE ELDERS SAITH UNTO ME, WEEP NOT; BEHOLD, THE LION THAT IS OF THE TRIBE OF JUDAH, THE ROOT OF DAVID, HATH OVERCOME TO OPEN THE BOOK AND THE SEVEN SEALS THEREOF.

While John was still a part of the church on earth engaged in the battle against sin ONE OF THE ELDERS, a representative of the church in heaven, the church victorious, brought him comfort. The assurance of salvation and eternal life comforts the Christian. The certainty of victory over sin, death and the grave that Christians have in Christ explains why we weep not as those who have no hope. The knowledge God has given to His people of the ultimate outcome of the conflict of the ages enables Christians to cope with life's experiences as "more than conquerors" Romans 8:37.

THE LION THAT IS OF THE TRIBE OF JUDAH and THE ROOT OF DAVID are Jewish titles of the Messiah. Jesus was the greatest member of the tribe of Judah. When Jacob called his sons together to tell them what would befall them in the latter days he said "Judah is a lion's whelp; From the prey, my son, thou art gone up: He stooped down, he sounded as a lion, And as a lioness; who shall rouse him up? The sceptre shall not depart from Judah, Nor the ruler's staff from between his feet. Until Shiloh come; And unto him shall the obedience of the people be" Genesis 49:9,10. THE ROOT OF DAVID is Jesus. "And there shall come forth a shoot out of the stock of Jesse, and a branch out of his roots shall bear fruit...And it shall come to pass in that day, that the root of Jesse, that standeth for an ensign of the peoples, unto him shall the nations seek; and his resting-place shall be glorious" Isaiah 11:1,10. "I Jesus have sent mine angel to testify unto you these things for the churches. I am the root and the off-spring of David, the bright, the morning star" Revelation 22:16.

HATH OVERCOME means Christ has conquered Satan. Jesus said to His disciples, "In the world ye have tribulation: but be of good cheer; I have overcome the world" John 16:33. In His death, burial and resurrection Christ gained the victory and accomplished that which was necessary for God to carry out His purpose for the ages to its final consummation.

5:6   AND I SAW IN THE MIDST OF THE THRONE AND OF THE FOUR LIVING CREATURES, AND IN THE MIDST OF THE ELDERS, A LAMB STANDING, AS THOUGH IT HAD BEEN SLAIN, HAVING SEVEN HORNS, AND SEVEN EYES, WHICH ARE THE SEVEN SPIRITS OF GOD, SENT FORTH INTO ALL THE EARTH.

When John looked to see a lion he saw a LAMB. LAMB is used to picture Christ many times in Revelation and elsewhere in scripture. It may appear unusual for a lamb to be standing and at the same time look as though it had been SLAIN. This picture calls attention to the fact of the risen Lord who was crucified for the sins of the world. "For the death that he died, he died unto sin once: but the life that he liveth, he liveth unto God. Even so reckon ye also yourselves to be dead unto sin, but alive unto God in Christ Jesus" Romans 6:10,11.

Seven horns symbolize omnipotence. "They that strive with Jehovah shall be broken to pieces: Against them will he thunder in heaven: Jehovah will judge the ends of the earth; And he will give strength unto his king, And exalt the horn of his anointed" 1 Samuel 2:10. "And his horns are the horns of the wild-ox: With them he shall push the peoples all of them, even the ends of the earth" Deuteronomy 33:17. SEVEN HORNS indicates perfect, complete, Divine power.

SEVEN EYES symbolize omniscience. Christ possessed the fullness of the Spirit as is indicated in identifying the SEVEN EYES with THE SEVEN SPIRITS OF GOD. The function of the Holy Spirit is to bear witness of Christ. Read John 15:26. Jesus ascended into heaven in order that the Holy Spirit might be SENT FORTH INTO ALL THE EARTH. Read John 16:7,8. The indwelling presence of the Holy Spirit in the life of the Christian is the fulfillment of the promise of Jesus "and lo, I am with you always" Matthew 28:20. Jesus intended that all the world should know Him through the witness of the Holy Spirit indwelling God's people.

Luke's account of the great commission is an interesting parallel to this sixth verse. "And he said unto them, Thus it is written that the Christ should suffer, and rise again from the dead the third day; and that repentance and remission of sins should be preached in his name unto all the nations, beginning from Jerusalem. Ye are witnesses of these things. And behold, I send forth the promise of my Father upon you: but tarry ye in the city, until ye be clothed with power from on high" Luke 24:46-49.

5:7   AND HE CAME, AND HE TAKETH IT OUT OF THE RIGHT HAND OF HIM THAT SAT ON THE THRONE.

Without any delay Jesus immediately took the scroll. It is not important to pinpoint the time in history when this actually happened. The emphasis in this vision is upon the fact of exercising the authority He possessed. "And Jesus came to them and spake unto them, saying, All authority hath been given unto me in heaven and on earth" Matthew 28:18. The action of verse seven takes place quickly as indicated by the verb tense.

5:8   AND WHEN HE HAD TAKEN THE BOOK, THE FOUR LIVING CREATURES AND THE FOUR AND TWENTY

ELDERS FELL DOWN BEFORE THE LAMB, HAVING EACH ONE A HARP, AND GOLDEN BOWLS FULL OF INCENSE, WHICH ARE THE PRAYERS OF THE SAINTS.

The taking of THE BOOK was the occasion of worship and praise on the part of all nature and all the people of God. Submission and the recognition of the sovereignty of the Lord is pictured in the posture assumed—FELL DOWN BEFORE THE LAMB. Christ is acknowledged as the King of kings and Lord of lords.

The HARP was frequently associated with praise and worship. "Sing praises unto Jehovah with the harp; With the harp and the voice of melody" Psalm 98:5. This is only one of several such scriptures. The HARP is also associated with prophets and prophecy. "I will open my dark saying upon the harp" Psalm 49:4. Read 1 Samuel 10:5; 1 Chronicles 25:1-3 and 2 Kings 3.

The symbolism of the INCENSE is clearly explained as THE PRAYERS OF THE SAINTS. Each morning at nine o'clock and each afternoon at three o'clock when the priests entered the Holy Place to offer incense unto God the people on the outside were praying. These were hours of prayer. "Let my prayer be set forth as incense before thee; The lifting up of my hands as the evening sacrifice" Psalm 141:2. Luke informs us of an experience Zacharias had while burning incense. "According to the custom of the priest's office, his lot was to enter into the temple of the Lord and burn incense. And the whole multitude of the people were praying without at the hour of incense" Luke 1:9,10.

Prayer is communion with God. It is an expression of devotion and dedication. We pray without ceasing by abiding in the will of God, living with a continual awareness of His presence and His will, ever seeking to honor Him with obedience.

5:9   AND THEY SING A NEW SONG, SAYING, WORTHY ART THOU TO TAKE THE BOOK, AND TO OPEN THE SEALS THEREOF: FOR THOU WAST SLAIN, AND DIDST PURCHASE UNTO GOD WITH THY BLOOD MEN OF EVERY TRIBE, AND TONGUE, AND PEOPLE, AND NATION.

This NEW SONG is not like other songs. It is NEW in the

sense that it possesses characteristics not known before. The theme of redemption is a new theme honoring THE Redeemer in a way not possible prior to His being SLAIN. Christ's redemptive power was the basis for the praise — WORTHY ART THOU!

Forgiveness is available to all men. Christ's BLOOD was shed for all people. "For God so loved the world, that he gave his only begotten Son, that whosoever believeth on him should not perish, but have eternal life" John 3:16.

MEN OF EVERY TRIBE indicates that not all men avail themselves of Christ's redemptive offer, but those who do come out of EVERY TRIBE, AND TONGUE, AND PEOPLE, AND NATION. It is appropriate that four designations are used for the peoples of the earth when four symbolizes the earth.

The PURCHASE Christ made at the cost of His life was for, UNTO GOD. "Ye were bought with a price: glorify God therefore in your body" 1 Corinthians 6:20. "And whatsoever ye do, in word or in deed, do all in the name of the Lord Jesus, giving thanks to God the Father through him" Colossians 3:17.

5:10   AND MADEST THEM TO BE UNTO OUR GOD A KINGDOM AND PRIESTS: AND THEY REIGN UPON THE EARTH.

Christians are royal people, a kingdom. Christ is King. The redeemed are His loyal subjects making up the kingdom. As a part of the kingdom of the Lord Christians reign with Christ. The verb REIGN is present active indicative. The futuristic use of this verb explains why some translations add the word "shall" REIGN. Indeed Christians shall REIGN with Christ. However, it is equally correct to say that Christians REIGN now with Christ. We must be careful not to think of reigning in a political or material way. We REIGN spiritually with Christ. "For if, by the trespass of the one, death reigned through the one; much more shall they that receive the abundance of grace and of the gift of righteousness reign in life through the one, even Jesus Christ" Romans 5:17. Read 2 Timothy 2:11,12 and 1 Peter 2:9.

The redeemed are PRIESTS of God. A Gentile might enter the court of Gentiles but he could go no further. A Jewess might pass through the court of Gentiles and enter the court of women. A Jew might walk both in the court of Gentiles and the court of women but he was privileged to go beyond into the court of Israel. But, only priests could go beyond all these courts into the court of priests and into the Holy Place. The concept of priesthood helps Christians understand their access to God directly through Jesus Christ, our High Priest. "But ye are an elect race, a royal priesthood, a holy nation, a people for God's own possession, that ye may show forth the excellencies of him who called you out of darkness into his marvelous light" 1 Peter 2:9.

5:11 AND I SAW, AND I HEARD A VOICE OF MANY ANGELS ROUND ABOUT THE THRONE AND THE LIVING CREATURES AND THE ELDERS; AND THE NUMBER OF THEM WAS TEN THOUSAND TIMES TEN THOUSAND, AND THOUSANDS OF THOUSANDS;

Mathematicians are not intended to work with these numbers to come up with a precise count. This is clearly the symbolism of a great host, so great that counting is impossible seemingly. Ten is a symbol of completeness, thus a multiple of ten gives even stronger emphasis to the idea of completeness.

Lest we forget that Revelation is a book of visions note that John first SAW and then he HEARD. John was impressed with the great host.

5:12 SAYING WITH A GREAT VOICE, WORTHY IS THE LAMB THAT HATH BEEN SLAIN TO RECEIVE THE POWER, AND RICHES, AND WISDOM, AND MIGHT, AND HONOR, AND GLORY, AND BLESSING.

The seven-fold doxology is by divine design. These seven attributes are all inclusive. They tell the whole story. The exalted state of the Lamb of God is emphatically acknowledged in this doxology. It is significant that seven attributes are listed in view of the symbolic meaning of the number.

5:13 AND EVERY CREATED THING WHICH IS IN THE HEAVEN, AND ON THE EARTH, AND UNDER THE EARTH, AND ON THE SEA, AND ALL THINGS THAT ARE IN THEM, HEARD I SAYING, UNTO HIM THAT SITTETH ON THE THRONE, AND UNTO THE LAMB, BE THE BLESSING, AND THE HONOR, AND THE GLORY, AND THE DOMINION, FOR EVER AND EVER.

Both God and Christ are praised which further emphasizes Christ's exaltation. It is not accidental that creation symbolized by the number four should offer a four-fold hymn of praise. John is not pictured as seeing but rather hearing all creation praise God and Christ. No part of creation is left out.

5:14 AND THE FOUR LIVING CREATURES SAID, AMEN. AND THE ELDERS FELL DOWN AND WORSHIPPED.

The rule and reign of God and Christ is universally acknowledged. The truth of the praise is verified and magnified in worship. Such a scene of thrilling triumph surely bolsters hope and courage in the lives of God's people. Indeed, God intended that it should be so. The Christians at the end of the first century and the years that followed needed the kind of encouragement that came through such scenes of divine power and sovereignty.

God grant that each of us might see clearly His majestic reign and as a result feel that magnetic tug within our hearts to assemble with the saints to adore Him who is omnipotent, omniscient, and full of grace.

Chapters four and five have provided the reader with the knowledge and understanding necessary to evaluate properly the events of history. To fail to see history as an unfolding of God's plan is to misunderstand and misinterpret history. That which follows is a description of the conflict of the ages as it continues to the time of final consumation.

JOURNEY TO JUDGMENT

CHAPTER SIX

6:1   AND I SAW WHEN THE LAMB OPENED ONE OF THE
       SEVEN SEALS, AND I HEARD ONE OF THE FOUR
       LIVING CREATURES SAYING AS WITH A VOICE OF
       THUNDER, COME.

With the assurance that God is on His throne and in complete control of all things we are now prepared for the breaking of the seals in order that we might see the events of history in light of God's sovereignty. The events of history illustrated in the breaking of the seals are factual but not decreed. God permits many things that He does not will. Both in that which God wills and that which God permits His plan is executed. In all history man is never robbed of his right and privilege to choose for himself. The numerous wrong decisions of man make up the tragedy of history. Much of this tragedy is portrayed in the book of Revelation.

THE SEVEN SEALS do not necessarily picture history chronologically. History has many parallels and the events pictured in some of the seals may occur repeatedly, such as war and famine. Keep in mind that the words of this chapter are enacting a drama, showing a vision. It is important to note the frequent use of the word AS to remind us that we are seeing a visual only, not that which is actually happening. To speak AS WITH A VOICE OF THUNDER suggests an impressive and strong voice. The directive to COME is a strong one.

The first four seals are similar in that a horse is manifested in each seal. Further on in our study we will be impressed with the similarity of the first four trumpets and the first four bowls. All of these similarities are by divine design. Careful consideration of this fact aids in understanding.

Do not assume that the red horse must follow the white horse and that the pale horse must follow the black horse. All four horses may appear at the same time or at different times. To make each horse represent a specific period of history creates many problems. It also tends to make one outline history in such a way as to determine the time of the Lord's return which the Lord clearly states cannot be known by man.

Jesus revealed what had previously been a guarded secret. This is the significance of opening the SEALS. Though there is nothing new about historic events as pictured by the first four seals it is noteworthy that God's people are protected and ultimately delivered from the consequences of sin. Man's punishment for sin is often wrapped up in his own sin so that God simply lets sinful man pursue his own course. From this point on in our study of Revelation we should see God at work in history to bring man to repentance and the folly of those who refuse to repent. When history comes to an end God is victorious and Satan is defeated. Chapter six is a brief map of the journey to judgment.

The imagery for the first part of this chapter is borrowed from Zechariah 1:7-17.

6:2   AND I SAW, AND BEHOLD, A WHITE HORSE, AND HE THAT SAT THEREON HAD A BOW; AND THERE WAS GIVEN UNTO HIM A CROWN: AND HE CAME FORTH CONQUERING, AND TO CONQUER.

John evidently had the words of Zechariah in mind when presenting the picture of the first four seals. "In the first chariot were red horses; and in the second chariot black horses; and in the third chariot white horses; and in the fourth chariot grizzled strong horses" Zechariah 6:2,3. Reading further in Zechariah is helpful. "Then I answered and said unto the angel that talked with me, What are these, my Lord? And the angel answered and said unto me, These are the four winds of heaven, which go forth from standing before the Lord of all the earth" Zechariah 6:4,5. The vision in Zechariah is one of judgment upon the heathen nations. "Wind" is a symbol of judgment. Keeping this in mind should be helpful in discerning the meaning of horses in the first four seals.

The symbolism of the HORSE must be understood in light of biblical usage and the thought it would have conveyed to the people of John's day. "The horse is prepared against the day of battle" Proverbs 21:31. This statement is in harmony with several other scriptures speaking of horses. The idea of war and conquest is probably to be understood by the figure of the HORSE. The colors will add detail to this basic concept.

WHITE is the color of victory. When a king had gained victory in battle it was a white horse that was riden in procession to celebrate the triumph.

The rider of the WHITE HORSE HAD A BOW. The BOW was an instrument used in battle. "He maketh wars to cease unto the end of the earth; He breaketh the bow, and cutteth the spear in sunder; He burneth the chariots in the fire" Psalm 46:9. A feared enemy of the Romans in the first century was the Parthian army. The Parthians were considered to be the greatest bowmen in the world at one time. In 62 A.D. the Parthians shamed the Romans in battle. The people of John's day may have called this to their attention in considering the meaning of the BOW possessed by the rider of the WHITE HORSE.

This rider also had a CROWN. It was not a royal crown. It was a victor's CROWN. This is appropriate in light of the fact that HE CAME FORTH CONQUERING, AND TO CONQUER. This rider intended to conquer and he did conquer. He fulfilled his purpose in conquest. Rome achieved great world power through conquest and the people of John's day were very much aware of this fact. The picture of conquest stands out in the symbolism of the WHITE HORSE and its rider.

Some have suggested that the rider of the WHITE HORSE is Christ. Christ is the rider of the white horse in chapter nineteen. That does not mean that He has to be the rider of this white horse. The seal of the WHITE HORSE may simply present the picture of conquest which occurs in history rather often.

6:3   AND WHEN HE OPENED THE SECOND SEAL, I HEARD THE SECOND LIVING CREATURE SAYING, COME.

Verses one, three, five and seven are alike in that they each call attention to the breaking of a seal. They inform us that each of the four living creatures participated in this part of the action.

6:4   AND ANOTHER HORSE CAME FORTH, A RED HORSE: AND TO HIM THAT SAT THEREON IT WAS GIVEN TO

67

TAKE PEACE FROM THE EARTH, AND THAT THEY SHOULD SLAY ONE ANOTHER: AND THERE WAS GIVEN UNTO HIM A GREAT SWORD.

RED is the color of fire and blood. "Jehovah thy God is a devouring fire, a jealous God" Deuteronomy 4:24. Paul pictures "the Lord Jesus from heaven with the angels of his power in flaming fire, rendering vengeance to them that know not God, and to them that obey not the gospel of our Lord Jesus: who shall suffer punishment, even eternal destruction from the face of the Lord and from the glory of his might" 2 Thessalonians 1:7-9. Anger is portrayed with RED the color of fire. That this symbolism is to include the idea of war is indicated in the remainder of this verse.

The rider of the RED HORSE possessed A GREAT SWORD with which he was able to TAKE PEACE FROM THE EARTH. With PEACE gone you are left with war and conflict. War and conflict are naturally associated with conquest. The sword was used to maintain Roman domination. Throughout history instruments of warfare have resulted in much bloodshed.

The rider received A GREAT SWORD but the slaying was done by others. Men do the slaughtering and the rider takes peace away.

6:5   AND WHEN HE OPENED THE THIRD SEAL, I HEARD THE THIRD LIVING CREATURE SAYING, COME. AND I SAW, AND BEHOLD, A BLACK HORSE; AND HE THAT SAT THERON HAD A BALANCE IN HIS HAND.

"Our skin is black like an oven, Because of the burning heat of famine" Lamentations 5:10. Calamity and famine are symbolized by the color BLACK. This is evidenced with A BALANCE IN HIS HAND. Perhaps scarcity fits the picture as well or better than famine. "They shall deliver your bread again by weight: and ye shall eat, and not be satisfied" Leviticus 26:26. The need to deliver food by weight suggests a rationing occasioned by scarcity and famine. Read Ezekiel 4:9-17.

6:6   AND I HEARD AS IT WERE A VOICE IN THE MIDST OF THE FOUR LIVING CREATURES SAYING, A MEASURE OF WHEAT FOR A SHILLING, AND THREE MEASURES OF BARLEY FOR A SHILLING: AND THE OIL AND THE WINE HURT THOU NOT.

The VOICE coming from the MIDST OF THE FOUR LIV-ING CREATURES may be the voice of nature crying out or it may have come from the throne. The price and the amount are equivalent to a day's wages purchasing a day's needs for one person. This leaves no money for anything else nor does it provide any food for the other members of the household for which the breadwinner must be responsible. The staple foods were scarce and very expensive compared to normal conditions. BARLEY was not as expensive as wheat and thus was usually used by the poor. A MEASURE was less than a quart but more than a pint. During this time of scarcity warning was given to do no harm to THE OIL AND THE WINE which were important liquid foods for the people.

A scarcity of food often results from conquest and war. Very often the shortage of food is not the result of inadequate supply but rather the consequence of inadequate distribution.

6:7   AND WHEN HE OPENED THE FOURTH SEAL, I HEARD THE VOICE OF THE FOURTH LIVING CREATURE SAYING, COME.

See comments on 6:3.

6:8   AND I SAW, AND BEHOLD, A PALE HORSE: AND HE THAT SAT UPON HIM, HIS NAME WAS DEATH; AND HADES FOLLOWED WITH HIM. AND THERE WAS GIVEN UNTO THEM AUTHORITY OVER THE FOURTH PART OF THE EARTH, TO KILL WITH SWORD, AND WITH FAMINE, AND WITH DEATH, AND BY THE WILD BEASTS OF THE EARTH.

PALE describes that which is an ashen or grey color. It is like the appearance of one who is said to be "white as a sheet" as a result of shock or fright. DEATH rides this horse and is the explanation of PALE. HADES is the abode of the dead and appropriately follows along behind DEATH. DEATH does not claim all who engage in conquest and war or who are victims of famine and pestilence. THE FOURTH PART OF THE EARTH conveys the thought of a limited number, a significant number but not a majority.

Again and again John's knowledge of the Old Testament surfaces. An important lesson is to be learned from this fact. God can and will use one who is filled with the knowledge of His will. We need to read, study and memorize scripture continually in order that we might be used of God to a greater degree. The last part of verse eight sounds much like Ezekiel 14:21 "For thus saith the Lord Jehovah: How much more when I send my four sore judgments upon Jerusalem, the sword, and the famine, and the evil beasts, and the pestilence, to cut off from it man and beast!"

Various applications of the symbolism in the first four seals have been made. Some see the first four seals as simply a picture of the events and experiences of men. Others would be a bit more specific and suggest that the rider of the white horse is Jesus and as a result of His ministry persecution of the saints results. Thus the last three horses picture the consequence of the first horse when understood in this light. Are we to understand the rider of the white horse as Jesus or are we simply to see that in all four seals a picture of God's judgment upon sinful man? In either case history is being described and God intends that the Christian shall not misunderstand or become frustrated when the events of history may seem to indicate the absence of God. God is alive and in control even when death, famine, pestilence, war, etc. are taking their toll on earth.

6:9   AND WHEN HE OPENED THE FIFTH SEAL, I SAW UNDERNEATH THE ALTAR THE SOULS OF THEM THAT HAD BEEN SLAIN FOR THE WORD OF GOD, AND FOR THE TESTIMONY WHICH THEY HELD:

The FIFTH SEAL presents us with a picture of martyred saints. No time is designated. This is probably a picture of martyred saints throughout the entirety of the Christian era. There is no apparent reason to believe otherwise.

Persecution of Christians is a reality in history, but this should not be a surprise. Jesus clearly warned, "If they persecuted me, they will also persecute you" John 15:20.

The fact that one cannot see SOULS should not be disturbing. This is a vision, a part of a spiritual experience. The purpose of the FIFTH SEAL is not to give us insight as to the abode of the righteous dead. Suffice it to say that Christians "are willing...to be absent from the body, and to be at home with the Lord" 2 Corinthians 5:8. The purpose of the FIFTH SEAL is to make us aware of the suffering of the saints, God's awareness of it and His control of it. It has never been easy for Christians to accept or understand suffering as a child of God in light of God's omnipotence.

THE ALTAR is a reference to the altar of burnt-offering. "And the priest shall put off the blood upon the horns of the altar of sweet incense before Jehovah, which is in the tent of meeting; and all the blood of the bullock shall he pour out at the base of the altar of burnt offering, which is at the door of the tent of meeting" Leviticus 4:7.

FOR THE WORD OF GOD is an expression of the loyalty of the saints. They were "steadfast, unmovable, always abounding in the work of the Lord" 1 Corinthians 15:58.

FOR THE TESTIMONY WHICH THEY HELD indicates that their good works shone as lights to men in darkness declaring the glory of God. They were not ashamed to confess Christ before men. "If a man suffer as a Christian, let him not be ashamed; but let him glorify God in this name" 1 Peter 4:16.

6:10   AND THEY CRIED WITH A GREAT VOICE, SAYING, HOW LONG, O MASTER, THE HOLY AND TRUE, DOST THOU NOT JUDGE AND AVENGE OUR BLOOD ON THEM THAT DWELL ON THE EARTH?

God is HOLY AND TRUE but the continuing persecution of the saints makes this difficult to understand, thus the cry for justice to vindicate righteousness. How much longer will God withhold judgment upon the wicked? Are we to understand that these martyrs desire to see the wicked punished? No. Rather, they desire to see God vindicated. They desire that the whole world shall be persuaded of the sovereignty of God. They do not understand why this has not already been done, thus the question, HOW LONG? Christians continue to ask this same question for the same reason. Read Psalm 79:5-10.

MASTER is the term used to designate one who has power over slaves. The cry recognizes God's power to act. "Avenge not yourselves, beloved, but give place unto the wrath of God: for it is written, Vengeance belongeth unto me; I will recompense, saith the Lord" Romans 12:19.

6:11   AND THERE WAS GIVEN THEM TO EACH ONE A

71

WHITE ROBE: AND IT WAS SAID UNTO THEM, THAT THEY SHOULD REST YET FOR A LITTLE TIME, UNTIL THEIR FELLOW-SERVANTS ALSO AND THEIR BRETHREN, WHO SHOULD BE KILLED EVEN AS THEY WERE, SHOULD HAVE FULFILLED THEIR COURSE.

A WHITE ROBE is symbolic of purity and holiness. The ROBE could also picture the victory they are experiencing in Christ. While persecution continues on earth the saints are to rest. God's purpose will not be changed nor His plan scrapped. The delay of judgment may be understood by the fact that God does not desire "that any should perish, but that all should come to repentance" 2 Peter 3:9. We are living in the longsuffering of God. Only mockers would suggest otherwise (2 Peter 3:3).

Justification and salvation are not earned. They are provided by God and this is suggested in the fact that A WHITE ROBE WAS GIVEN TO EACH.

6:12   AND I SAW WHEN HE OPENED THE SIXTH SEAL, AND THERE WAS A GREAT EARTHQUAKE; AND THE SUN BECAME BLACK AS SACKCLOTH OF HAIR, AND THE WHOLE MOON BECAME AS BLOOD;

The awfulness of judgment upon wicked men is vividly pictured in THE SIXTH SEAL as affecting various elements of nature as well as various classes of men. The coming of the Lord in judgment is described in this kind of language in the Old Testament as well as here in Revelation. Joel describes the coming judgment of the Lord apocalyptically. "The earth quaketh before them; the heavens tremble; the sun and the moon are darkened, and the stars withdraw their shining" Joel 2:10. "And I will show wonders in the heavens and in the earth: blood, and fire, and pillars of smoke. The sun shall be turned into darkness, and the moon into blood, before the great and terrible day of Jehovah cometh" Joel 2:30,31. Jesus described the days of judgment upon Judiasm that came with the destruction of the temple in 70 A.D. with similarly vivid language. "The sun shall be darkened, and the moon shall not give her light, and the stars shall fall from heaven, and the powers of the heavens shall be shaken" Matthew 24:29.

72

A GREAT EARTHQUAKE symbolizes great changes, revolutions, agitations and upheavals. We are not told whether they are civil, religious, racial, social or perhaps a combination of all these plus other areas of upsetting circumstances. The crumbling of governmental powers and the collapse of big business may illustrate that which is symbolized by the EARTHQUAKE.

SACKCLOTH was cloth used for making sacks. It was a coarse material, black in color, made of goat's hair. In addition to its use in sacks it was used for straining and worn as a mourning garment. Appropriately it symbolizes a time of sadness and tragedy.

The darkness created by the SUN wearing a mourners garment and the MOON becoming as BLOOD is terrifying. "I clothe the heavens with blackness, and I make sackcloth their covering" Isaiah 50:3. Such language portrays a time of moral and spiritual decay and distress.

In an effort to discern the meaning of this kind of language we are aided by the words of Peter, who, on the day of Pentecost, said, "this is that which hath been spoken through the prophet Joel" Acts 2:16. He then quoted from the second chapter of Joel those verses so similar to this verse we are now studying. It is difficult if not impossible to find a literal understanding to the fulfillment of Joel's prophecy. Thus we look for its symbolic meaning to understand the word of Peter "this is that."

Some suggest that THE SIXTH SEAL pictures judgment upon wicked men preceding the time of the final judgment, whereas others see in this a portrayal of the final judgment. There are good reasons for both points of view. In either case the lot of the wicked is to be avoided. The judgment of the Lord is always terrible.

6:13   AND THE STARS OF THE HEAVEN FELL UNTO THE EARTH, AS A FIG TREE CASTETH HER UNRIPE FIGS WHEN SHE IS SHAKEN OF A GREAT WIND.

A chaotic condition is described here. The cosmic disturbances suggest that there is nothing for the ungodly to depend upon any longer. STARS may symbolize leaders. Thus, a part of the terrible picture of judgment may be seen in the falling apart of organizational structures and the loss of power and influence on the part of those in positions of importance. Whatever the specific application may be it is true that the things of this world will come to an end and those who plan their future only on the basis of this world make a terrible and fatal mistake. Jesus said, "heaven and earth shall pass away, but my words shall not pass away" Matthew 24:35.

6:14 AND THE HEAVEN WAS REMOVED AS A SCROLL WHEN IT IS ROLLED UP; AND EVERY MOUNTAIN AND ISLAND WERE MOVED OUT OF THEIR PLACES.

"And all the host of heaven shall be dissolved, and the heavens shall be rolled together as a scroll" Isaiah 34:4. Peter tells us that "the day of the Lord will come as a thief; in the which the heavens shall pass away with a great noise, and the elements shall be dissolved with fervent heat, and the earth and the works that are therein shall be burned up" 2 Peter 3:10.

Jesus once rebuked His disciples for their little faith, saying, "If ye have faith as a grain of mustard seed, ye shall say unto this mountain, Remove hence to yonder place; and it shall remove; and nothing shall be impossible unto you" Matthew 17:20. The moving of mountains is a symbol of impossibility for men. Only God can do this and He may choose to empower His people to do so. At a time when not one mountain but EVERY MOUNTAIN AND ISLAND is moved the danger and insecurity of ungodly men is dramatically underscored. Great is the judgment of God upon the wicked. There is no safety outside the will of God.

6:15 AND THE KINGS OF THE EARTH, AND THE PRINCES, AND THE CHIEF CAPTAINS, AND THE RICH, AND THE STRONG, AND EVERY BONDMAN AND FREEMAN, HID THEMSELVES IN THE CAVES AND IN THE ROCKS OF THE MOUNTAINS;

There is no occupation or social status or economic condition that can provide escape for the ungodly. Frantic and futile will be all their efforts to escape the wrath of God occasioned by their sin. The courage of the brave, the armies of the kings, the strength of the great, the possessions of the rich, the provisions of the slave, the liberty of the free are all without value in the face of divine judgment. Every effort to hide in the only places they knew to find hiding is vain.

6:16   AND THEY SAY TO THE MOUNTAINS AND TO THE
        ROCKS, FALL ON US, AND HIDE US FROM THE FACE
        OF HIM THAT SITTETH ON THE THRONE, AND
        FROM THE WRATH OF THE LAMB:

Wicked men do not like to face the reality of their own sins. "And this is the judgment, that the light is come into the world, and men loved the darkness rather than the light; for their works were evil" John 3:19. Those who live in sin would rather die than meet God. To confront God is to see yourself as you really are. Only the blood of Jesus Christ can cleanse adequately for the presence of God to be a blessing and privilege.

Note that those who seek hiding are aware of God and of the Lamb. "Knowing God, they glorified him not as God, neither gave thanks; but became vain in their reasonings, and their senseless heart was darkened. Professing themselves to be wise, they became fools" Romans 1:21,22. This is the tragic story of the godless.

The necessity of receiving Jesus as Saviour explains the WRATH OF THE LAMB to those who have rejected Him, for "in none other is there salvation: for neither is there any other name under heaven, that is given among men, wherein we must be saved" Acts 4:12.

6:17   FOR THE GREAT DAY OF THEIR WRATH IS COME;
        AND WHO IS ABLE TO STAND?

"Wail ye; for the day of Jehovah is at hand; as destruction from the Almighty shall it come. Therefore shall all hands be feeble, and every heart of man shall melt: and they shall be dismayed; pangs and sorrows shall take hold of them; they shall be in pain as a woman in travail: they shall look in amazement one at another; their faces shall be faces of flame. Behold, the day of Jehovah cometh, cruel, with wrath and fierce anger; to make the land a desolation, and to destroy the sinners thereof out of it" Isaiah 13:6-9. These words of Isaiah should be read in the light of the rest of the chapter which speaks of the judgment upon Babylon. The book of Revelation often borrows pictures of judgment from the Old Testament to picture the future judgment of God upon wicked men. THE GREAT DAY OF THEIR WRATH is the day when it is no longer possible for the wicked to obtain redemption and salvation. It is the day when their condemnation is inevitable and their salvation impossible. It is the point of no return the sinner ultimately passes by continually rejecting Jesus as Saviour. It has been a journey to judgment.

WHO IS ABLE TO STAND? Only the child of God will be able to stand. Jesus said, "watch ye at every season, making supplication, that ye may prevail to escape all these things that shall come to pass, and to stand before the Son of man" Luke 21:36. "Wherefore, my beloved brethren, be ye steadfast, unmovable, always abounding in the work of the Lord, forasmuch as ye know that your labor is not in vain in the Lord" 1 Corinthians 15:58. "For freedom did Christ set us free: stand fast therefore" Galatians 5:1. "Finally, be strong in the Lord, and in the strength of his might. Put on the whole armor of God, that ye may be able to stand against the wiles of the devil" Ephesians 6:10,11.

A WORD OF ENCOURAGEMENT

CHAPTER SEVEN

7:1   AFTER THIS I SAW FOUR ANGELS STANDING AT THE FOUR CORNERS OF THE EARTH, HOLDING THE FOUR WINDS OF THE EARTH, THAT NO WIND SHOULD BLOW ON THE EARTH, OR ON THE SEA, OR UPON ANY TREE.

AFTER THIS suggests a change of scene but not necessarily that which follows chronologically. Revelation contains many scenes describing the same period of time. The student must be careful not to be misled by a preconceived idea that each scene in the book necessarily follows the preceding one in time. The seven seals, the seven trumpets, and the seven bowls of wrath cover the same span of history, each in a different way. Having said this it should be further noted that there is progression in the book of Revelation with regard to intensity and urgency.

Chapter seven is a break in the action. Instead of introducing the next and final seal two different pictures are presented to give encouragement to the Christian. The purpose of this interlude in the drama is to underscore the victory of the church throughout the human struggle. In spite of Satanic efforts, as effective as they may seem to be, the church of Jesus Christ will continue to reign victoriously.

John SAW FOUR ANGELS STANDING AT THE FOUR CORNERS OF THE EARTH. The angels are agents of God. The entirety of the earth is indicated by the four directions, here specified as CORNERS. These angels are seen HOLDING THE FOUR WINDS. "The wind bloweth where it will, and thou hearest the voice thereof, but knowest not whence it cometh, and whither it goeth: so is every one that is born of the Spirit" John 3:8. We will better understand the meaning of the winds from Jeremiah 51:1 "Thus saith Jehovah: Behold, I will raise up against

Babylon, and against them that dwell in Lebkamai, a destroying wind." "And upon Elam will I bring the four winds from the four quarters of heaven, and will scatter them toward all those winds; and there shall be no nation whither the outcasts of Elam shall not come" Jeremiah 49:36. WINDS symbolize judgment and divine visitation. The HOLDING of the winds suggests a controlling and hindering of judgment. God's omnipotence is demonstrated in this action. The TREE would present the most visible evidence of the withholding of the wind upon the earth and sea. Absolutely nothing in history will prevent God's making His people safe in the struggle against sin and Satan.

7:2   AND I SAW ANOTHER ANGEL ASCEND FROM THE SUNRISING, HAVING THE SEAL OF THE LIVING GOD: AND HE CRIED WITH A GREAT VOICE TO THE FOUR ANGELS TO WHOM IT WAS GIVEN TO HURT THE EARTH AND THE SEA,

Several verses may suggest a significance to THE SUNRISING. "And Jehovah God planted a garden eastward, In Eden; and there he put the man whom he had formed" Genesis 2:8. "And, behold, the glory of the God of Israel came from the way of the east:..." Ezekiel 43:2. "Now when Jesus was born in Bethlehem of Judaea in the days of Herod the king, behold, Wisemen from the east came to Jerusalem, saying, Where is he that is born King of the Jews? for we saw his star in the east, and are come to worship him" Matthew 2:1,2.

THE SEAL OF THE LIVING GOD is the identification of the Christian. This imagery is borrowed from Ezekiel 9:1-8. The man who had the writer's inkhorn by his side was instructed to "go through the midst of the city, through the midst of Jerusalem, and set a mark upon the foreheads of the men that sigh and that cry over all the abominations that are done in the midst thereof" Ezekiel 9:4. The six men with slaughtering weapons were instructed to smite each person who did not have the mark.

Several scriptures speak of the seal as the Christian's identification. "And grieve not the Holy Spirit of God, in whom ye were sealed unto the day of redemption" Ephesians 4:30. "Howbeit the firm foundation of God standeth, having this seal, The Lord knoweth them that are his: and, Let every one that nameth the name of

78

the Lord depart from unrighteousness; 2 Timothy 2:19. "In whom ye also, having heard the word of the truth, the gospel of your salvation,—in whom, having also believed, ye were sealed with the Holy Spirit of promise" Ephesians 1:13. See also 2 Corinthians 1:21,22.

The Christian's God is LIVING in contradistinction to the pagan gods that were and are dead.

The urgency and importance of what the angel cried is noted with A GREAT VOICE. IT WAS GIVEN indicates that someone other than the angels was in control. HURT suggests the kind of picture seen in the first four seals of the preceding chapter.

7:3   SAYING, HURT NOT THE EARTH, NEITHER THE SEA, NOR THE TREES, TILL WE SHALL HAVE SEALED THE SERVANTS OF OUR GOD ON THEIR FOREHEADS.

The identification of the Christian is conspicuous as indicated by placing the seal ON THEIR FOREHEADS. Jesus said, "By this shall all men know that ye are my disciples, if ye have love one to another" John 13:35. Jesus taught, "Therefore by their fruits ye shall know them" Matthew 7:20. Paul informs us that "the fruit of the Spirit is love, joy, peace, longsuffering, kindness, goodness, faithfulness, meekness, selfcontrol; against such there is no law" Galatians 5:22,23. On the day of Pentecost Peter stated that those who obeyed the Lord would "receive the gift of the Holy Spirit" Acts 2:38b. Each of these verses helps us appreciate the distinctives of the Christian's identity as God's child and bond servant.

7:4   AND I HEARD THE NUMBER OF THEM THAT WERE SEALED, A HUNDRED AND FORTY AND FOUR THOUSAND, SEALED OUT OF EVERY TRIBE OF THE CHILDREN OF ISRAEL:

The indwelling presence of the Holy Spirit is evidence that they WERE SEALED. A HUNDRED AND FORTY AND FOUR THOUSAND is the numerical designation for all of God's people living on the earth. This number is the result of multiplying the number twelve and the number ten. Twelve symbolizes God's people and ten symbolizes completeness. Twelve multiplied by twelve may indicate Jew and Gentile or it may indicate God's peo-

ple under both covenants. The verses that follow make it clear
that this numerical symbol of A HUNDRED AND FORTY AND
FOUR THOUSAND indicates God's people on earth as contrasted with God's people who have left the earthly scene who
are noted in the last half of this chapter.

THE CHILDREN OF ISRAEL must be understood in light
of the New Testament teaching. This is not a reference to national Israel. "For ye are all sons of God, through faith, in Christ
Jesus. For as many of you as were baptized into Christ did put on
Christ. There can be neither Jew nor Greek, there can be neither
bond nor free, there can be no male and female; for ye all are one
in Christ Jesus. And if ye are Christ's, then are ye Abraham's
seed, heirs according to promise" Galatians 3:26-29. "For he is not
a Jew who is one outwardly; neither is that circumcision which is
outward in the flesh: but he is a Jew who is one inwardly; and circumcision is that of the heart, in the spirit not in the letter;
whose praise is not of men, but of God" Romans 2:28,29. "For they
are not all Israel, that are of Israel" Romans 9:6b.

7:5　OF THE TRIBE OF JUDAH WERE SEALED TWELVE
THOUSAND: OF THE TRIBE OF REUBEN TWELVE
THOUSAND: OF THE TRIBE OF GAD TWELVE THOU-
SAND:

7:6　OF THE TRIBE OF ASHER TWELVE THOUSAND: OF
THE TRIBE OF NAPHTALI TWELVE THOUSAND: OF
THE TRIBE OF MANASSEH TWELVE THOUSAND:

7:7　OF THE TRIBE OF SIMEON TWELVE THOUSAND: OF
THE TRIBE OF LEVI TWELVE THOUSAND: OF THE
TRIBE OF ISSACHAR TWELVE THOUSAND:

7:8　OF THE TRIBE OF ZEBULUN TWELVE THOUSAND:
OF THE TRIBE OF JOSEPH TWELVE THOUSAND: OF
THE TRIBE OF BENJAMIN WERE SEALED TWELVE
THOUSAND.

There is no other listing of the twelve tribes in the scriptures that is identical to this list. Though Reuben was the oldest
Judah is listed first. This may be due to the fact that Jesus was
born of the tribe of Judah. Levi is listed in place of Dan. Levi was
the priestly tribe and thus separate from the others. Ephraim
and Manasseh, the two sons of Joseph, would ordinarily be listed,

80

but in this instance Joseph is listed in place of Ephraim. The several questions raised in this listing stresses the fact that this is not to be understood literally. Questions regarding this peculiar listing need no answer if we accept the fact that the twelve tribes simply combine together to picture God's people on earth. Verse three indicates that these are all servants of God.

TWELVE THOUSAND symbolizes God's people. That there should be an identical number in each tribe further emphasizes the symbolism of the number. The fact that each of the twelve tribes is listed enforces the idea of protection of all of God's people.

7:9   AFTER THESE THINGS I SAW, AND BEHOLD, A GREAT MULTITUDE, WHICH NO MAN COULD NUMBER, OUT OF EVERY NATION AND OF ALL TRIBES AND PEOPLES AND TONGUES, STANDING BEFORE THE THRONE AND BEFORE THE LAMB, ARRAYED IN WHITE ROBES, AND PALMS IN THEIR HANDS:

This verse begins the second of two pictures in this chapter of the servants of God. In the first eight verses we are presented with a picture of God's people on earth, alive and involved in world evangelism. Beginning with verse nine we see God's people triumphant and victorious, having completed their earthly service. They are seen STANDING BEFORE THE THRONE AND BEFORE THE LAMB. In a sense we may say that both pictures in this chapter portray the same people, but under different conditions and circumstances.

AFTER THESE THINGS indicates a change of scenery. Having seen God's people on earth we are shown now God's people in heaven. Seeing the future joy of the Christian would be an encouragement to those engaged in the present conflict.

Jesus said, "Blessed are the pure in heart: for they shall see God" Matthew 5:8. Purity is symbolized with white. Appropriately the glorious state of the Christian is pictured as CLOTHED IN WHITE ROBES. Victory over sin and death is celebrated with the PALM BRANCHES...IN THEIR HANDS. The joyful Feast of Tabernacles provides a helpful background for appreciating the meaning of the PALM BRANCHES.

When one feels all alone it is comforting to be made aware of A GREAT MULTITUDE, WHICH NO ONE COULD NUMBER, who are all on the Lord's side. Barriers of race and color are broken and destroyed in Christ, for God's people come FROM EVERY NATION.

7:10 AND THEY CRY WITH A GREAT VOICE, SAYING, SALVATION UNTO OUR GOD WHO SITTETH ON THE THRONE, AND UNTO THE LAMB.

The saints are united and emphatic in giving praise to God and Christ for salvation. God is identified as "our Saviour" in 1 Timothy 1:1 and 2:3 as well as in many other scriptures. "And we have beheld and bear witness that the Father hath sent the Son to be the Saviour of the world" 1 John 4:14. CRY is in the present tense indicating continuous praise on the part of the saints.

7:11 AND ALL THE ANGELS WERE STANDING ROUND ABOUT THE THRONE, AND ABOUT THE ELDERS AND THE FOUR LIVING CREATURES; AND THEY FELL BEFORE THE THRONE ON THEIR FACES, AND WORSHIPPED GOD,

There is no one prescribed posture for prayer and worship. The nature of our prayers suggests the proper posture. When expressing praise to God for His power and salvation it is appropriate that we express our submission with the bended knee or prostration. It is fitting that they FELL ON THEIR FACES BEFORE THE THONE AND WORSHIPPED GOD, in light of the doxology that follows.

7:12 SAYING, AMEN: BLESSING, AND GLORY, AND WISDOM, AND THANKSGIVING, AND HONOR, AND POWER, AND MIGHT, BE UNTO OUR GOD FOR EVER AND EVER. AMEN.

It is significant, in light of the symbolism of the number seven, that this is a sevenfold doxology. Each word of this doxology is packed with meaning and speaks of the greatness of our God. The verity of this praise is enforced with the AMEN, meaning, so be it.

7:13 AND ONE OF THE ELDERS ANSWERED, SAYING UNTO ME, THESE THAT ARE ARRAYED IN THE WHITE ROBES, WHO ARE THEY, AND WHENCE CAME

THEY?

It is important that John and the readers of Revelation understand who the saints of glory are and how they arrived in this glorious state. This dialogue is intended to emphasize the greatness of salvation through Christ. The question and answer method is an effective teaching tool.

7:14   AND SAY UNTO HIM, MY LORD, THOU KNOWEST. AND HE SAID TO ME, THESE ARE THEY THAT COME OUT OF THE GREAT TRIBULATION, AND THEY WASHED THEIR ROBES, AND MADE THEM WHITE IN THE BLOOD OF THE LAMB.

LORD means sir. This is a title of respect. John is confident that the elder has the answer to his own question. COME OUT indicates that they are continuing to come. THE GREAT TRIBU-LATION is emphasized at certain times in history, such as in the days of Antiochus Epiphanes (168-165 A.B.) and in the days of the Jewish Wars (66-70 A.D.) culminating in the destruction of the temple and the city of Jerusalem, but it is not to be limited to any brief duration. THE GREAT TRIBULATION is an expression in-cluding all the sufferings of the saints throughout history. When all the suffering of God's people throughout time is seen as a unit it is GREAT! This is not to be confused with the great tribulation of Matthew 24:21 that is explained by what took place in 70 A.D. However, that great tribulation along with all other tribulations combine to explain the thought of this verse. See Acts 14:22.

All God's people before and after the cross have been and are saved by the blood of Jesus Christ. "For it is impossible that the blood of bulls and goats should take away sins" Hebrews 10:4. "But if we walk in the light, as he is in the light, we have fellow-ship one with another, and the blood of Jesus his Son cleanseth us from all sin. If we say that we have no sin, we deceive ourselves, and the truth is not in us. If we confess our sins, he is faithful and righteous to forgive us our sins, and to cleanse us from all un-righteousness" 1 John 1:7-9.

7:15   THEREFORE ARE THEY BEFORE THE THRONE OF GOD: AND THEY SERVE HIM DAY AND NIGHT IN HIS TEMPLE: AND HE THAT SITTETH ON THE THRONE SHALL SPREAD HIS TABERNACLE OVER THEM.

THEREFORE refers to the cleansing received in the blood of the Lamb. BEFORE THE THRONE indicates direct access to God. Service is a privilege for God's people throughout eternity. IN HIS TEMPLE is explained in chapter 21:22, "And I saw no temple therein: for the Lord God the Almighty, and the Lamb, are the temple thereof." SHALL SPREAD HIS TABERNACLE OVER THEM is an expression of God's presence with His people. "And I will set my tabernacle among you: and my soul shall not abhor you. And I will walk among you, and will be your God, and ye shall be my people" Leviticus 26:11,12.

7:16   THEY SHALL HUNGER NO MORE, NEITHER THIRST ANY MORE; NEITHER SHALL THE SUN STRIKE UPON THEM, NOR ANY HEAT:

"They shall not hunger nor thirst; neither shall the heat nor sun smite them: for he that hath mercy on them will lead them, even by springs of water will he guide them" Isaiah 49:10. The absence of two strong appetites, hunger and thirst, characterizes the future state of the Christian. The language ought to destroy materialistic concepts of future glory. "Blessed are they that hunger and thirst after righteousness: for they shall be filled" Matthew 5:6. "But whosoever drinketh of the water that I shall give him shall never thirst; but the water that I shall give him shall become in him a well of water springing up unto eternal life" John 4:14. "Jesus said unto them, I am the bread of life: he that cometh to me shall not hunger, and he that believeth on me shall never thirst" John 6:35. Present discomforts are unknown in heaven.

7:17   FOR THE LAMB THAT IS IN THE MIDST OF THE THRONE SHALL BE THEIR SHEPHERD, AND SHALL GUIDE THEM UNTO FOUNTAINS OF WATERS OF LIFE: AND GOD SHALL WIPE AWAY EVERY TEAR FROM THEIR EYES.

"Now the God of peace, who brought again from the dead the great shepherd of the sheep with the blood of an eternal covenant, even our Lord Jesus, make you perfect in every good thing to do his will, working in us that which is well-pleasing in his sight, through Jesus Christ; to whom be the glory for ever and ever. Amen" Hebrews 13:20,21.

The absence of all sorrow and the causes of sorrow accounts for the absence of tears. The rewards of eternity with God give encouragement to the Christian while he lives in anticipation of this reality.

Chapter seven is intended to assure and encourage the Christian. It is a word of encouragement.

TRUMPETS WARN

CHAPTERS EIGHT AND NINE

8:1　AND WHEN HE OPENED THE SEVENTH SEAL, THERE FOLLOWED A SILENCE IN HEAVEN ABOUT THE SPACE OF HALF AN HOUR.

The SILENCE may be explained as a dramatic pause or as a time of delayed judgment. SILENCE draws attention to what has just happened and to what is about to happen. Another possible explanation of this SILENCE is the reverence associated with prayer as noted in the verses that follow preceding the sounding of the trumpets. Read Habakkuk 2:20.

The action that was interrupted at the end of chapter six is now resumed. Again, it should be noted that this chapter does not follow chapter six chronologically. The seventh seal includes the seven trumpets. The seven trumpets cover the same time period of the seven seals. John saw the seals. He heard the trumpets. Trumpets warn. Warnings are needed in the presence of danger. Sin is always dangerous and deadly. While sin persists warnings are needed.

8:2　AND I SAW THE SEVEN ANGELS THAT STAND BEFORE GOD; AND THERE WERE GIVEN UNTO THEM SEVEN TRUMPETS.

"Blow ye the trumpet in Zion, and sound an alarm in my holy mountain; let all the inhabitants of the land tremble: for the day of Jehovah cometh, for it is nigh at hand;" Joel 2:1. The trumpets will break the silence. The contents of chapters eight and nine will make it clear that the trumpets are calls to repentance.

8:3　AND ANOTHER ANGEL CAME AND STOOD OVER THE ALTAR, HAVING A GOLDEN CENSER: AND THERE WAS GIVEN UNTO HIM MUCH INCENSE THAT HE SHOULD ADD IT UNTO THE PRAYERS OF ALL THE SAINTS UPON THE GOLDEN ALTAR WHICH WAS BEFORE THE THRONE.

86

ANOTHER distinguishes this angel from the seven in verse two. Priests offered incense to God each morning at nine o'clock and each afternoon at three o'clock. While the priest was in the temple offering incense to God the people outside were praying. These were designated as hours of prayer. There has always been a close association of incense with prayer. "Let my prayer be set forth as incense before thee; The lifting up of my hands at the evening sacrifice" Psalm 141:2.

The altar of the fifth seal (6:9) is understood in light of the altar of sacrifice. Here the ALTAR is explained by the altar of incense located in the Holy Place of the temple, immediately before the veil and the Holy of Holies. This altar was made of gold. It was eighteen inches square and stood three feet high.

8:4   AND THE SMOKE OF THE INCENSE, WITH THE PRAYERS OF THE SAINTS, WENT UP BEFORE GOD OUT OF THE ANGEL'S HAND.

This verse indicates that God heard the prayers of the saints. The answers would follow. The angel offered assistance but did not serve as mediator. "For there is one God, one mediator also between God and men, himself man, Christ Jesus" 1 Timothy 2:5.

8:5   AND THE ANGEL TAKETH THE CENSER; AND HE FILLED IT WITH THE FIRE OF THE ALTAR, AND CAST IT UPON THE EARTH: AND THERE FOLLOWED THUNDERS, AND VOICES, AND LIGHTNINGS, AND AN EARTHQUAKE.

"And he spake unto the man clothed in linen, and said, Go in between the whirling wheels, even under the cherubim, and fill both thy hands with coals of fire from between the cherubim, and scatter them over the city" Ezekiel 10:2. God answers the prayers of the saints with punishment upon the wicked. God's love for His people is magnified by His wrath against those who have rejected Him.

THUNDERS, AND VOICES, AND LIGHTNINGS, AND AN EARTHQUAKE all vividly describe God's wrath, the terror of His judgments upon wicked men. They are not the judgments but symbolically point to them.

FIRE calls several scriptures to our attention. In the Old

Testament we are reminded of the fire that was used of God to devour Nadab and Abihu in punishment for their disobedience. See Leviticus 10:1,2. In the New Testament we have the word of Jesus, "I came to cast fire upon the earth;" Luke 12:49a. The Hebrew writer reminds us that "if we sin wilfully after that we have received the knowledge of the truth, there remaineth no more a sacrifice for sins, but a certain fearful expectation of judgment, and a fierceness of fire which shall devour the adversaries" Hebrews 10:26,27.

When Elijah prayed the fire fell from above to consume his sacrifice proving Jehovah alone is God. The false prophets were killed. Perhaps we can draw a comparison with Elijah's experience on Mt. Carmel and the experience related in this verse.

8:6 AND THE SEVEN ANGELS THAT HAD THE SEVEN TRUMPETS PREPARED THEMSELVES TO SOUND.

The TRUMPETS are raised to their lips ready for sounding. Each trumpet in a unique and special way will warn sinful man of his need to repent and get right with God. The first four trumpets are similar in that they affect the physical surroundings of man. In this respect we are reminded of the first four seals and a bit later in our study we'll note the strong resemblance to the first four bowls of wrath. Also, the first four trumpets will be strikingly different from the last three. Throughout history God repeatedly warns man of the inevitable consequences of sin.

8:7 AND THE FIRST SOUNDED, AND THERE FOLLOWED HAIL AND FIRE, MINGLED WITH BLOOD, AND THEY WERE CAST UPON THE EARTH: AND THE THIRD PART OF THE EARTH WAS BURNT UP, AND THE THIRD PART OF THE TREES WAS BURNT UP, AND ALL GREEN GRASS WAS BURNT UP.

THE THIRD PART is a large part. Thus, this cannot be understood for the final judgment, for it will be total. Keep in mind throughout the study of this book that the truth is being presented to us in signs. Do not confuse the sign with the truth signified. The earth is affected in such a way as to call man's attention to his need for God.

The plagues inflicted upon the Egyptians in the days of Moses aid us in understanding the language employed by John.

"And Moses stretched forth his rod toward heaven: and Jehovah sent thunder and hail, and fire ran down unto the earth; and Jehovah rained hail upon the land of Egypt. So there was hail, and fire mingled with the hail, very grievous, such as had not been in all the land of Egypt since it became a nation" Exodus 9:23,24.

"Jehovah also thundered in the heavens, And the Most High uttered his voice, Hailstones and coals of fire" Psalm 18:13.

HAIL AND FIRE were destructive forces in nature. MINGLED WITH BLOOD may indicate the death of people due to natural calamities. All nature is at God's disposal in the administration of judgment against sin.

8:8   AND THE SECOND ANGEL SOUNDED, AND AS IT WERE A GREAT MOUNTAIN BURNING WITH FIRE WAS CAST INTO THE SEA: AND THE THIRD PART OF THE SEA BECAME BLOOD:

8:9   AND THERE DIED THE THIRD PART OF THE CREATURES WHICH WERE IN THE SEA, EVEN THEY THAT HAD LIFE; AND THE THIRD PART OF THE SHIPS WAS DESTROYED.

AS IT WERE makes it clear that this is not to be understood literally. The destructive power that manifests itself upon the sea affects both the fish in the water and the ships that sail upon the water. We assume that the waters of the sea are polluted in some way and are disturbed by tempests. The fishing industry would be adversely affected in both cases.

"And Moses and Aaron did so, as Jehovah commanded; and he lifted up the rod, and smote the waters that were in the river, in the sight of Pharaoh, and in the sight of his servants; and all the waters that were in the river were turned to blood. And the fish that were in the river died; and the river became foul, and the Egyptians could not drink water from the river; and the blood was throughout all the land of Egypt" Exodus 7:20,21.

The Christian need not fear the judgments of God upon the wicked. "God is our refuge and strength, A very present help in trouble. Therefore will we not fear, though the earth do change, And though the mountains be shaken into the heart of the seas: Though the waters thereof roar and be troubled, Though the mountains tremble with the swelling thereof" Psalm 46:1-3.

A kingdom may be represented symbolically with the word MOUNTAIN. SEA may speak of a state of confusion.

8:10　AND THE THIRD ANGEL SOUNDED, AND THERE FELL FROM THE HEAVEN A GREAT STAR, BURNING AS A TORCH, AND IT FELL UPON THE THIRD PART OF THE RIVERS, AND UPON THE FOUNTAINS OF THE WATERS:

8:11　AND THE NAME OF THE STAR IS CALLED WORMWOOD: AND THE THIRD PART OF THE WATERS BECAME WORMWOOD: AND MANY MEN DIED OF THE WATERS, BECAUSE THEY WERE MADE BITTER.

That which is essential to sustain life, water, is polluted to the point that many died from drinking it. WORMWOOD symbolized the bitterness of judgment. "Therefore thus saith Jehovah of hosts, the God of Israel, Behold, I will feed them, even this people with wormwood, and give them water of gall (poison) to drink" Jeremiah 9:15. "He hath filled me with bitterness, he hath sated me with wormwood" Lamentations 3:15.

The fact that STAR may symbolize a ruler should be considered carefully before reaching a conclusion as to the full meaning of the third trumpet.

8:12　AND THE FOURTH ANGEL SOUNDED, AND THE THIRD PART OF THE SUN WAS SMITTEN, AND THE THIRD PART OF THE MOON, AND THE THIRD PART OF THE STARS; THAT THE THIRD PART OF THEM SHOULD BE DARKENED, AND THE DAY SHOULD NOT SHINE FOR THE THIRD PART OF IT, AND THE NIGHT IN LIKE MANNER.

The source of light and energy proves inadequate for all. "And Jehovah said unto Moses, Stretch out thy hand toward heaven, that there may be darkness over the land of Egypt, even darkness which may be felt. And Moses stretched forth his hand toward heaven; and there was a thick darkness in all the land of Egypt three days;" Exodus 10:21,22. "For the stars of heaven and the constellations thereof shall not give their light; the sun shall be darkened in its going forth, and the moon shall not cause its light to shine" Isaiah 13:10.

90

Nature most noticeably and essentially a part of man's basic needs is used to express the mercy of God in His effort to prove that He is not willing for men to be lost, but wills their repentance. Though many will not repent, none will be able to hold God accountable for his condemnation.

8:13   AND I SAW, AND I HEARD AN EAGLE, FLYING IN MID HEAVEN, SAYING WITH A GREAT VOICE, WOE, WOE, WOE, FOR THEM THAT DWELL ON THE EARTH, BY REASON OF THE OTHER VOICES OF THE TRUMPET OF THE THREE ANGELS, WHO ARE YET TO SOUND.

"Set the trumpet to thy mouth. As an eagle he cometh against the house of Jehovah, because they have transgressed my covenant, and trespassed against my law" Hosea 8:1. "They fly as an eagle that hasteth to devour" is the descriptive language used in Habakkuk 1:8 to describe the Chaldeans who were raised up to punish Judah. The EAGLE is seen FLYING IN MID HEAVEN where every one can see and hear. This is where the sun is in the middle of the day. The EAGLE is a bird of prey and thus a fit harbinger for disaster.

Verse thirteen is a parenthetical scene in the drama of Revelation. It prepares us for the remaining trumpets in such a way as to dread hearing them sound.

WOE is a dreadful word. Observe its frequent use by the Lord in Matthew 23 in denouncing the hypocrisy of the scribes and Pharisees. The meaning of this word is illustrated in the words of Matthew 11:20-24. "Then began he to upbraid the cities wherein most of his mighty works were done, because they repented not. Woe unto thee, Chorazin! woe unto thee, Bethsaida! for if the mighty works had been done in Tyre and Sidon which were done in you, they would have repented long ago in sackcloth and ashes. But I say unto you, it shall be more tolerable for Tyre and Sidon in the day of judgment, than for you. And thou, Capernaum, shalt thou be exalted unto heaven? thou shalt go down unto Hades: for if the mighty works had been done in Sodom which were done in thee, it would have remained until this day. But I say unto you that it shall be more tolerable for the land of Sodom in the day of judgment, than for thee." It is a serious thing to be the object of the Lord's woe! Great affliction and grief await those who have failed to properly respond to the mercy of God, the warning of the trumpets.

The intensity of the warning increases in chapter nine. Three trumpets are yet to sound. WOE, WOE, WOE.

9:1   AND THE FIFTH ANGEL SOUNDED, AND I SAW A STAR FROM HEAVEN FALLEN UNTO THE EARTH: AND THERE WAS GIVEN TO HIM THE KEY OF THE PIT OF THE ABYSS.

When the seventy returned and reported their power over the demonic forces, Jesus replied, "I beheld Satan fallen as lightning from heaven" Luke 10:18. Some suggest the STAR FROM HEAVEN is Satan. Others conclude it is a fallen angel. John does not see the fall. He simply notes that the fall had taken place at an earlier time. The STAR did not have authority of his own, but THERE WAS GIVEN TO HIM THE KEY. KEY is a symbol of authority. The ABYSS is a place of great depth, sometimes described as bottomless. The PIT is the long shaft that provides entrance to the ABYSS.

With the sounding of the fifth trumpet a movement is made away from the natural world to the spirit world. Satan and demonic spirits have their abode in the ABYSS.

9:2   AND HE OPENED THE PIT OF THE ABYSS; AND THERE WENT UP SMOKE OUT OF THE PIT, AS THE SMOKE OF A GREAT FURNACE; AND THE SUN AND THE AIR WERE DARKENED BY REASON OF THE SMOKE OF THE PIT.

This is a graphic picture of demonic forces released upon the earth. God permits hellish influences to work in another effort to bring man to repentance. The ABYSS is the abode of evil spirits. SMOKE, FURNACE, DARKENED are all key words in identifying this picture as Satanic. "Put on the whole armor of God, that ye may be able to stand against the wiles of the devil. For our wrestling is not against flesh and blood, but against the principalities, against the powers, against the world-rulers of this darkness, against the spiritual hosts of wickedness in the heavenly places" Ephesians 6:11,12.

9:3   AND OUT OF THE SMOKE CAME FORTH LOCUSTS

UPON THE EARTH; AND POWER WAS GIVEN THEM,
AS THE SCORPIONS OF THE EARTH HAVE POWER.

The first two chapters of Joel should be read to see the many similarities with this portion of Revelation. LOCUSTS symbolize destructive power. POWER WAS GIVEN THEM indicates that they were not almighty. It must always be remembered that almighty is a word that belongs to God only. God is always in control throughout history. Everything that has happened or will happen falls into one of two areas—either what God wills or what God permits. God is just as much in control of what He permits as He is in what He wills. Christians, take comfort in this truth.

The sting of SCORPIONS is intensely painful though usually not fatal. LOCUSTS represent demonic forces at work in the minds of sinful men which God uses in another effort to bring men to repentance.

9:4   AND IT WAS SAID UNTO THEM THAT THEY
      SHOULD NOT HURT THE GRASS OF THE EARTH,
      NEITHER ANY GREEN THING, NEITHER ANY TREE,
      BUT ONLY SUCH MEN AS HAVE NOT THE SEAL OF
      GOD ON THEIR FOREHEADS.

The power of the locusts was limited. Ordinarily locusts totally destroy all the grass, the leaves of the trees and leave an area as if it had been burned. They hurt SUCH MEN AS HAVE NOT THE SEAL OF GOD ON THEIR FOREHEADS. Christians are protected from their destructive power. This is important to remember in seeking the meaning of this passage. It is helpful to recall the days of Moses when the plagues inflicted the Egyptians but did not bother the Israelites. Satan's agents can work on the lives of non-Christians in a way in which they cannot touch the Christian.

Observe that as the first four trumpets were physical in nature the fifth trumpet is spiritual as noted above. The Christian will not escape the consequences of natural and spiritual calamities, but the consequences are not the same for the Christian. The Christian may suffer physical and mental anguish as the result of living in a world of sin but he is not conquered by sin. In Christ the Christian is "free from the law of sin and of death" Romans 8:2b. The affliction of the Christian is nothing compared to the affliction of the wicked. The wicked will suffer anquish for eternity. Not so for the Christian. "For our light affliction, which is for the moment, worketh for us more and more exceedingly an eternal weight of glory; while we look not at the things which are seen, but at the things which are not seen: for the things which are seen are temporal; but the things which are not seen are eternal" 2 Corinthians 4:17,18.

THE SEAL OF GOD ON THEIR FOREHEADS indicates the obvious and clear identification of the Christians. "Even so let your light shine before men; that they may see your good works, and glorify your Father who is in heaven" Matthew 5:16.

9:5 AND IT WAS GIVEN THEM THAT THEY SHOULD NOT KILL THEM, BUT THAT THEY SHOULD BE TORMENTED FIVE MONTHS: AND THEIR TORMENT WAS AS THE TORMENT OF A SCORPION, WHEN IT STRIKETH A MAN.

The life span of a locust is about five months. FIVE MONTHS indicates a limited time, perhaps a brief period. The acute pain inflicted upon sinful man may be both physical and mental. The consequences of sin provide numerous illustrations.

9:6 AND IN THOSE DAYS MEN SHALL SEEK DEATH, AND SHALL IN NO WISE FIND IT; AND THEY SHALL DESIRE TO DIE, AND DEATH FLEETH FROM THEM.

The desire to die demonstrates the intensity of the pain. However, the nature of the hurt is such that death, if possible, would bring no relief. Job speaks of those "who long for death, but it cometh not" Job 3:21.

9:7 AND THE SHAPES OF THE LOCUSTS WERE LIKE UNTO HORSES PREPARED FOR WAR; AND UPON THEIR HEADS AS IT WERE CROWNS LIKE UNTO GOLD, AND THEIR FACES WERE AS MEN'S FACES.

AS IT WERE reminds us that we are dealing with symbolism. The description of the locusts is intended to add vividness and terror to this judgment on wickedness. CROWNS are not the kind worn by kings but rather those worn by victors. The word may suggest the idea of helmets. AS MEN'S FACES may suggest intelligence like to that of man.

9:8 AND THEY HAD HAIR AS THE HAIR OF WOMEN,

AND THEIR TEETH WERE AS THE TEETH OF LIONS.

HAIR OF WOMEN may imply long hair. TEETH OF LIONS may speak of greed and strength.

9:9   AND THEY HAD BREASTPLATES, AS IT WERE BREASTPLATES OF IRON; AND THE SOUND OF THEIR WINGS WAS AS THE SOUND OF CHARIOTS, OF MANY HORSES RUSHING TO WAR.

Each time the word AS appears we are reminded of a similarity. Their BREASTPLATES were not made OF IRON and the SOUND was not OF CHARIOTS or of HORSES. The picture indicates a preparation for conflict.

9:10   AND THEY HAVE TAILS LIKE UNTO SCORPIONS, AND STINGS; AND IN THEIR TAILS IS THEIR POWER TO HURT MEN FIVE MONTHS.

Locusts are born in the early spring and die in the early fall which is a period of about five months. It has been suggested that the description of these verses points up the glamour and attractiveness of sin which in the end does its hurt and brings destruction. IN THEIR TAILS IS THEIR POWER TO HURT MEN. Sin is deceptive and always destructive and hurtful. The tail is the important part of this entire picture as it speaks of the real nature of the locust.

9:11   THEY HAVE OVER THEM AS KING THE ANGEL OF THE ABYSS: HIS NAME IN HEBREW IS ABADDON, AND IN THE GREEK TONGUE HE HATH THE NAME APOLLYON.

"The locusts have no king, Yet go they forth all of them by bands;" Proverbs 30:27. Since this is just an imaginary picture there is no need to be restricted by reality. The picture is painted to illuminate the truth.

ABADDON means destruction APPOLLYON means destroyer. The meaning of the name speaks clearly concerning the nature of work accomplished by the plague of locusts.

The fifth trumpet speaks of the suffering experienced by those who are not identified as the people of God. This, therefore, is understood as evil at work in the lives of people. "Whoso despiseth the word bringeth destruction on himself;...the way of the transgressor is hard" Proverbs 13:15b. "For many walk, of whom I told you often, and now tell you even weeping, that they are the enemies of the cross of Christ: whose end is perdition, whose god is the belly, and whose glory is in their shame, who mind earthly things" Philippians 3:18,19. Consider the many diseases, crimes, heartaches, and severe sufferings that are the direct result of sin, yet the very sin that brought these results appeared initially attractive. This is a warning to sinful man!

THE ANGEL OF THE ABYSS is not identified except by name. The lesson of the fifth trumpet is clear without further identity.

9:12　THE FIRST WOE IS PAST: BEHOLD, THERE COME YET TWO WOES HEREAFTER.

This is a reminder of what was made very clear in 8:13 by an eagle flying in mid heaven. John is keeping count of these final three woes.

9:13　AND THE SIXTH ANGEL SOUNDED, AND I HEARD A VOICE FROM THE HORNS OF THE GOLDEN ALTAR WHICH IS BEFORE GOD,

The sixth trumpet is the warning of God coming in response to the prayers of the saints. THE GOLDEN ALTAR was introduced to us in 8:3. THE HORNS refer to the projections at the four corners of the altar which were primarily decorative on the altar of incense. This is the same altar where prayers and incense were offered. John keeps the power of prayer before our attention.

9:14　ONE SAYING TO THE SIXTH ANGEL THAT HAD THE TRUMPET, LOOSE THE FOUR ANGELS THAT ARE BOUND AT THE GREAT RIVER EUPHRATES.

In 7:1 we were introduced to four angels holding the four winds at the four corners of the earth. Here FOUR ANGELS ARE BOUND AT THE GREAT RIVER EUPHRATES. In each instance the angels are agents of God used in the administration of His anger and wrath. BOUND suggests a restraint of divine judgment. LOOSE indicates the execution of judgment.

THE GREAT RIVER EUPHRATES was a boundary line beyond which were the enemies. "In that day Jehovah made a covenant with Abram, saying, Unto thy seed have I given this land, from the river of Egypt unto the great river, the river

Euphrates;" Genesis 15:18. "By the rivers of Babylon, There we sat down, yea, we wept, When we remembered Zion. Upon the willows in the midst thereof We hanged up our harps. For there they that led us captive required of us songs, And they that wasted us required of us mirth, saying, Sing us one of the songs of Zion" Psalm 137:1-3. The Assyrians, beyond the river, captured the northern kingdom. The Parthians, beyond the river, presented a real threat to the Roman Empire.

The invasion of an enemy power is suggested by the loosing of the angels at the Euphrates river.

9:15   AND THE FOUR ANGELS WERE LOOSED, THAT HAD BEEN PREPARED FOR THE HOUR AND DAY AND MONTH AND YEAR, THAT THEY SHOULD KILL THE THIRD PART OF MEN.

A specific time indicated points to the plan and control of God in the affairs of the universe and man. The definite article THE appears before the word HOUR but not before DAY, MONTH or YEAR. When an event is pinpointed to the very hour it is usually regarded as important, more important than those events that are remembered by the day, month and year.

THE THIRD PART OF MEN identifies this as one of the trumpets and distinguishes it from the fourth seal which was limited to the fourth part of the earth. The death of men is a warning for those who live. Both the fifth and sixth trumpets directly affect the person, one with destruction and the other with death. Each is designed to bring man to repentance.

9:16   AND THE NUMBER OF THE ARMIES OF THE HORSE-MEN WAS TWICE TEN THOUSAND TIMES TEN THOUSAND: I HEARD THE NUMBER OF THEM.

Two hundred million is a great number both literally and figuratively. John receives his information by sound, not by sight. A number so vast would make any resistance virtually impossible. Nothing shall prevent this trumpet from sounding. Man will be warned in this dramatic way.

9:17   AND THUS I SAW THE HORSES IN THE VISION, AND THEM THAT SAT ON THEM, HAVING BREAST-PLATES AS OF FIRE AND OF HYACINTH AND OF BRIMSTONE: AND THE HEADS OF THE HORSES ARE

97

AS THE HEADS OF LIONS; AND OUT OF THEIR MOUTHS PROCEEDETH FIRE AND SMOKE AND BRIMSTONE.

HYACINTH was an opaque stone described as purple or dark blue-violet. BRIMSTONE was a sulphuric mineral substance. "Then Jehovah rained upon Sodom and upon Gomorrah brimstone and fire from Jehovah out of heaven;" Genesis 19:24. Red, blue and yellow are the general colors of the BREASTPLATES, HEADS OF LIONS make the HORSES all the more terrifying.

FIRE AND SMOKE AND BRIMSTONE are destructive agents and symbolize the means by which death is brought upon the third part of men. "But I will send a fire into the house of Hazael, and it shall devour the palaces of Benhadad" Amos 1:4. "Upon the wicked he will rain snares; Fire and brimstone and burning wind shall be the portion of their cup" Psalm 11:6.

9:18 BY THESE THREE PLAGUES WAS THE THIRD PART OF MEN KILLED, BY THE FIRE AND THE SMOKE AND THE BRIMSTONE, WHICH PROCEEDED OUT OF THEIR MOUTHS.

The same language used to describe the manner in which God dealt with the Egyptians just prior to His deliverance of the Israelites from their bondage (PLAGUES), and the words used to describe hell and the punishment OF THE WICKED (FIRE, SMOKE, BRIMSTONE), are here employed to make this trumpet warning vivid and meaningful. Certainly a warning so terrifying as pictured here should bring sinful man to his senses.

OUT OF THEIR MOUTHS reminds us that this is a demonic activity.

9:19 FOR THE POWER OF THE HORSES IS IN THEIR MOUTH, AND IN THEIR TAILS: FOR THEIR TAILS ARE LIKE UNTO SERPENTS, AND HAVE HEADS: AND WITH THEM THEY HURT.

Satan is designated as a serpent. This is important to keep in mind in studying this verse. HEADS may refer to intelligence. Satan is very clever and powerful. He may appear as an angel of light (2 Corinthians 11:14) or as a roaring lion (1 Peter 5:8). The MOUTH may imply the means by which Satanic power is exerted, whereas the TAILS may suggest the results and the terrible consequences of sin.

Throughout the history of the Old Testament era God disciplined His people and punished the wicked with foreign powers invading, capturing and killing. God continues to warn through such means as history verifies.

9:20 AND THE REST OF MANKIND, WHO WERE NOT KILLED WITH THESE PLAGUES, REPENTED NOT OF THE WORKS OF THEIR HANDS, THAT THEY SHOULD NOT WORSHIP DEMONS, AND THE IDOLS OF GOLD, AND OF SILVER, AND OF BRASS AND OF STONE, AND OF WOOD; WHICH CAN NEITHER SEE, NOR HEAR, NOT WALK:

THE REST OF MANKIND, who should have learned an important lesson REPENTED NOT, that is, they did not change their minds nor their lives, but continued in sin. In this respect mankind is not different from the Pharaoh of Egypt in the days of Moses. Pharaoh let the plagues harden his heart rather than submit to the will of God. Stubborn rebellion marks the wicked throughout history.

"Wherefore should the nations say, Where is now their God? But our God is in the heavens: He hath done whatsoever he pleased. Their idols are silver and gold, The work of men's hands. They have mouths, but they speak not; Eyes have they, but they see not; They have ears, but they hear not; Noses have they, but they smell not; They have hands, but they handle not; Feet have they, but they walk not: Neither speak they through their throat. They that make them shall be like unto them; Yea, every one that trusteth in them" Psalm 115:2-8. In the song of Moses we read, "They sacrificed unto demons, which were no God, To gods that they knew not, To new gods that came up of late, Which your fathers dreaded not" Deuteronomy 32:17. The apostle Paul speaks clearly on this issue. "But I say, that the things which the Gentiles sacrifice, they sacrifice to demons, and not to God: and I would not that ye should have communion with demons. Ye cannot drink the cup of the Lord, and the cup of demons: ye cannot partake of the table of the Lord, and of the table of demons. Or do we provoke the Lord to jealousy? are we stronger than he" 1 Corinthians 10:20-22? "Yet the people have not turned unto him that smote them, neither have they sought Jehovah of hosts" Isaiah 9:13.

9:21 AND THEY REPENTED NOT OF THEIR MURDERS, NOR OF THEIR SORCERIES, NOR OF THEIR FORNICATION, NOR OF THEIR THEFTS.

Romans 1:18-32 reinforces the attitude of God toward sinful man, where sin is identified similarly as it is in these two verses that conclude chapter nine. SORCERIES comes from a Greek word from which we derive our word pharmacies.

God's attitude toward sorcery was made clear to the children of Israel. "When thou art come into the land which Jehovah thy God giveth thee, thou shalt not learn to do after the abominations of those nations. There shall not be found with thee any one that maketh his son or his daughter to pass through the fire, one that useth divination, one that practiceth augury, or an enchanter, or a sorcerer, or a charmer, or a consulter with a familiar spirit, or a wizard, or a necromancer" Deuteronomy 18:9-11.

The sins of murder, immorality, and theft were clearly condemned in the ten commandments. However, we may understand the full significance of this verse by making both literal and spiritual application of these words, for in both areas men sin against God.

Reflecting back on the exemption of those who have God's seal we are reminded of the words of Jesus, "And be not afraid of them that kill the body, but are not able to kill the soul: but rather fear him who is able to destroy both soul and body in hell" Matthew 10:28.

TRUTH TRIUMPHS

CHAPTERS TEN AND ELEVEN

10:1 AND I SAW ANOTHER STRONG ANGEL COMING DOWN OUT OF HEAVEN, ARRAYED WITH A CLOUD; AND THE RAINBOW WAS UPON HIS HEAD, AND HIS FACE WAS AS THE SUN, AND HIS FEET AS PILLARS OF FIRE;

We do not read of the sounding of the seventh trumpet until we read chapter eleven, verse fifteen. Chapter ten and the first portion of chapter eleven are intended to do between the sixth and seventh trumpets what chapter seven did between the sixth and seventh seals — make the security and safety of the Christians known for their encouragement in the human predicament. This section (10:1-11:13) is another interlude in this drama of God's omnipotence. Following this break the action will resume with the sounding of the final trumpet. This is the longest interlude in the book of Revelation.

ANOTHER STRONG ANGEL places this angel in the category with the angel in 5:2 and 18:2. COMING DOWN OUT OF HEAVEN indicates that he has come from the presence of God. The CLOUD is often associated with heavenly beings. We are reminded that Jesus ascended in a cloud and will return in like manner. While the children of Israel journeyed through the wilderness "Jehovah went before them by day in a pillar of cloud, to lead them the way, and by night in a pillar of fire, to give them light; that they might go by day and by night: the pillar of cloud by day, and the pillar of fire by night, departed not from before the people" Exodus 13:21,22. It has been suggested that the CLOUD is a symbol of divine majesty.

THE RAINBOW speaks of God's grace and faithfulness. Read Genesis 9:12-17. THE RAINBOW suggests that this angel comes with mercy and good news in contrast with the angels who brought judgment. HIS FACE WAS AS THE SUN, speaking of his glory. HIS FEET AS PILLARS OF FIRE pictures his power over the enemies of the church.

10:2　AND HE HAD IN HIS HAND A LITTLE BOOK OPEN:
　　　AND HE SET HIS RIGHT FOOT UPON THE SEA, AND
　　　HIS LEFT UPON THE EARTH;

The entire universe is indicated by THE SEA AND THE
EARTH. FOOT UPON suggests submission. "For he must reign,
till he hath put all his enemies under his feet" 1 Corinthians 15:25.
"And he put all things in subjection under his feet" Ephesians
1:22a. Apparently the message contained in the LITTLE BOOK is
for all people. The fact that this BOOK is IN HIS HAND is in contrast with the book of chapter five which was on his hand. The
Greek text brings out this distinction, though the English version
may use the word IN both times. The fact that this is a LITTLE
BOOK may indicate that only a small portion of God's revelation
is included in its contents or that the message is for a limited
period of time.

10:3　AND HE CRIED WITH A GREAT VOICE, AS A LION
　　　ROARETH: AND WHEN HE CRIED, THE SEVEN
　　　THUNDERS UTTERED THEIR VOICES.

John borrowed his language from Hosea 11:10 "They shall
walk after Jehovah, who will roar like a lion; for he will roar, and
the children shall come trembling from the west." AS A LION
ROARETH adds emphasis to the GREAT VOICE with which the
angel CRIED. The voice of the angel is not to be confused with
the voices of the SEVEN THUNDERS.

THE SEVEN THUNDERS UTTERED THEIR VOICES in
response to the angel's strong cry. In Psalm 29 the voice of God is
likened unto thunder with seven different attributes of His voice
enumerated. The setting of thunder in John's gospel record may
be valuable to our understanding of its meaning here. Jesus said,
"Father, glorify thy name. There came therefore a voice out of
heaven, saying, I have both glorified it, and will glorify it again.
The multitude therefore, that stood by, and heard it, said that it
had thundered: others said, An angel hath spoken to him. Jesus
answered and said, This voice hath not come for my sake, but for
your sakes. Now is the judgment of this world: now shall the
prince of this world be cast out" John 12:28-31.

Thunder is symbolic of God's judgment and serves as a warning from God. In light of the frequent uses of the number SEVEN in Revelation it is not without significance that there were SEVEN THUNDERS. SEVEN has been regarded as both a sacred and complete number. It might be added that it is a number that identifies God as the author of this book.

10:4 AND WHEN THE SEVEN THUNDERS UTTERED THEIR VOICES, I WAS ABOUT TO WRITE: AND I HEARD A VOICE FROM HEAVEN SAYING, SEAL UP THE THINGS WHICH THE SEVEN THUNDERS UTTERED, AND WRITE THEM NOT.

WRITE THEM NOT is not a new directive for God to give. "But thou, O Daniel, shut up the words, and seal the book, even to the time of the end:" Daniel 12:4a. What John heard he was not privileged or allowed to share with others. Paul had a similar experience which he wrote about in 2 Corinthians 12:1-4. John may have lived at a time and in a place under proper circumstances for a revelation meaningful only to him.

There is an important lesson to be learned from the fact that the THINGS WHICH THE SEVEN THUNDERS UTTERED were sealed up. This ought to be a warning for us not to pretend that we have all the answers to what has happened, is happening and may yet happen in the future. We do not have all the information John had. God, in His infinite wisdom, may have seen the inability of man to cope with the utterance of the SEVEN THUNDERS.

We must never lose sight of the fact that God has adequately informed us for all our needs. Remember the words of Paul to Timothy. "Every scripture inspired of God is also profitable for teaching, for reproof, for correction, for instruction which is in righteousness: that the man of God may be complete, furnished completely unto every good work" 2 Timothy 3:16, 17.

10:5 AND THE ANGEL THAT I SAW STANDING UPON THE SEA AND UPON THE EARTH LIFTED UP HIS RIGHT HAND TO HEAVEN,

10:6 AND SWARE BY HIM THAT LIVETH FOR EVER AND EVER, WHO CREATED THE HEAVEN AND THE THINGS THAT ARE THEREIN, AND THE EARTH AND THE THINGS THAT ARE THEREIN, AND THE

SEA AND THE THINGS THAT ARE THEREIN, THAT
THERE SHALL BE DELAY NO LONGER:

It is not uncommon that one should lift his hand in taking an oath. Daniel wrote, "And I heard the man clothed in linen, who was above the waters of the river, when he held up his right hand and his left hand unto heaven, and sware by him that liveth for ever..." Daniel 12:7.

HIM WHO LIVES FOREVER is a clear reference to God. THERE SHALL BE DELAY NO LONGER is an answer to the question asked in 6:10, "How long, O Master, the holy and true, dost thou not judge and avenge our blood on them that dwell on the earth?" The next verse gives further indication that the delay will end with the sounding of the seventh trumpet. DELAY is the proper word, not time as some versions record. When the circumstances are right the end will come without DELAY. God knows the proper time. He is in control.

This interlude (10:1-11:13), though recorded between the sixth and seventh trumpets, is not to be regarded as coming chronologically at the end of the sixth trumpet. Further study of this section will make it clear that the events described take place during the Christian age and are not restricted to any time period within the Christian age.

10:7 BUT IN THE DAYS OF THE VOICE OF THE SEVENTH
      ANGEL, WHEN HE IS ABOUT TO SOUND, THEN IS
      FINISHED THE MYSTERY OF GOD, ACCORDING TO
      THE TIDINGS WHICH HE DECLARED TO HIS SER-
      VANTS THE PROPHETS.

Because man refused to repent after the sounding of six trumpets there is no need for further delay. The sounding of the seventh trumpet would bring the completion of the MYSTERY OF GOD.

MYSTERY refers to God's revelation, that knowledge we have because God has made it known to us. MYSTERY may refer to the entirety of the Christian message or it may refer to a specific doctrine. The SOUND OF THE SEVENTH ANGEL will bring that portion of God's revelation that had not yet been made known and could not be known apart from God's announcement of it.

John included himself in the term SERVANTS in the very begining of the Revelation. All God's people are God's slaves. The basic function of the prophet is to speak for another, thus prophets were spokesmen. God gave His revelation to the prophets in order that they might proclaim it to others.

10:8 AND THE VOICE WHICH I HEARD FROM HEAVEN, I HEARD IT AGAIN SPEAKING WITH ME, AND SAYING, GO, TAKE THE BOOK WHICH IS OPEN IN THE HAND OF THE ANGEL THAT STANDETH UPON THE SEA AND UPON THE EARTH.

THE VOICE FROM HEAVEN has the authority of God. This is the same voice heard in verse four. TAKE THE BOOK requires effort on the part of John. God does not force His will upon man; man must receive God's message of his own volition. The symbolism for this section comes from Ezekiel 2:28-3:3.

10:9 AND I WENT UNTO THE ANGEL, SAYING UNTO HIM THAT HE SHOULD GIVE ME THE LITTLE BOOK. AND HE SAITH UNTO ME, TAKE IT, AND EAT IT UP; AND IT SHALL MAKE THY BELLY BITTER, BUT IN THY MOUTH IT SHALL BE SWEET AS HONEY.

EAT IT UP indicates that the message must be assimilated into his very life. Jeremiah said, "Thy words were found, and I did eat them; and thy words were unto me a joy and the rejoicing of my heart:" Jeremiah 15:16. God's messenger is not an effective proclaimer of the truth until he has personally digested it and given it application in his own life.

IT SHALL MAKE THY BELLY BITTER may refer to the suffering of the Christian and the pain of self-denial. It may also refer to the judgment upon sinful man. There is no joy in proclaiming the wrath of God, but it is essential. It wasn't easy for Jesus to go to the cross, but it was necessary for the redemption of man.

BUT IN THY MOUTH IT SHALL BE SWEET AS HONEY. "The ordinances of Jehovah are true and righteous altogether. More to be desired are they than gold, yea, than much fine gold; Sweeter also than honey and the droppings of the honeycomb" Psalm 19:9b,10. "How sweet are thy words unto my taste! Yea, sweeter than honey to my mouth" Psalm 119:103!

10:10 AND I TOOK THE LITTLE BOOK OUT OF THE AN-
GEL'S HAND, AND ATE IT UP; AND IT WAS IN MY
MOUTH SWEET AS HONEY: AND WHEN I HAD
EATEN IT, MY BELLY WAS MADE BITTER.

John found the results to be just exactly as he had been told.
God's mercy is sweet; His judgment is bitter. God's messenger
has both sweet and bitter experiences in digesting the message
and in propagating it.

10:11 AND THEY SAY UNTO ME, THOU MUST PROPHESY
AGAIN OVER MANY PEOPLES AND NATIONS AND
TONGUES AND KINGS.

MUST indicates necessity. John MUST make known the
message of THE LITTLE BOOK. AGAIN looks ahead to chapter
twelve where a new set of prophecies begins. If the book of
Revelation were divided into two parts the division would take
place between chapters eleven and twelve. The message is intended for all PEOPLES, NATIONS, TONGUES, AND KINGS.
It is universal in its application as further emphasized in the symbolism of the number four. The mention of KINGS in this list of
four may intend to remind us that no one ever reaches such a
lofty or important position that exempts them from the need of
God's prophetic message.

11:1 AND THERE WAS GIVEN ME A REED LIKE UNTO A
ROD: AND ONE SAID, RISE, AND MEASURE THE
TEMPLE OF GOD, AND THE ALTAR, AND THEM
THAT WORSHIP THEREIN.

Ezekiel used a reed for measuring purposes "to make a
separation between that which was holy and that which was common" Ezekiel 42:20b. This is the purpose for measuring the temple. The effect of measuring is the same as that of sealing in chapter seven. It is a symbolic means of identifying the people of God,
distinguishing them from the peoples of the world who stand in
need of repentance.

Herod's temple was destroyed in 70 A.D, thus the reference
here is not to a literal temple. "Know ye not that ye are a temple
of God, and that the Spirit of God dwelleth in you" 1 Corinthians
3:16? "So then ye are no more strangers and sojourners, but ye
are fellow-citizens with the saints, and of the household of God,

being built upon the foundation of the apostles and prophets, Christ Jesus himself being the chief corner stone: in whom each several building, fitly framed together, groweth into a holy temple in the Lord; in whom ye also are builded together for a habitation of God in the Spirit" Ephesians 2:19-22.

God's people are given three designations—THE TEMPLE OF GOD, THE ALTAR, AND THOSE WHO WORSHIP IN IT. TEMPLE refers only to the temple proper, not including all the courts that surround the temple. ALTAR alludes to the character of Christian service. "I beseech you therefore, brethren, by the mercies of God, to present your bodies a living sacrifice, holy acceptable to God, which is your spiritual service" Romans 12:1.

The ROD which is used as a measuring instrument is at the same time a symbol of power and authority. This adds weight to the truth being illustrated. It is by God's authority and power that His people are safe and secure.

11:2   AND THE COURT WHICH IS WITHOUT THE TEMPLE LEAVE WITHOUT, AND MEASURE IT NOT; FOR IT HATH BEEN GIVEN UNTO THE NATIONS: AND THE HOLY CITY SHALL THEY TREAD UNDER FOOT FORTY AND TWO MONTHS.

The largest court area surrounding the temple was the Gentile court. All people could enter this court, but Gentiles could go no further into the temple. THE COURT is used to symbolize all those who are not in the church of Jesus. It may imply a special emphasis upon those who think they are saved but are not because of close proximity to THE TEMPLE itself. Jesus aid, "Not every one that saith unto me, Lord, Lord, shall enter into the kingdom of heaven; but he that doeth the will of my Father who is in heaven" Matthew 7:21. Many may appear to be in the church but God knows they are not. God notes the difference. Jesus asked, "And why call ye me, Lord, Lord, and do not the things which I say?" Luke 6:46. MEASURE IT NOT stresses the fact that those who are not Christians have no security.

THE HOLY CITY contains both the TEMPLE and THE COURT. TREAD UNDER FOOT calls to mind the words of Jesus, "and Jerusalem shall be trodden down of the Gentiles, until the times of the Gentiles be fulfilled" Luke 21:24b. Oppression will come both to the righteous and the unrighteous but it will not destroy the church. "And I also say unto thee, that thou art Peter, and upon this rock I will build my church; and the gates of Hades shall not prevail against it" Matthew 16:18. THE TEMPLE of God has been measured and is safe. Those outside the TEMPLE have no security.

FORTY AND TWO MONTHS is equivalent to A THOUSAND TWO HUNDRED AND THREESCORE DAYS. Both time designations equal three and a half years. This length of time may have brought several pictures to the minds of those who lived at the end of the first century. This is the period of time that it did not rain in the days of Elijah. This is the period of time (June, 168 - December, 165 B.C.) when Antiochus Epiphanes appeared to be doing well in his effort to stamp out Judaism. Symbolically it speaks of an undefined (so far as man is concerned) period of time, a time of uncertainty. Of course God knows the limitation of this time period but has not revealed it to man. Those living in this time period do not know when it will end and may be anxious about this.

The various designations of three and a half years in the book of Revelation help us synchronize these sections of the book. For example, the two witnesses prophesy during the same period of time that the nations tread under foot the holy city. FORTY AND TWO MONTHS speak of evil at work, whereas A THOUSAND TWO HUNDRED AND THREESCORE DAYS speak of good at work. This obscure period of time may describe the duration of time between Christ's first and second comings The length of the Christian era cannot be known in light of scripture. Jesus said, "Watch therefore: for ye know not on what day your Lord cometh" Matthew 24:42.

11:3　AND I WILL GIVE UNTO MY TWO WITNESSES, AND THEY SHALL PROPHESY A THOUSAND TWO HUNDRED AND THREESCORE DAYS, CLOTHED IN SACKCLOTH.

MY TWO WITNESSES is to be understood as the strong Christian witness, the number having a symbolic meaning rather than a numeric value. "One witness shall not rise up against a man for any iniquity, or for any sin, in any sin that he sinneth: at the mouth of two witnesses, or at the mouth of three witnesses, shall a matter be established" Deuteronomy 19:15. TWO may suggest the inclusion of Jew and Gentile, the combination of God's people under the Old Testament and those under the New Testament. It is the function of the church to PROPHESY, that is, be spokesmen for God. Paul stated that it was "through the church the manifold wisdom of God" was to be made known "according to the eternal purpose which he purposed in Christ Jesus our Lord" Ephesians 3:10,11.

The TWO WITNESSES are CLOTHED IN SACKCLOTH, a mourner's garment. This is an expression of the genuine concern the church has for the lost world. "Cast away from you all your transgressions, wherein ye have transgressed; and make you a new heart and a new spirit: for why will ye die, O house of Israel? For I have no pleasure in the death of him that dieth, saith the Lord Jehovah: wherefore turn yourselves, and live" Ezekiel 18:31,32. "And the people of Nineveh believed God; and they proclaimed a fast, and put on sackcloth, from the greatest of them even to the least of them" Jonah 3:5. The church is portrayed as penitential in the wearing of SACKCLOTH. The association of sackcloth with repentance is noted in the words of Jesus, "Woe unto thee, Chorazin! woe unto thee, Bethsaida! for if the mighty works had been done in Tyre and Sidon, which were done in you, they would have repented long ago, sitting in sackcloth and ashes" Luke 10:13. SACKCLOTH was a coarse material used in making sacks. This does not mean that the Christian loses his joy in serving Jesus. We are reminded of the experience of Jesus who faced the cross with joy. See Hebrews 12:2.

Because the church is to continue her ministry till Jesus comes we conclude that A THOUSAND TWO HUNDRED AND THREESCORE DAYS is a symbolic designation for the Christian era.

11:4   THESE ARE THE TWO OLIVE TREES AND THE TWO
        CANDLESTICKS, STANDING BEFORE THE LORD OF
        THE EARTH.

THESE refers to the TWO WITNESSES. In chapter one we were informed that the "seven candlesticks are seven churches" 1:20. This gives added evidence to the conclusion that the TWO

WITNESSES designate the church. CANDLESTICKS are better understood as lampstands in view of the fact they did not have candles in John's day. Olive trees supplied oil for the lamps. The Christian is not a light, he contains the light. TWO OLIVE TREES may refer to the Holy Spirit who indwells the Christian and gives life and light through the word. Read Zechariah 4 for background material regarding the symbolism of the TWO OLIVE TREES. See Acts 1:8. The fact that the TWO WITNESS- ES are also TWO OLIVE TREES and TWO CANDLESTICKS should serve as a reminder that this is figurative language.

11:5   AND IF ANY MAN DESIRETH TO HURT THEM, FIRE PROCEEDETH OUT OF THEIR MOUTH AND DE- VOURETH THEIR ENEMIES: AND IF ANY MAN SHALL DESIRE TO HURT THEM, IN THIS MANNER MUST HE BE KILLED.

"Wherefore thus saith Jehovah, the God of hosts, Because ye speak this word, behold, I will make my words in thy mouth fire, and this people wood, and it shall devour them" Jeremiah 5:14. Elijah responded to the men sent by Ahaziah both with words and fire from heaven. "And Elijah answered and said to the cap- tain of fifty, If I be a man of God, let fire come down from heaven, and consume thee and thy fifty. And there came down fire from heaven, and consumed him and his fifty" 2 Kings 1:10. Though in- dividual Christians may be harmed nothing shall destroy the church of Jesus Christ and nothing shall prevent the gospel from accomplishing its purpose. Read Matthew 16:18. "So shall my word be that goeth forth out of my mouth: it shall not return unto me void, but it shall accomplish that which I please, and it shall prosper in the thing whereto I sent it" Isaiah 55:11.

The scripture in Jeremiah is more relevant to the under- standing of this verse than the passage in 2 Kings, because the FIRE PROCEEDETH OUT OF THEIR MOUTH. The word of God is the weapon that will ultimately totally defeat the enemy. "The word of God is living, and active, and sharper than any two- edged sword, and piercing even to the dividing of soul and spirit, of both joints and marrow, and quick to discern the thoughts and intents of the heart" Hebrews 4:12. Jesus said, "In the world ye have tribulation: but be of good cheer; I have overcome the world" John 16:33b.

11:6   THESE HAVE THE POWER TO SHUT THE HEAVEN,
        THAT IT RAIN NOT DURING THE DAYS OF THEIR
        PROPHECY: AND THEY HAVE POWER OVER THE
        WATERS TO TURN THEM INTO BLOOD, AND TO
        SMITE THE EARTH WITH EVERY PLAGUE, AS OF-
        TEN AS THEY SHALL DESIRE.

THE POWER TO SHUT THE HEAVEN is a reference to
Elijah's experience and the POWER OVER THE WATERS TO
TURN THEM INTO BLOOD along with EVERY PLAGUE is a
reference to Moses' experiences with the Pharoah of Egypt. Each
of these historical events illustrates the power of the Christian
witness. "Elijah was a man of like passions with us, and he prayed
fervently that it might not rain; and it rained not on the earth for
three years and six months" James 5:17.

The church has power, power superior to that of the opposition. Truth is stronger than falsehood. Life is stronger than
death. "But ye shall receive power, when the Holy Spirit is come
upon you: and ye shall be my witnesses both in Jerusalem, and in
all Judaea and Samaria, and unto the uttermost part of the earth"
Acts 1:8. Not only is the church empowered with the Holy Spirit
but also with the power of the word. Paul testified, "For I am not
ashamed of the gospel: for it is the power of God unto salvation to
everyone that believeth; to the Jew first, and also to the Greek"
Romans 1:16.

11:7   AND WHEN THEY SHALL HAVE FINISHED THEIR
        TESTIMONY, THE BEAST THAT COMETH UP OUT OF
        THE ABYSS SHALL MAKE WAR WITH THEM, AND
        OVERCOME THEM, AND KILL THEM.

Nothing will prevent the church from accomplishing her
God-given task. Jesus announced that "this gospel of the kingdom
shall be preached in the whole world for a testimony unto all the
nations; and then shall the end come" Matthew 24:14. He was
speaking of the end of the temple and the events that transpired
in 70 A.D. Prior to 70 A.D. Paul wrote to the Colossians, "the gospel which ye heard, which was preached in all creation under heaven; whereof I Paul was made a minister" Colossians 1:23b. Satan
was unable to prevent the coming of the Messiah. He was unable

111

to keep Him in the tomb. He was unable to prevent the completion of the sacred canon. He has been and will continue to be unable to stop the growth and witness of the church. "Wherefore, my beloved brethren, be ye steadfast, unmovable, always abounding in the work of the Lord, forasmuch as ye know that your labor is not vain in the Lord" 1 Corinthians 15:58.

THE BEAST is not Satan but certainly one of his chief agents. This is a wild beast. It is suggested that the word BEAST symbolizes Satanic power as it shows itself through men of power in high positions in government, such as the Caesars who insisted upon being worshipped by the people. In every age there have been those who served Satan's purpose in persecuting the church. The leaders in antichristian activity may be referred to collectively as the BEAST.

The emperor of Rome, with all his armies and power, could not stop the growth of the early church, but he was able to inflict terrible persecutions and make it look as if the Christians had been overcome and killed.

"But we have this treasure in earthen vessels, that the exceeding greatness of the power may be of God, and not from ourselves; we are pressed on every side, yet not straitened; perplexed, yet not unto despair; pursued, yet not forsaken; smitten down, yet not destroyed; always bearing about in the body the dying of Jesus, that the life also of Jesus may be manifested in our body. For we who live are always delivered unto death for Jesus' sake, that the life also of Jesus may be manifested in our mortal flesh" 2 Corinthians 4:7-11.

The ABYSS is a designation for a hellish place.

11:8   AND THEIR DEAD BODIES LIE IN THE STREET OF THE GREAT CITY, WHICH SPIRITUALLY IS CALLED SODOM AND EGYPT, WHERE ALSO THEIR LORD WAS CRUCIFIED.

The church appears defeated. Beware of appearances. Your eyes can deceive you if you are not careful. Do not stop your reading with verse eight.

THE GREAT CITY is described as a place of sin, bondage and apostasy. SODOM intimates the degree of sin that brings the judgment of God upon her. EGYPT points to the degree of bondage that brings the power of God to rescue His people from it. Obviously sin and bondage are brought to mind with the mention of SODOM and EGYPT. The LORD WAS CRUCIFIED in Jerusalem, however, this could be understood in light of Hebrews 6:4-6 "For as touching those who were once enlightened and tasted of the heavenly gift, and were made partakers of the Holy Spirit, and tasted the good word of God, and the powers of the age to come, and then fell away, it is impossible to renew them again unto repentance; seeing they crucify to themselves the Son of God afresh, and put him to an open shame." In John's day Rome could fit this description as THE GREAT CITY. However, symbolism would not limit this designation to any one city.

It was the custom of the Jews to bury their dead on the day of the death. When a dead body was not given a burial insult was intended. The severity of persecution against the church is pictured as DEAD BODIES IN THE STREET. Certainly the words of Jesus come true. "And ye shall be hated of all men for my name's sake: but he that endureth to the end, the same shall be saved" Matthew 10:22.

11:9   AND FROM AMONG THE PEOPLES AND TRIBES AND TONGUES AND NATIONS DO MEN LOOK UPON THEIR DEAD BODIES THREE DAYS AND A HALF, AND SUFFER NOT THEIR DEAD BODIES TO BE LAID IN A TOMB.

Nothing pleases the BEAST any more than for the whole world to see what he has done to the church. Sinful men cannot leave the church and the word of God alone. Even when it appears dead they continue to be aware of it by LOOKING UPON THEIR DEAD BODIES. There's an intersting story in 1 Kings 13 of a man whose body was left, for a time, in the street to be seen as a dead body. "The blood have they shed like water round about Jerusalem; And there was none to bury them" Psalm 79:3.

THREE DAYS AND A HALF is a short period of time whose length is not known by man. Some have likened this period of time to the time that Jesus was in the tomb. Just as the tomb could not keep Jesus prisoner, neither can Satan destroy the church. THREE...AND A HALF describe a time of anxiety, frustration, persecution, etc. whether it be short as indicated by

113

DAYS or long as indicated by YEARS.

11:10 AND THEY THAT DWELL ON THE EARTH REJOICE
OVER THEM, AND MAKE MERRY; AND THEY SHALL
SEND GIFTS ONE TO ANOTHER: BECAUSE THESE
TWO PROPHETS TORMENTED THEM THAT DWELL
ON THE EARTH.

THEY THAT DWELL ON THE EARTH refer to those who
are not God's people. THEY REJOICE AND MAKE MERRY because there is no one to make them feel ill at ease in their
sins—THEY are no longer TORMENTED. THESE TWO PRO-
PHETS shed the light of truth upon their wickedness. "And this
is the judgment, that the light is come into the world, and men
loved the darkness rather than the light; for their works were
evil" John 3:19. Really wicked people hate really righteous people
for the really righteous people make the really wicked people see
how really wicked they really are. Truth torments those who live
a lie.

The extent to which sin perverts people is symbolized by the
sending of GIFTS ONE TO ANOTHER on the occasion of death.

11:11 AND AFTER THREE DAYS AND A HALF THE
BREATH OF LIFE FROM GOD ENTERED INTO THEM,
AND THEY STOOD UPON THEIR FEET; AND GREAT
FEAR FELL UPON THEM THAT BEHELD THEM.

Ezekiel's vision of dry bones in Ezekiel 37:1-14 assists our understanding of this verse. What appeared to be dead is very much
alive. GOD gives LIFE to His people. "The word of God...liveth
and abideth...the word of the Lord abideth forever" 1 Peter
1:23,25.

The GREAT FEAR is presented in complete contrast with
the making MERRY of the preceding verse. This FEAR is to be
understood in light of the sixth seal. "It is a fearful thing to fall
into the hands of the living God" Hebrews 10:31. The victory of
the church is visible—they BEHELD THEM!

11:12 AND THEY HEARD A GREAT VOICE FROM HEAVEN
SAYING UNTO THEM, COME UP HITHER. AND THEY
WENT UP INTO HEAVEN IN THE CLOUD; AND
THEIR ENEMIES BEHELD THEM.

This speaks of the end of the Christian era when the Christian witness is removed from the earth and no opportunity remains for sinful man to repent, but sinful man will be very much aware of the victory of the church, for THEIR ENEMIES BEHELD THEM. THEY WENT UP INTO HEAVEN IN THE CLOUD. At the time of Jesus' ascension, when "a cloud received him out of their sight. And while they were looking steadfastly into heaven as he went, behold two men stood by them in white apparel; who also said, Ye men of Galilee, why stand ye looking into heaven? this Jesus, who was received up from you into heaven, shall so come in like manner as ye beheld him going into heaven" Acts 1:9-11. "For the Lord himself shall descend from heaven, with a shout, with the voice of the archangel, and with the trump of God: and the dead in Christ shall rise first; then we that are alive, that are left, shall together with them be caught up in the clouds, to meet the Lord in the air: and so shall we ever be with the Lord" 1 Thessalonians 4:16, 17.

"Faithful is the saying: For if we died with him, we shall also live with him:" 2 Timothy 2:11. "The Spirit himself beareth witness with our spirit, that we are children of God; and if children, then heirs; heirs of God, and joint-heirs with Christ; if so be that we suffer with him, that we may be also glorified with him" Romans 8:17.

11:13 AND IN THAT HOUR THERE WAS A GREAT EARTHQUAKE, AND THE TENTH PART OF THE CITY FELL; AND THERE WERE KILLED IN THE EARTHQUAKE SEVEN THOUSAND PERSONS: AND THE REST WERE AFFRIGHTED AND GAVE GLORY TO THE GOD OF HEAVEN.

Literally and figuratively A GREAT EARTHQUAKE speaks of the power of God. Here it symbolizes a great upheaval. The vividness of the scene is magnified by the destruction and death that resulted from the GREAT EARTHQUAKE. SEVEN THOUSAND designates the completeness of God's judgment. SEVEN is a sacred number suggesting completeness. Any multiple of ten magnifies the thought of completeness.

It is not known whether the giving of GLORY TO THE GOD OF HEAVEN was a manifestation of genuine repentance (probably not) or simply the result of their great fear. This is the first time since the breaking of the first seal that we have seen this kind of reaction on the part of sinful man. It is not uncommon in history for man to turn to God in times of great disasters. This is not to suggest that all of those who turn to God as a result of being scared are truly converted. GOD is glorified when His omnipotence is recognized and confessed whether or not man properly responds through submission to His will. Read Philippians 2:9-11.

11:14 THE SECOND WOE IS PAST: BEHOLD, THE THIRD WOE COMETH QUICKLY.

The interlude is completed and the final WOE is to come QUICKLY. There will be no more delay. There is no doubt left concerning the victory and security of the saints of God. With this assurance attention is now given to the final trumpet.

11:15 AND THE SEVENTH ANGEL SOUNDED; AND THERE FOLLOWED GREAT VOICES IN HEAVEN, AND THEY SAID, THE KINGDOM OF THE WORLD IS BECOME THE KINGDOM OF OUR LORD, AND OF HIS CHRIST: AND HE SHALL REIGN FOR EVER AND EVER.

All the kingdoms of the world are viewed as one world KINGDOM and it is surrendered to THE KINGDOM OF OUR LORD, the KINGDOM that is not of this world (John 18:36). The seventh ANGEL sounds the note of victory for Christ and His church! This is indeed WOE for the world that rejected Christ, for Christ's victory is Satan's defeat. Eternal condemnation is this final WOE for the non-Christian.

11:16 AND THE FOUR AND TWENTY ELDERS, WHO SIT BEFORE GOD ON THEIR THRONES, FELL UPON THEIR FACES AND WORSHIPPED GOD,

We were introduced to the FOUR AND TWENTY ELDERS in chapter four and both times they are seen praising God. They are representatives of all God's people.

11:17 SAYING, WE GIVE THEE THANKS, O LORD GOD, THE ALMIGHTY, WHO ART AND WHO WAST: BECAUSE THOU HAST TAKEN THY GREAT POWER, AND DIDST REIGN.

The ELDERS express gratitude for the entire church. In the battle with Satan it is well to keep in mind that God is AL-

MIGHTY. God has now demonstrated His GREAT POWER by reigning. Truth triumphs!

11:18 AND THE NATIONS WERE WROTH, AND THY WRATH CAME, AND THE TIME OF THE DEAD TO BE JUDGED, AND THE TIME TO GIVE THEIR REWARD TO THY SERVANTS THE PROPHETS, AND TO THE SAINTS, AND TO THEM THAT FEAR THY NAME, THE SMALL AND THE GREAT: AND TO DESTROY THEM THAT DESTROY THE EARTH.

This is a fulfillment of Psalm 2:2,5 "The kings of the earth set themselves, And the rulers take counsel together, Against Jehovah, and against his anointed,...Then will he speak unto them in his wrath, And vex them in his sore displeasure." "He will bless them that fear Jehovah, Both small and great" Psalm 115:13.

All men will be judged. This means condemnation for those THAT DESTROY THE EARTH. "Be not deceived; God is not mocked: for whatsoever a man soweth, that shall he also reap. For he that soweth unto his own flesh shall of the flesh reap corruption; but he that soweth unto the Spirit shall of the Spirit reap eternal life" Galatians 6:7,8. It is important for us to note that sin destroys and sinful men's activities are regarded as destructive of THE EARTH. A REWARD awaits all those who FEAR God—SERVANTS, SAINTS. This same thought will be stated again in chapter twenty. SMALL AND GREAT include every one.

11:19 AND THERE WAS OPENED THE TEMPLE OF GOD THAT IS IN HEAVEN; AND THERE WAS SEEN IN HIS TEMPLE THE ARK OF HIS COVENANT; AND THERE FOLLOWED LIGHTNINGS, AND VOICES, AND THUNDERS, AND AN EARTHQUAKE, AND GREAT HAIL.

The TEMPLE OF GOD was opened in order that we might see THE ARK OF HIS COVENANT, a symbol of God's presence and promise. God is faithful to do all He has promised. God's judgment upon sin is portrayed with the words LIGHTNINGS, VOICES, THUNDERS, EARTHQUAKE, and HAIL. God's plan has now been completed. The seventh trumpet sound comes to an end with the defeat of evil. Majesty and power are ascribed to God through this symbolism.

This ends the first half of the book of Revelation. In a sense the record is complete within the first eleven chapters. What follows, beginning with chapter twelve, covers the same time period from a different perspective and couches the truth with different imagery. The difference between the two halves of Revelation is immediately discerned, yet the unity of the entire book is likewise evident.

OVERCOMERS IN CONFLICT

12:1 AND A GREAT SIGN WAS SEEN IN HEAVEN: A WO-
MAN ARRAYED WITH THE SUN, AND THE MOON
UNDER HER FEET, AND UPON HER HEAD A CROWN
OF TWELVE STARS:

This is A GREAT SIGN pointing to a great truth. The WO-
MAN is a sign of the church. In the second major section of Revelation God's people are portrayed as a woman and as a city. The
city is the new Jerusalem. Satan's people are also portrayed as a
woman and as a city. The woman is the harlot and the city is
Babylon. There is a great contrast between the two women and
between the two cities as we shall note in our further study.

The garment of the woman speaks of the glory of the church.
Paul pictures the church as "a glorious church, not having spot or
wrinkle...holy and without blemish" Ephesians 5:27. SUN is an appropriate symbol for those whom Jesus said "are the light of the
world" Matthew 5:14. The light of truth and righteousness garbs
the Christian. THE MOON UNDER HER FEET gives added emphasis to her exalted position. Her CROWN is one of victory.
TWELVE is symbolic of God's people. STARS are sometimes
symbols of great leaders. The church is portrayed as glorious and
exalted, exercising dominion and power and achieving victory
over opposition.

12:2 AND SHE WAS WITH CHILD; AND SHE CRIETH OUT,
TRAVAILING IN BIRTH, AND IN PAIN TO BE DE-
LIVERED.

"Be in pain, and labor to bring forth, O daughter of Zion, like
a woman in travail" Micah 4:10a. The WOMAN is here presented
as the people of God throughout the Old Testament era. She is
pregnant, about ready to deliver the Messiah. We recall the first
promise of the Messiah in Genesis 3:15 "and I will put enmity between thee and the woman, and between thy seed and her seed:
he shall bruise thy head, and thou shalt bruise his heel." This

promise was renewed to Abram in Genesis 12:1-3 "Now Jehovah said unto Abram, Get thee out of the country, and from thy kindred, and from thy father's house, unto the land that I will show thee: and I will make of thee a great nation, and I will bless thee, and make thy name great; and be thou a blessing: and I will bless them that bless thee, and him that curseth thee will I curse: and in thee shall all the families of the earth be blessed."

The CHILD is Jesus.

12:3   AND THERE WAS SEEN ANOTHER SIGN IN HEAVEN: AND BEHOLD, A GREAT RED DRAGON, HAVING SEVEN HEADS AND TEN HORNS, AND UPON HIS HEADS SEVEN DIADEMS.

The Greek word John uses for SIGN is his favorite word in his gospel record for describing the miracles of Jesus. John saw each of the miracles to be signs pointing to important truths. Here John sees A GREAT RED DRAGON as a SIGN. Verse nine makes it clear that this DRAGON is Satan. RED, the color of blood, is probably selected to symbolize the destructive power of the DRAGON. SEVEN HEADS speak of great wisdom. TEN HORNS speak of great power. SEVEN DIADEMS speak of great authority. Each of these are characteristics of Satan. The DRAGON is an ugly monster. It would be difficult to imagine a greater contrast than that which is set forth here in the two signs seen IN HEAVEN.

12:4   AND HIS TAIL DRAWETH THE THIRD PART OF THE STARS OF HEAVEN, AND DID CAST THEM TO THE EARTH: AND THE DRAGON STANDETH BEFORE THE WOMAN THAT IS ABOUT TO BE DELIVERED, THAT WHEN SHE IS DELIVERED HE MAY DEVOUR HER CHILD.

TAIL is a symbol of destructive power. This was noted in the sixth trumpet in chapter nine. See 9:19. THE THIRD PART OF THE STARS is a large part and thus the power of the DRAGON is made impressive. The DRAGON intends to terrify THE WOMAN with brute strength and world power. The object of his attack is the CHILD. If Satan can prevent Jesus from giving His life a ransom for many he will be able to maintain his possession of mankind. Jesus is the target of Satan's attack in this verse. An in-

120

teresting way to study the Old Testament is to note the numerous attempts of Satan to destroy the seed to prevent the birth of the Messiah and the fulfillment of God's promise of the Messiah.

12:5 AND SHE WAS DELIVERED OF A SON, A MAN CHILD, WHO IS TO RULE ALL THE NATIONS WITH A ROD OF IRON: AND THE CHILD WAS CAUGHT UP UNTO GOD, AND UNTO HIS THRONE.

The events in the life of Christ between His birth and ascension are skipped over since they are not pertinent to the picture here. The point is that Satan was unable to prevent Christ's birth and was unable to keep him from His THRONE.

The RULE WITH A ROD OF IRON symbolizes a firm, loving rule of a good shepherd, not that of a dictator. The Greek word for RULE gives us the shepherd image. "Thou shalt break them with a rod of iron; Thou shalt dash them in pieces like a potter's vessel" Psalm 2:9. The power of the gospel is symbolized with A ROD OF IRON.

12:6 AND THE WOMAN FLED INTO THE WILDERNESS, WHERE SHE HAD A PLACE PREPARED OF GOD, THAT THERE THEY MAY NOURISH HER A THOUSAND TWO HUNDRED AND THREESCORE DAYS.

A THOUSAND TWO HUNDRED AND THREESCORE DAYS is the same period of time the two witnesses prophesied. See 11:3. This symbolizes the Christian era. The Christian's sojourn upon this earth may be likened unto the journey of the children of Israel through the wilderness on their way to the Promised Land. God provided for the Israelites during this time in sending manna. Though they faced many trials and temptations God was clearly with His people. In like manner God is with His church and provides for their nourishment. We are to feed upon the word of God. "Man shall not live by bread alone, but by every word that proceedeth out of the mouth of God" Matthew 4:4. Jesus said, "He that eateth my flesh and drinketh my blood hath eternal life; and I will raise him up at the last day. For my flesh is meat indeed, and my blood is drink indeed. He that eateth my flesh and drinketh my blood abideth in me, and I in him" John 6:54-56. THEY that do the nourishing may refer to the prophets and apostles used of God in giving the church the living word.

A PLACE PREPARED OF GOD symbolizes the will of God, for to live in His will is to be assured of His protection. "Thy word have I laid up in my heart, That I might not sin against thee" Psalm 119:11.

12:7 AND THERE WAS WAR IN HEAVEN: MICHAEL AND HIS ANGELS GOING FORTH TO WAR WITH THE DRAGON; AND THE DRAGON WARRED AND HIS ANGELS,

We appreciate the ministry of MICHAEL from Daniel 12:1a "And at that time shall Michael stand up, the great prince who standeth for the children of thy people." MICHAEL fights for God's people. "But Michael the archangel, when contending with the devil he disputed about the body of Moses, durst not bring against him a railing judgment, but said, The Lord rebuke thee" Jude 9.

While the battle rages upon the earth it also is seen raging IN HEAVEN. Observe the past tense of the verb. THERE WAS WAR IN HEAVEN. This describes a battle prior to Christ's death. Until the death of Christ the sins of man were not forgiven. "For it is impossible that the blood of bulls and goats should take away sins" Hebrews 10:4. Bulls and goats were the sin offerings offered each year on the annual day of atonement. Until Christ's death Satan claimed all men, even those men of faith in the Old Testament era. HEAVEN would be understood as the place of the departed saints but should not be confused with that place prepared for the eternal abode of the church.

12:8 AND THEY PREVAILED NOT, NEITHER WAS THEIR PLACE FOUND ANY MORE IN HEAVEN.

"Who shall lay anything to the charge of God's elect? It is God that justifieth; who is he that condemneth? It is Christ Jesus that died, yea rather, that was raised from the dead, who is at the right hand of God, who also maketh intercession for us" Romans 8:33,34. Satan and his angels are defeated and have no more PLACE IN HEAVEN. The victory came at Calvary. Read Hebrews 9:16-28.

12:9 AND THE GREAT DRAGON WAS CAST DOWN, THE OLD SERPENT, HE THAT IS CALLED THE DEVIL AND SATAN, THE DECEIVER OF THE WHOLE

WORLD; HE WAS CAST DOWN TO THE EARTH, AND HIS ANGELS WERE CAST DOWN WITH HIM.

When was the DRAGON CAST DOWN? "And the seventy returned with joy, saying, Lord, even the demons are subject unto us in thy name. And he said unto them, I beheld Satan fallen as lightning from heaven" Luke 10:17,18. Jesus saw the victory over demons as a victory over Satan. The certainty of this victory is viewed as an accomplished fact though Jesus had not yet gone to Calvary where the final devastating blow would be delivered. Notice how the defeat of Satan is tied in with the death of Christ in John 12:31-33. "Now is the judgment of this world: now shall the prince of this world be cast out. And I, if I be lifted up from the earth, will draw all men unto myself. But this is said, signifying by what manner of death he should die."

Four designations are given for Satan in this verse. Each designation describes a specific manner of operation. When you speak of Satan's seemingly overwhelming power and strength, as may be manifested in pagan world powers, it is fitting to call him the DRAGON. "Thus said the Lord Jehovah: Behold, I am against thee, Pharaoh king of Egypt, the great monster (DRAGON) that lieth in the midst of his rivers, that hath said, My river is mine own, and I have made it for myself" Ezekiel 29:3. "Nebuchadrezzar the king of Babylon hath devoured me, he hath crushed me, he hath made me an empty vessel, he hath, like a monster (DRAGON), swallowed me up, he hath filled his maw with my delicacies; he hath cast me out" Jeremiah 51:34.

When you refer to Satan's deceptive qualities you may call him a SERPENT. It was the serpent that told Eve she would not die from eating the fruit of the tree in the midst of the garden. See Genesis 3:1-5. "But I fear, lest by any means, as the serpent beguiled Eve in his craftiness, your minds should be corrupted from the simplicity and the purity that is toward Christ...And no marvel; for even Satan fashioneth himself into an angel of light" 2 Corinthians 11:3,14. The SERPENT plants doubts and lies in the hearts of men to accomplish his purpose. He uses false propaganda effectively. "He is a liar" John 8:44.

DEVIL means false accuser or slanderer. SATAN is the adversary, the enemy of God. Other designations are recorded in

123

scripture, such as "the prince of this world" John 12:31. Perhaps the significance of the multiple designations in verse nine is to emphasize the effort put forth to avoid being defeated and CAST DOWN.

12:10 AND I HEARD A GREAT VOICE IN HEAVEN, SAYING, NOW IS COME THE SALVATION, AND THE POWER, AND THE KINGDOM OF OUR GOD, AND THE AUTHORITY OF HIS CHRIST: FOR THE ACCUSER OF OUR BRETHREN IS CAST DOWN, WHO ACCUSETH THEM BEFORE OUR GOD DAY AND NIGHT.

OUR BRETHREN who are accused DAY AND NIGHT is a reference to all those identified as God's people throughout the Old Testament period of time. At the cross they received the pardon of their sins, but prior to that time the lack of full pardon gave opportunity for the ACCUSER to accuse THEM.

Our hope in Christ is the theme of this victorious message. The victory is the Lord's. SALVATION is the deliverance of the woman from the dragon, the deliverance of the church from the power of evil, the freedom from sin the Christian has in Christ. POWER is an important word throughout the book of Revelation and to those in history who are deceived by Satanic power. All powers are nothing when compared to the POWER of God. The victory in the conflict of the ages is the great demonstration of this POWER. THE KINGDOM OF OUR GOD is a repetition of the thought expressed in 11:15.

12:11 AND THEY OVERCAME HIM BECAUSE OF THE BLOOD OF THE LAMB, AND BECAUSE OF THE WORD OF THEIR TESTIMONY; AND THEY LOVED NOT THEIR LIFE EVEN UNTO DEATH.

OVERCAME suggests effort and struggle. The battle against Satan is won by Christ at the cross and by the Christian in the surrender of his life to Christ. "He that loveth his life loseth it; and he that hateth his life in this world shall keep it unto life eternal" John 12:25. "Knowing that ye were redeemed, not with corruptible things, with silver or gold, for your vain manner of life handed down from your fathers; but with precious blood, as of a lamb without blemish and without spot, even the blood of Christ" 1 Peter 1:18,19. Christians share in the struggle and vic-

124

tory through confession. Jesus said, "Every one therefore who shall confess me before men, him will I also confess before my Father who is in heaven" Matthew 10:32.

12:12 THEREFORE REJOICE, O HEAVENS, AND YE THAT DWELL IN THEM. WOE FOR THE EARTH AND FOR THE SEA: BECAUSE THE DEVIL IS GONE DOWN UNTO YOU, HAVING GREAT WRATH, KNOWING THAT HE HATH BUT A SHORT TIME.

"Rejoice in the Lord always: again I will say, "Rejoice" Philippians 4:4. Here is a special reason for rejoicing. Satan has been cast out of heaven. But the blessing for the HEAVENS is WOE FOR THE EARTH AND FOR THE SEA. Satan is angry. The only sphere for his labors is the EARTH, that is, the people who dwell on the earth. KNOWING of his limitation both of space and time he does not give up but continues to manifest GREAT WRATH. A SHORT TIME is the same as FORTY TWO MONTHS. Time is a relative term. "But forget not this one thing, beloved, that one day is with the Lord as a thousand years, and a thousand years as one day" 2 Peter 3:8. EARTH AND SEA designate all the area where God's people are to be found, for they are the object of Satan's wrath.

12:13 AND WHEN THE DRAGON SAW THAT HE WAS CAST DOWN TO THE EARTH, HE PERSECUTED THE WOMAN THAT BROUGHT FORTH THE MAN CHILD.

Though Satan cannot do any damage to the MAN CHILD he can persecute THE WOMAN, the church. This he does. In John's day the people may have recalled the persecution under Nero as well as their current persecution under Domitian. Throughout the Christian era Christ's people have been persecuted. "If the world hateth you, ye know that it hath hated me before it hated you. If ye were of the world, the world would love its own: but because ye are not of the world, but I chose you out of the world, therefore the world hateth you" John 15:18,19. "Beloved, think it not strange concerning the fiery trial among you, which cometh upon you to prove you, as though a strange thing happened unto you: but insomuch as ye are partakers of Christ's sufferings, rejoice, that at the revelation of his glory also ye may rejoice with exceeding joy. If ye are reproached for the name of Christ, blessed are ye; because the Spirit of glory and the Spirit of God resteth upon you" 1 Peter 4:12-14.

12:14 AND THERE WERE GIVEN TO THE WOMAN THE TWO WINGS OF THE GREAT EAGLE, THAT SHE MIGHT FLY INTO THE WILDERNESS UNTO HER PLACE, WHERE SHE IS NOURISHED FOR A TIME, AND TIMES, AND HALF A TIME, FROM THE FACE OF THE SERPENT.

The DRAGON of the preceding verse is now the SERPENT. This may indicate a change of tactics in administering persecution against THE WOMAN. This is suggested by verse fifteen. THE SERPENT deceives with lies.

THE TWO WINGS OF THE GREAT EAGLE will support the church against the enemy. "They that wait for Jehovah shall renew their strength; they shall mount up with wings as eagles; they shall run, and not be weary; they shall walk, and not faint" Isaiah 40:31. God instructed Moses to inform the people: "Ye have seen what I did unto the Egyptians, and how I bare you on eagles' wings, and brought you unto myself" Exodus 19:4. God protects and cares for His people. This enables His people to be overcomers in conflict.

12:15 AND THE SERPENT CAST OUT OF HIS MOUTH AFTER THE WOMAN WATER AS A RIVER, THAT HE MIGHT CAUSE HER TO BE CARRIED AWAY BY THE STREAM.

Why didn't the SERPENT go into the wilderness to get THE WOMAN? He couldn't. The WILDERNESS is the will of God, where the Christian resides and is nourished of God. So long as the Christian abides in God's will the SERPENT is powerless against him. Jesus said, "My sheep hear my voice, and I know them, and they follow me: and I give unto them eternal life; and they shall never perish, and no one shall snatch them out of my hand" John 27,28. "There hath no temptation taken you but such as man can bear: but God is faithful, who will not suffer you to be tempted above that ye may be able to endure it" 1 Corinthians 10:13.

THE SERPENT makes an effort to remove THE WOMAN by casting OUT OF HIS MOUTH A RIVER of lies. This was the manner in which the SERPENT successfully drove man from the Garden of Eden. Satan floods the scene with false propaganda, heresy, false doctrine, etc. in an effort to remove THE WOMAN from the WILDERNESS of God's will. "If any man preacheth unto you any gospel other than that which ye received, let him be anathema" Galatians 1:9b.

12:16 AND THE EARTH HELPED THE WOMAN, AND THE EARTH OPENED HER MOUTH AND SWALLOWED UP THE RIVER WHICH THE DRAGON CAST OUT OF HIS MOUTH.

"And the earth opened its mouth, and swallowed them up, and their households, and all the men that appertained unto Korah, and all their goods" Numbers 16:32. The waters of the Red Sea closed in on the Egyptian army to give protection to the children of Israel. Nature is always on God's side. Ultimately every lie will be proved to be just that — a lie. "For the fearful, and unbelieving, and abominable, and murderers, and fornicators and sorcerers, and idolators, and all liars, their part shall be in the lake that burneth with fire and brimstone; which is the second death" 21:8. Satan will be just as powerless against the church as he was against Christ. Read Matthew 16:18.

12:17 AND THE DRAGON WAXED WROTH WITH THE WOMAN, AND WENT AWAY TO MAKE WAR WITH THE REST OF HER SEED, THAT KEEP THE COMMANDMENTS, OF GOD, AND HOLD THE TESTIMONY OF JESUS:

A distinction is made between THE WOMAN and THE REST OF HER SEED. We have indicated that THE WOMAN symbolizes the church. THE REST OF HER SEED symbolizes individual Christians as is indicated in the phrase KEEP THE COMMANDMENTS OF GOD and HOLD THE TESTIMONY OF JESUS. Though Satan cannot destroy the church he can be successful in his attack against individual Christians. God supplies adequate power for the salvation of every Christian but the Christian may refuse to avail himself of that power, he may reject Jesus as his Saviour. This is understood in light of the warnings against falling away from the faith. "For as touching those who were once enlightened and tasted of the heavenly gift, and were made partakers of the Holy Spirit, and tasted the good word of God, and the powers of the age to come, and then fell away, it is impossible to renew them again unto repentance; seeing they crucify to themselves the Son of God afresh, and put him to an open shame" Hebrews 6:4-6. "For if we sin willfully after that we have received the knowledge of the truth, there remaineth no more a sacrifice for sins, but a certain fearful expectation of judgment, and a fierceness of fire which shall devour the adversaries" Hebrews 10:26,27.

Christians are identified as those who KEEP THE COMMANDMENTS OF GOD. Jesus said, If ye love me, ye will keep my commandments" John 14:15. "He that saith, I know him, and keepeth not his commandments, is a liar, and the truth is not in him; but whoso keepeth his word, in him verily hath the love of God been perfected. Hereby we know that we are in him: he that saith he abideth in him ought himself also to walk even as he walked" 1 John 2:4-6.

Christians are identified as those who HOLD THE TESTIMONY OF JESUS. Jesus said, "ye shall be my witnesses" Acts 1:8. "Be not ashamed therefore of the testimony of our Lord, nor of me his prisoner," said Paul, "but suffer hardship with the gospel according to the power of God" 2 Timothy 1:8.

THE ENEMY

CHAPTER THIRTEEN

13:1   AND HE STOOD UPON THE SAND OF THE SEA. AND I
       SAW A BEAST COMING UP OUT OF THE SEA,
       HAVING TEN HORNS AND SEVEN HEADS, AND ON
       HIS HORNS TEN DIADEMS, AND UPON HIS HEADS
       NAMES OF BLASPHEMY.

This is a wild BEAST. The BEAST is not Satan but it is an agent of Satan. The BEAST symbolizes world power as used by Satan. TEN HORNS speak of great power. SEVEN HEADS symbolize great wisdom. TEN DIADEMS represent great authority — political authority. SEA may symbolize pagan nations. "But the wicked are like the troubled sea; for it cannot rest, and its waters cast up mire and dirt. There is no peace, saith my God, to the wicked" Isaiah 57:20,21. The NAMES OF BLASPHEMY UPON HIS HEADS identify the BEAST with Satan in an effort to usurp the power of God. More than anything else Satan would like to prove himself more powerful than God, but his attempts are vain.

This chapter explains two principle ways Satan wars against the church.

In John's day the Roman empire fit this picture well. Domitian insisted upon being recognized and addressed as Lord and God. This is blasphemous. Throughout history there have been similar applications of this picture of the BEAST.

13:2   AND THE BEAST WHICH I SAW WAS LIKE UNTO A
       LEOPARD, AND HIS FEET WERE AS THE FEET OF A
       BEAR, AND HIS MOUTH AS THE MOUTH OF A LION:
       AND THE DRAGON GAVE HIM HIS POWER, AND HIS
       THRONE, AND GREAT AUTHORITY.

THE DRAGON GAVE HIM HIS POWER explains the source and nature of the BEAST'S strength and authority. We understand the meaning of this imagery with the aid of Daniel.

129

"These great beasts, which are four, are four kings, that shall arise out of the earth. But the saints of the Most High shall receive the kingdom, and possess the kingdom for ever, even for ever and ever. Then I desired to know the truth concerning the fourth beast, which was diverse from all of them, exceeding terrible, whose teeth were of iron, and its nails of brass; which devoured, brake in pieces, and stamped the residue with its feet: and concerning the ten horns that were on its head" etc... "Thus he said, The fourth beast shall be a fourth kingdom upon earth,....And as for the ten horns, out of this kingdom shall ten kings arise:...And the kingdom and the dominion, and the greatness of the kingdoms under the whole heaven, shall be given to the people of the saints of the Most High: his kingdom is an everlasting kingdom, and all dominions shall serve and obey him. Here is the end of the matter" Daniel 7:17-20,23,24,27,28. The fourth beast is probably the Roman empire. Earlier in Daniel 7 he speaks of the characteristics of the lion, bear and leopard as descriptive of the world powers. This language adds terror to this wild BEAST. We have missed the point John is making if we fail to see the enemy of the church as anything less than threatening and horrible.

13:3 AND I SAW ONE OF HIS HEADS AS THOUGH IT HAD BEEN SMITTEN UNTO DEATH; AND HIS DEATH-STROKE WAS HEALED: AND THE WHOLE EARTH WONDERED AFTER THE BEAST;

At the end of the first century there were those who believed that Domitian was Nero come back to life. Satan mimicked the death, burial and resurrection of Christ. It has been true throughout history that powers that seemed to be dead were revived. When this happens it arouses the wonder of the people. The effectiveness of Satan's work through the BEAST is indicated by the fact that the WHOLE EARTH WONDERED AFTER THE BEAST. "Men loved the darkness rather than the light; for their works were evil" John 3:19b.

13:4 AND THEY WORSHIPPED THE DRAGON, BECAUSE HE GAVE HIS AUTHORITY UNTO THE BEAST; AND THEY WORSHIPPED THE BEAST, SAYING, WHO IS LIKE UNTO THE BEAST? AND WHO IS ABLE TO WAR WITH HIM?

All idolatry is a worship of Satan. Caesar worship would fit this category in John's day. Appreciation of and respect for the BEAST is expressed in the confident saying, WHO IS LIKE UNTO THE BEAST? Again, Satan tries to take the place of God. "Who is like unto thee, O Jehovah, among the gods? Exodus 15:11a. To make this question apply to the BEAST is blasphemy. His power appears to be invincible. WHO IS ABLE TO WAR WITH HIM?

All that is said with regard to this BEAST is not in contradiction with what Paul wrote to the Romans. "Let every soul be in subjection to the higher powers: for there is no power but of God; and the powers that be are ordained of God" Romans 13:1. Let it be understood that anything that God has made and ordained is good. However, that which is good may be perverted by Satan. What we see in this chapter is both a perversion of power and of truth — the perversion of truth will be presented in the imagery of the second beast.

13:5   AND THERE WAS GIVEN TO HIM A MOUTH SPEAKING GREAT THINGS AND BLASPHEMIES; AND THERE WAS GIVEN TO HIM AUTHORITY TO CONTINUE FORTY AND TWO MONTHS.

"And the king shall do according to his will; and he shall exalt himself and magnify himself above every god and shall speak marvellous things against the God of gods; and he shall prosper till the indignation be accomplished; for that which is determined shall be done" Daniel 11:36. The "man of sin" is described by Paul as "he that opposeth and exalteth himself against all that is called God or that is worshipped; so that he sitteth in the temple of God, setting himself forth as God" 2 Thessalonians 2:4.

WAS GIVEN TO HIM indicates the power of Satan behind the BEAST. Satan uses every one whom he can to accomplish his work against God. BLASPHEMIES are understood as those things that are injurious and hurtful, spoken against the holy God of heaven.

The duration of this blasphemous activity is equal to the length of the Christian era. Again note that FORTY AND TWO MONTHS denotes an evil time, or a time when evil is at work.

13:6 AND HE OPENED HIS MOUTH FOR BLASPHEMIES AGAINST GOD, TO BLASPHEME HIS NAME, AND HIS TABERNACLE, EVEN THEM THAT DWELL IN THE HEAVEN.

HIS NAME not only designates God but includes all that is involved in His character. This is true of the word NAME, not only in the book of Revelation but throughout scripture. Ascribing to man what is due God alone is blasphemy. The blasphemy does not stop with God but includes God's people also. This verse is a further amplification of verse five. Emperor worship in the first century was an example of what is here being described.

13:7 AND IT WAS GIVEN UNTO HIM TO MAKE WAR WITH THE SAINTS, AND TO OVERCOME THEM: AND THERE WAS GIVEN TO THEM AUTHORITY OVER EVERY TRIBE AND PEOPLE AND TONGUE AND NATION.

This picture is similar to that of chapter eleven, verses eight and nine. There are reoccuring times in history when it appears as if the church is being crushed out of existence. What chance does the church have for survival when pagan governments seek to crush her to death? Revelation provides the answer to the riddle of history. Appearances may be and sometimes are deceptive. Learn the truth about history through the study of God's word. As this verse states non-Christian world powers will appear to overcome in the conflict of the ages, but this verse is not the end of the story.

13:8 AND ALL THAT DWELL ON THE EARTH SHALL WORSHIP HIM, EVERY ONE WHOSE NAME HATH NOT BEEN WRITTEN FROM THE FOUNDATION OF THE WORLD IN THE BOOK OF LIFE OF THE LAMB THAT HATH BEEN SLAIN.

The ALL is explained by the exception of those WHOSE NAME HATH NOT BEEN WRITTEN IN THE BOOK OF LIFE. SHALL WORSHIP indicates that this will be the case as long as the battle against Satan continues. We should not be surprised by the great number who WORSHIP the BEAST. Jesus said, "broad is the way, that leadeth to destruction, and many are they that enter thereby" Matthew 7:13b.

132

FROM THE FOUNDATION OF THE WORLD refers to the record of the names of the saints. This is in keeping with Paul's words in Ephesians 1:4 "even as he chose us in him before the foundation of the world, that we should be holy and without blemish before him in love." However, the grammar of the text allows for this to refer to THE LAMB THAT HATH BEEN SLAIN. In this event it would be in harmony with the words of Peter, "but with precious blood, as of a lamb without blemish and without spot, even the blood of Christ: who was foreknown indeed before the foundation of the world, but was manifested at the end of the times for your sake" 1 Peter 1:19,20. This verse gives emphasis to those whose names are recorded in THE BOOK OF LIFE. This is God's record of His people. It may prove to be a startling revelation to someday see the difference between God's record and the local church membership records on earth. THE BOOK OF LIFE is mentioned five times in this book.

13:9   IF ANY MAN HATH AN EAR, LET HIM HEAR.

This injunction adds seriousness to what has just been said and to what is about to be said. The power of the BEAST must not be regarded lightly. Great pressure is exerted on the Christian when it looks as if he is standing all alone. There is always the strong temptation to go along with the crowd. Be warned against giving in to this temptation.

Furthermore, do not misunderstand what has just been said with regard to that which happened FROM THE FOUNDATION OF THE WORLD. This does not suggest that God has predestined some to be saved and others to be lost. It is simply an indication of His foreknowledge. It also indicates that God has a plan and purpose and history, rightly understood, is the execution of this plan and the carrying out of this purpose.

13:10 IF ANY MAN IS FOR CAPTIVITY, INTO CAPTIVITY HE GOETH: IF ANY MAN SHALL KILL WITH THE SWORD, WITH THE SWORD MUST HE BE KILLED. HERE IS THE PATIENCE AND THE FAITH OF THE SAINTS.

"And it shall come to pass, when they say unto thee, Whither shall we go forth? then thou shalt tell them, Thus saith Jehovah: Such as are for death, to death; and such as are for the sword, to

133

the sword; and such as are for the famine, to the famine; and such as are for captivity, to captivity" Jeremiah 15:2. "Then saith Jesus unto him, Put up again thy sword into its place: for all they that take the sword shall perish with the sword" Matthew 26:52. The Christian must be careful not to lay aside the "sword of the Spirit, which is the word of God" (Ephesians 6:17) for the sword of steel. There are times when there will be no way for the Christian to escape the persecution if he remains faithful to God. PATIENCE means steadfast endurance. The PATIENCE and FAITH OF THE SAINTS is demonstrated in their resistance to the powers of the BEAST. The Christian shows himself strong in the Lord through his never-ending trust in God and his willingness to endure affliction for the cause of Christ. The Christian is admonished to "be steadfast, unmovable, always abounding in the work of the Lord" 1 Corinthians 15:58a.

13:11 AND I SAW ANOTHER BEAST COMING UP OUT OF THE EARTH; AND HE HAD TWO HORNS LIKE UNTO A LAMB, AND HE SPAKE AS A DRAGON.

Jesus said, "Beware of false prophets, who come to you in sheep's clothing, but inwardly are ravening wolves" Matthew 7:15. This second BEAST is called the "false prophet" in 19:20. Though his looks deceive, his voice gives him away. He has the appearance of a LAMB but his voice is that of the DRAGON. The first BEAST was political. This BEAST is religious. False religions, pagan religions, serve Satan's purpose. This BEAST gives the appearance of being your friend, harmless, but this is hypocrisy. This BEAST wears a mask for the purpose of deceiving.

13:12 AND HE EXERCISETH ALL THE AUTHORITY OF THE FIRST BEAST IN HIS SIGHT. AND HE MAKETH THE EARTH AND THEM THAT DWELL THEREIN TO WORSHIP THE FIRST BEAST, WHOSE DEATH-STROKE WAS HEALED.

Any philosophy or religion that is not in total accord with pure Christianity is an instrument of the second BEAST and serves the purpose of the first BEAST. A definite relationship is indicated between Satan's power and satanic religion. The priests of the emperor cult in John's day served the emperor by bringing the people to worship the emperor. The HEALED

134

DEATH-STROKE suggests a revival or a resurrection of the FIRST BEAST. Of course this is a mimicry of Christ's resurrection. Non-Christians have been impressed with a revival of power that suggests permanency.

13:13 AND HE DOETH GREAT SIGNS, THAT HE SHOULD EVEN MAKE FIRE TO COME DOWN OUT OF HEAVEN UPON THE EARTH IN THE SIGHT OF MEN.

The devil does a good job of imitating the miraculous. Elijah called upon God to prove Himself by sending fire down from heaven. The fire fell. Here is an effort to duplicate this feat. "For there shall arise false Christs, and false prophets, and shall show great signs and wonders; so as to lead astray, if possible, even the elect" Matthew 24:24. "And then shall be revealed the lawless one, whom the Lord Jesus shall slay with the breath of his mouth, and bring to nought by the manifestation of his coming; even he, whose coming is according to the working of Satan with all power and signs and lying wonders" 2 Thessalonians 2:8,9. The Bible does not equate the SIGNS of the devil with the miracles of God. It is important to remember that the devil's power is in his deceptive ability. These SIGNS seem to be as great as those of God. Because the word "miracle" is used rather casually and carelessly today to refer to many things that are not technically miraculous we must be careful in assessing the SIGNS of the devil. Clever works of magic illustrate man's ability to make you believe something that is not true.

13:14 AND HE DECEIVETH THEM THAT DWELL ON THE EARTH BY REASON OF THE SIGNS WHICH IT WAS GIVEN TO HIM TO DO IN THE SIGHT OF THE BEAST; SAYING TO THEM THAT DWELL ON THE EARTH, THAT THEY SHOULD MAKE AN IMAGE TO THE BEAST WHO HATH THE STROKE OF THE SWORD AND LIVED.

"If there arise in the midst of thee a prophet, or a dreamer of dreams, and he give thee a sign or a wonder, and the sign or the wonder come to pass, whereof he spake unto thee, saying, Let us go after other gods, which thou hast not known, and let us serve them; thou shalt not harken unto the words of that prophet, or unto that dreamer of dreams: for Jehovah your God proveth you,

135

to know whether ye love Jehovah your God with all your heart and with all your soul. Ye shall walk after Jehovah your God, and fear him, and keep his commandments, and obey his voice, and ye shall serve him and cleave unto him" Deuteronomy 13:1-4.

"And the beast was taken, and with him the false prophet that wrought the signs in his sight, wherewith he deceived them that had received the mark of the beast and them that worshipped his image: they two were cast alive into the lake of fire that burneth with brimstone:...And the devil that deceived them was cast into the lake of fire and brimstone, where are also the beast and the false prophet; and they shall be tormented day and night for ever and ever" 19:20; 20:10.

AN IMAGE OF THE BEAST may refer to a painting, the imprint on a coin, a bust of stone, or any other likeness of the emperor before which man might bow. The decalogue clearly records, "Thou shalt not make unto thee a graven image, nor any likeness of anything that is in heaven above, or that is in the earth beneath, or that is in the water under the earth: thou shalt not bow down thyself unto them, nor serve them; for I, Jehovah, thy God, am a jealous God, visiting the iniquity of the fathers upon the children, and upon the third and upon the fourth generation of them that hate me" Deuteronomy 5:8,9.

Faithfulness to God in prayer, Bible study and Christian service will prevent the Christian from being deceived by satanic efforts.

13:15 AND IT WAS GIVEN UNTO HIM TO GIVE BREATH TO IT, EVEN TO THE IMAGE OF THE BEAST, THAT THE IMAGE OF THE BEAST SHOULD BOTH SPEAK, AND CAUSE THAT AS MANY AS SHOULD NOT WORSHIP THE IMAGE OF THE BEAST SHOULD BE KILLED.

The death of Antipas (2:13) may have been the result of his refusal to worship the IMAGE OF THE BEAST. The magical abilities make the IMAGE impressive for deceptive purposes. The killing of those who do NOT WORSHIP THE IMAGE is intended to strengthen the cause of the BEAST, but the Christian has nothing to fear from those who can only kill the body. Death is Satan's weapon.

IT WAS GIVEN is another of the several reminders of Satan's power behind the work of the two beasts. Only God can give life, but Satan's deceptive work seems to be able TO GIVE BREATH to the IMAGE OF THE BEAST.

13:16 AND HE CAUSETH ALL, THE SMALL AND THE GREAT, AND THE RICH AND THE POOR, AND THE FREE AND THE BOND, THAT THERE BE GIVEN THEM A MARK ON THEIR RIGHT HAND, OR UPON THEIR FOREHEAD:

Identification marks on hands and foreheads were not uncommon in John's day. Soldiers were identified. Slaves were identified. The Pharisees wore phylacteries on their foreheads and on their arms. The seal of God was placed upon the forehead. See 7:3.

HE CAUSETH ALL to be identified. The non-Christian is just as certainly identified with the devil as the Christian is with God. The non-Christian's identity is noted in his speech, his habits, his way of living, his character, his deeds, etc. Jesus had no trouble making this distinction, even when talking with those who claimed to be God's people. "Ye are of your father the devil, and the lusts of your father it is your will to do. He was a murderer from the beginning, and standeth not in the truth, because there is no truth in him. When he speaketh a lie, he speaketh not in the truth, because there is no truth in him. When he speaketh a lie, he speaketh of his own: for he is a liar, and the father thereof" John 8:44.

Satan's people are made up of people from every step on the social ladder and from every economic level. Sin is no respector of persons. "Be sure your sin will find you out" Numbers 32:23b.

13:17 AND THAT NO MAN SHOULD BE ABLE TO BUY OR TO SELL, SAVE HE THAT HATH THE MARK, EVEN THE NAME OF THE BEAST OR THE NUMBER OF HIS NAME.

Real pressure is brought to bear upon the Christian when his rights to BUY OR TO SELL are taken away unless he denies his faith in God and surrenders to the BEAST by receiving his MARK. HIS NUMBER is an identification of his NAME. The reference is to a form of discrimination that results in the persecution and suffering of the saints. Forms of ostracism have been inflicted upon groups from time to time. Examples of this may be seen in the history of the Jews and more recently with the blacks in the United States. Here the discrimination is against the Christians. The victory of faith is made abundantly clear in circumstances like these.

13:18 HERE IS WISDOM. HE THAT HATH UNDERSTANDING, LET HIM COUNT THE NUMBER OF THE BEAST; FOR IT IS THE NUMBER OF A MAN: AND HIS NUMBER IS SIX HUNDRED AND SIXTY AND SIX.

Numbers are used frequently in this book to signify identity. God's people are signfied by "a hundred and forty and four thousand" (7:4). It should not be considered strange that non-Christians should likewise be identified with a number. SIX is the number of creation. It falls short of the sacred and complete number—SEVEN. It is an appropriate numerical designation for those who "fall short of the glory of God" Romans 3:23b. The triple use of this number may indicate repeated failures of man to measure up to the will of God.

The cryptic aspect of this verse is indicated with the words, HERE IS WISDOM. When making an interpretation of the symbols of Revelation we must be careful to ask if we have the proper key for understanding this code language. Consider the meaning which is consistent with the rest of scripture but be cautious in being too dogmatic with your conclusion.

Men have reached varied conclusions by giving each letter of the alphabet a numeric value. The numeric value you select for each letter will determine whether or not you can come up with the sum 666. Avoid this!

All men who fall short of God's will are symbolized with the number SIX. To fall short of God's will places man in Satan's camp. Three sixes make an unholy trinity in opposition to God.

:

BLESSED ASSURANCE

CHAPTER FOURTEEN

14:1 AND I SAW, AND BEHOLD, THE LAMB STANDING ON THE MOUNT ZION, AND WITH HIM A HUNDRED AND FORTY AND FOUR THOUSAND, HAVING HIS NAME, AND THE NAME OF HIS FATHER, WRITTEN ON THEIR FOREHEADS.

This verse presents a complete contrast with the final verses of chapter thirteen. THE LAMB is Jesus Christ. MOUNT ZION is a designation for Jerusalem, this being the principal hill in the city. A HUNDRED AND FORTY AND FOUR THOUSAND designates symbolically the people of God. See chapter seven for more details regarding this number. Chapter seven also speaks concerning the identity of God's people, a conspicuous and obvious identification, WRITTEN ON THEIR FOREHEADS.

It is appropriate in light of the dark picture in chapter thirteen that we should not be encouraged with the message of hope and blessed assurance. By the way, assurance is a vital part of Christian hope. This book is designed to accentuate the Christian's assurance throughout the struggle against the forces of evil. After showing the seeming triumph of sin the real victory of righteousness is portrayed. Our experience in witnessing the divine drama of Revelation may be likened unto the experience Elisha had with his servant. His servant arose early one morning and looked outside to see that the city was surrounded with a great host of horses and chariots. "And his servant said unto him, Alas, my master! How shall we do? And he answered, Fear not; for they that are with us are more than they that are with them. And Elisha prayed, and said, Jehovah, I pray thee, open his eyes, that he may see. And Jehovah opened the eyes of the young man; and he saw: and behold, the mountain was full of horses and chariots of fire round about Elisha" 2 Kings 6:15-17. Our eyes are opened with this verse to show us the greater power of God and the security of those whose names are recorded in the BOOK OF

LIFE.

14:2 AND I HEARD A VOICE FROM HEAVEN, AS THE
VOICE OF MANY WATERS, AND AS THE VOICE OF A
GREAT THUNDER: AND THE VOICE WHICH I HEARD
WAS AS THE VOICE OF HARPERS HARPING WITH
THEIR HARPS:

The sound is both strong and beautiful, both loud and sweet.
Apparently this is the voice of the redeemed.

14:3 AND THEY SING AS IT WERE A NEW SONG BEFORE
THE THRONE, AND BEFORE THE FOUR LIVING
CREATURES AND THE ELDERS: AND NO MAN
COULD LEARN THE SONG SAVE THE HUNDRED
AND FORTY AND FOUR THOUSAND, EVEN THEY
THAT HAD BEEN PURCHASED OUT OF THE EARTH.

Some things are only learned by experience. The uniqueness
of the experience of the HUNDRED AND FORTY AND FOUR
THOUSAND enabled them to LEARN THE SONG. Their experience was that of having BEEN PURCHASED OUT OF THE
EARTH. "For ye were bought with a price: glorify God therefore
in your body" 1 Corinthians 7:23. Not until man has a new heart
and a new life can he sing this NEW SONG, which is undoubtedly
a song of praise to God, a song of victory, like that of Moses or
Deborah.

14:4 THESE ARE THEY THAT WERE NOT DEFILED WITH
WOMEN; FOR THEY ARE VIRGINS. THESE ARE
THEY THAT FOLLOW THE LAMB WHITHERSOEVER
HE GOETH. THESE WERE PURCHASED FROM
AMONG MEN, TO BE THE FIRSTFRUITS UNTO GOD
AND UNTO THE LAMB.

NOT DEFILED WITH WOMEN symbolizes the purity that
results when one has been cleansed by the blood of Christ. It also
speaks of the faithfulness of the Christian to Christ, for THEY
FOLLOW THE LAMB WITHERSOEVER HE GOETH. Certainly
this describes those who are pure from physical adultery but also
those free from spiritual adultery. This meaning is enforced with
the word VIRGIN. Paul said, "For I am jealous over you with a
godly jealousy: for I espoused you to one husband, that I might
present you as a pure virgin to Christ" 2 Corinthians 11:2.

It is a mistake to regard this language literally. Celibacy is not regarded as a holier state than marriage in scripture. "For this cause shall a man leave his father and mother, and shall cleave to his wife; and the two shall become one flesh? So that they are no more two, but one flesh. What therefore God hath joined together, let not man put asunder" Matthew 19:5,6. "Let marriage be had in honor among all, and let the bed be undefiled: for fornicators and adulterers God will judge" Hebrews 13:4. Read Ephesians 5:22,23.

Jesus appealed to man, "Come ye after me" Matthew 4:19a. "For hereunto were ye called: because Christ also suffered for you, leaving you an example, that ye should follow his steps" 1 Peter 2:21. "My sheep hear my voice, and I know them, and they follow me" John 10:27. Following Jesus is not to be regarded lightly as Jesus made clear to a scribe, who said, "Teacher, I will follow thee whithersoever thou goest. And Jesus saith unto him, The foxes have holes, and the birds of the heaven have nests; but the Son of man hath not where to lay his head" Matthew 8:19,20.

FIRSTFRUITS were regarded holy to God. "Israel was holiness unto Jehovah, the firstfruits of his increase" Jeremiah 2:3a. "Of his own will he brought us forth by the word of truth, that we should be a kind of firstfruits of his creatures" James 1:18. The first part of the harvest was called FIRSTFRUITS.

14:5   AND IN THEIR MOUTH WAS FOUND NO LIE: THEY
       ARE WITHOUT BLEMISH.

During the time of trials and persecutions there is a strong temptation to LIE in an effort to avoid suffering. "Who is the liar but he that denieth that Jesus is the Christ? This is the antichrist, even he that denieth the Father and the Son" 1 John 2:22. "If a man say, I love God, and hateth his brother, he is a liar" 1 John 4:20a. "If we say that we have fellowship with him and walk in the darkness, we lie, and do not the truth" 1 John 1:6. "Now unto him that is able to guard you from stumbling, and to set you before the presence of his glory without blemish in exceeding joy, to the only God our Saviour, through Jesus Christ our Lord be glory, majesty, dominion and power, before all time, and now, and for evermore. Amen" Jude 24. Christians are known for telling the truth. The LIE is the devil's weapon and the Christian should have nothing to do with any thing that is less than honest. Each falsehood is a BLEMISH.

14:6 AND I SAW ANOTHER ANGEL FLYING IN MID HEAVEN, HAVING ETERNAL GOOD TIDINGS TO PROCLAIM UNTO THEM THAT DWELL ON THE EARTH, AND UNTO EVERY NATION AND TRIBE AND TONGUE AND PEOPLE;

Good news is for all men. Jesus commissioned that the gospel should be preached to all nations. See Mark 16:15. God's good news is ETERNAL. It is beneficial now and forever. ANGEL means messenger. ETERNAL GOOD TIDINGS are intended to be made known. What a joy to PROCLAIM good news! Though the message is to be embodied it is also to be proclaimed. All people are the object of God's love and grace. Those who need the gospel are given four designations, the symbolic number for the earth. This follows the pattern of numeric symbolism in Revelation.

14:7 AND HE SAITH WITH A GREAT VOICE, FEAR GOD, AND GIVE HIM GLORY; FOR THE HOUR OF HIS JUDGMENT IS COME: AND WORSHIP HIM THAT MADE THE HEAVEN AND THE EARTH AND THE SEA AND FOUNTAINS OF WATERS.

Three things are required of all those who would escape the JUDGMENT of God—FEAR GOD, GIVE HIM GLORY and WORSHIP HIM. We FEAR God when we give Him proper respect and reverence Him. We do this through submission and obedience. We GIVE HIM GLORY when we regard Him with praise and magnify Him with honor. We are to glorify HIM with our whole person—body, soul and spirit. We WORSHIP HIM because He is the Creator of the universe.

THE HOUR OF HIS JUDGMENT IS COME. "And this is the judgment, that the light is come into the world, and men loved the darkness rather than the light; for their works were evil" John 3:19. "Now is the judgment of this world" John 12:31a. "And Jesus said, For judgment came I into this world, that they that see not may see; and that they that see may become blind. Those of the Pharisees who were with him heard these things, and said unto him, Are we also blind? Jesus said unto them, if ye were blind, ye would have no sin: but now ye say, We see: your sin remaineth" John 9:39-41.

This verse covers the time period of the Christian era. It is man's acceptance or rejection of the gospel that determines his judgment. "For he saith, At an acceptable time I hearkened unto thee, And in a day of salvation did I succor thee: behold, now is the acceptable time, behold, now is the day of salvation" 2 Corinthians 6:2. "And if any man hear my sayings, and keep them not, I judge him not: for I came not to judge the world, but to save the world. He that rejecteth me, and receiveth not my sayings, hath one that judgeth him: the word that I spake, the same shall judge him in the last day" John 12:47,48.

14:8   AND ANOTHER, A SECOND ANGEL, FOLLOWED, SAYING, FALLEN, FALLEN IS BABYLON THE GREAT, THAT HATH MADE ALL THE NATIONS TO DRINK OF THE WINE OF THE WRATH OF HER FORNICATION.

It is likely that BABYLON was regarded as synonomous with Rome in the first century mind. Peter speaks of BABYLON in his first epistle (5:13), but this could not be the historic Babylon, for it was destroyed, never to be builded again. It is only fair to be informed that some Bible scholars do believe the BABYLON in 1 Peter refers to the historic location. BABYLON is used in Revelation to symbolize Satan's people. It was stated earlier that the church is symbolized by a woman and a city and Satan's people are symbolized by a woman and a city — BABYLON is the city.

BABYLON had not yet FALLEN, but the fall was so certain that it was viewed as an accomplished fact. Long ago, Isaiah wrote, "Fallen, fallen is Babylon" Isaiah 21:9b. Later, Jeremiah recorded, "Babylon is suddenly fallen and destroyed" Jeremiah 51:8a. In both instances these were words of prediction that literally came true. What happened to historic Babylon is symbolic of what will inevitably happen to all who reject Christ as Saviour.

BABYLON is called THE GREAT! Historic Babylon was a great city. This was acknowledged by Daniel when he interpreted the king's dream by calling Babylon the "head of gold" Daniel 2:38. Historical accounts verify the greatness of this city. BABY-

LON, referring to the pagan world, appears to be GREAT, and is thus signified here. GREAT is the pride of men who live in heathen wickedness. Indeed their effort will all come to nought.

The wickedness of BABYLON is signified with drunkenness and immorality. She HATH MADE ALL THE NATIONS TO DRINK OF THE WINE OF THE WRATH OF HER FORNICATION. Once intoxicating the NATIONS with her WINE she then engages them in FORNICATION. God's wrath is incurred upon those who have surrendered their lives to impurity.

The certain destruction and fall of all sin gives the Christian great hope. This is always important to remember, particularly when pagan power seems to be all powerful.

14:9 AND ANOTHER ANGEL, A THIRD, FOLLOWED THEM, SAYING WITH A GREAT VOICE, IF ANY MAN WORSHIPPETH THE BEAST AND HIS IMAGE, AND RECEIVETH A MARK ON HIS FOREHEAD, OR UPON HIS HAND

14:10 HE ALSO SHALL DRINK OF THE WINE OF THE WRATH OF GOD, WHICH IS PREPARED UNMIXED IN THE CUP OF HIS ANGER: AND HE SHALL BE TORMENTED WITH FIRE AND BRIMSTONE IN THE PRESENCE OF THE HOLY ANGELS, AND IN THE PRESENCE OF THE LAMB:

This is the other side of the picture than was seen in chapter thirteen, verses fifteen and seventeen. UNMIXED means full strength. "For in the hand of Jehovah there is a cup, and the wine foameth; It is full of mixture, and he poureth out the same: Surely the dregs thereof, all the wicked of the earth shall drain them, and drink them" Psalm 75:8. "For thus saith Jehovah, the God of Israel, unto me: Take this cup of the wine of wrath at my hand, and cause all the nations, to whom I send thee, to drink it. And they shall drink, and reel to and fro, and be mad, because of the sword that I will send among them" Jeremiah 25:15,16.

FIRE AND BRIMSTONE may be understood figuratively in light of what actually happened to Sodom and Gomorrah. See Genesis 19:24.

IN THE PRESENCE OF THE HOLY ANGELS AND OF THE LAMB is not to suggest that there is any joy in witnessing the punishment of the wicked. It is a contrast with the picture in chapter eleven, verses eight through ten. A punishment is always accentuated and aggravated when others stand by looking on. Thus, the picture is one of intense punishment as an expression of the WRATH OF GOD. A suffocating odor accompanies the burning of BRIMSTONE which was sulphuric.

14:11 AND THE SMOKE OF THEIR TORMENT GOETH UP FOR EVER AND EVER: AND THEY HAVE NO REST DAY AND NIGHT, THEY THAT WORSHIP THE BEAST AND HIS IMAGE, AND WHOSO RECEIVETH THE MARK OF HIS NAME.

This is strong language and intended to be as strong as man can comprehend in order to show the folly of following the BEAST and the wisdom of enduring for Christ. Ponder each word — SMOKE, TORMENT, NO REST — and then add the words FOR EVER AND EVER, DAY AND NIGHT. "It is a fearful thing to fall into the hands of the living God" Hebrews 10:31. THE MARK is that which clearly identifies one with Satan. The purpose of this vivid and horrible picture is to shock, if need be, a person into his senses lest he identify himself with Satan rather than with God. There simply is no more important decision that man can make in his entire lifetime than the decision he makes for God. Rejecting God not only has eternal consequences; these consequences are frightening and severe.

14:12 HERE IS THE PATIENCE OF THE SAINTS, THEY THAT KEEP THE COMMANDMENTS OF GOD, AND THE FAITH OF JESUS.

Wicked conditions upon the earth present a real challenge to the Christian to remain faithful unto death. Those who obey Christ and remain faithful to him steadfastly endure throughout the struggle. These are those who have not become "weary in well-doing: for in due season we shall reap, if we faint not" Galatians 6:9.

It is comforting to know that our patience in Christ is not in vain. The Christian is challenged to live so that he may testify with Paul, "I have fought the good fight, I have finished the course, I have kept the faith: henceforth there is laid up for me the crown of righteousness, which the Lord, the righteous judge, shall give to me at that day; and not to me only, but also to all them that have loved his appearing" 2 Timothy 4:7,8.

14:13 AND I HEARD A VOICE FROM HEAVEN SAYING, WRITE, BLESSED ARE THE DEAD WHO DIE IN THE LORD FROM HENCEFORTH: YEA, SAITH THE SPIRIT, THAT THEY MAY REST FROM THEIR LABORS; FOR THEIR WORKS FOLLOW WITH THEM.

Death is not to be feared by the Christian. "We are of good courage, I say, and are willing rather to be absent from the body, and to be at home with the Lord" 2 Corinthians 5:8. "For to me to live is Christ, and to die is gain" Philippians 1:21.

BLESSED is that state of joy based upon our relationship with God, not upon uncertain and changing circumstances. "For the Lord himself shall descend from heaven, with a shout, with the voice of the archangel, and with the trump of God: and the dead in Christ shall rise first" 1 Thessalonians 4:16.

REST means to be refreshed. A distinction is to be noted between LABORS and WORKS. LABORS refer to the suffering and hardship endured by good soldiers of Christ Jesus (2 Timothy 2:3). WORKS refer to acts of righteousness which bring glory to God (Matthew 5:16). Jesus said, "Come unto me, all ye that labor and are heavy laden, and I will give you rest" Matthew 11:28. THEIR WORKS FOLLOW WITH THEM as a basis upon which God rewards His people (Luke 6:35). God honors Christian work.

14:14 AND I SAW, AND BEHOLD, A WHITE CLOUD; AND ON THE CLOUD I SAW ONE SITTING LIKE UNTO A SON OF MAN, HAVING ON HIS HEAD A GOLDEN CROWN, AND IN HIS HAND A SHARP SICKLE.

God's judgment is pictured in the verses that remain in this chapter. These verses picture the end of time as we know it upon the earth, just as was the case in the sixth seal in chapter six. Judgment for God's people will be like the harvesting of grain, but for the others it will be like being thrown in the wine press to be trampled upon.

WHITE symbolizes purity and holiness. The CLOUD was symbolic of the vehicle used for heavenly transportation. The language of this verse is borrowed from Daniel 7:13 "And I saw in the night visions, and, behold, there came with the clouds of heaven one like unto a son of man, and he came even to the ancient of days, and they brought him near before him."

SON OF MAN is a designation Jesus frequently used of Himself. Jesus said, "The foxes have holes, and the birds of the heaven have nests; but the Son of man hath not where to lay his head" Matthew 8:20. The GOLDEN CROWN is the victor's crown, appropriately worn at the end of the conflict to make distinct the omnipotence of God and the victory that is assured the child of God through Jesus Christ. GOLDEN emphasizes the value and preciousness of our victory in Christ — it is eternal.

The SHARP SICKLE is the instrument used for reaping. He is not using a sword at this time, for the victory has been won, the battle is over. Now is the time for rewarding the saints. The language is similar to that of Joel. "Put ye in the sickle; for the harvest is ripe: come, tread ye; for the winepress is full, the vats overflow; for their wickedness is great" Joel 3:13. Jesus said, "So is the kingdom of God, as if a man should cast seed upon the earth; and should sleep and rise night and day, and the seed should spring up and grow, he knoweth not how. The earth beareth fruit of herself; first the blade, then the ear, then the full grain in the ear. But when the fruit is ripe, straightway he putteth forth the sickle, because the harvest is come" Mark 4:26-29.

14:15 AND ANOTHER ANGEL CAME OUT FROM THE TEMPLE, CRYING WITH A GREAT VOICE TO HIM THAT SAT ON THE CLOUD, SEND FORTH THY SICKLE, AND REAP: FOR THE HOUR TO REAP IS COME; FOR THE HARVEST OF THE EARTH IS RIPE.

ANOTHER ANGEL is understood in light of verses six, eight and nine. FROM THE TEMPLE indicates from the presence of God. THE HOUR TO REAP IS COME. Jesus' disciples asked for an explanation of the parable of the tares. "And he answered and said, He that soweth the good seed is the Son of man; and the field is the world; and the good seed, these are the sons of the kingdom; and the tares are the sons of the evil one; and the enemy that sowed them is the devil: and the harvest is the end of the world; and the reapers are angels" Matthew 13:37-39. Later Jesus said, "And he shall send forth his angels with a great sound of a trumpet, and they shall gather together his elect from the four winds, from one end of heaven to the other" Matthew 24:31. During His ministry Jesus said, "Say not ye, There are yet four months, and then cometh the harvest? behold, I say unto you, Lift up your eyes, and look on the fields, that they are white already unto harvest. He that reapeth receiveth wages, and gathereth fruit unto life eternal; that he that soweth and he that reapeth may rejoice together" John 4:35,36. The harvesting is done through evangelism throughout the last days which are equated in scripture with the Christian era. Read Hebrews 1:1,2.

14:16 AND HE THAT SAT ON THE CLOUD CAST HIS SICKLE UPON THE EARTH; AND THE EARTH WAS REAPED.

THE EARTH WAS REAPED indicates the salvation of the redeemed. The harvesting of grain would have been understood as a reference to the ultimate blessings of the Christians. When John announced the beginning of Jesus' ministry upon the earth he made a similar reference. "John answered, saying unto them all, I indeed baptize you with water; but there cometh he that is mightier than I, the latchet of whose shoes I am not worthy to unloose: he shall baptize you in the Holy Spirit and in fire: whose fan is in his hand, thoroughly to cleanse his threshing-floor, and to gather the wheat into his garner; but the chaff he will burn up with unquenchable fire" Luke 3:16,17.

This verse expresses the obedience of God's order. "Jesus saith unto them, My meat is to do the will of him that sent me, and to accomplish his work" John 4:34.

14:17 AND ANOTHER ANGEL CAME OUT FROM THE TEMPLE WHICH IS IN HEAVEN, HE ALSO HAVING A SHARP SICKLE.

AND ANOTHER ANGEL suggests yet another picture. This is no thought of suggesting a time difference, rather a different view of judgment—this time as it relates to the wicked. FROM THE TEMPLE means that God is still in control. God's power is manifested just as surely in the condemnation of the wicked as it is in the salvation of the righteous. A SHARP SICKLE is an instrument that will be effective in accomplishing the purpose of God.

14:18 AND ANOTHER ANGEL CAME OUT FROM THE AL-

TAR, HE THAT HATH POWER OVER FIRE; AND HE
CALLED WITH A GREAT VOICE TO HIM THAT HAD
THE SHARP SICKLE, SAYING, SEND FORTH THY
SHARP SICKLE, AND GATHER THE CLUSTERS OF
THE VINE OF THE EARTH: FOR HER GRAPES ARE
FULLY RIPE.

THE ALTAR is not identified. If we identify this altar with
that of the fifth seal we may understand this verse to be an answer to the question, "How long, O Master, the holy and true,
dost thou not judge and avenge our blood on them that dwell on
the earth?" (6:10). But if we identify this altar with the golden altar seen in the introduction of the seventh seal we may think this
verse to be a response to the prayers of the saints. In either instance the truth is clear—God exercises judgment upon sinful
men.

POWER OVER FIRE symbolizes authority to execute judgment. A GREAT VOICE gives emphasis to the directive.
GRAPES symbolize wicked men. The remaining verses will make
this clear.

14:19 AND THE ANGEL CAST HIS SICKLE INTO THE
EARTH, AND GATHERED THE VINTAGE OF THE
EARTH, AND CAST IT INTO THE WINEPRESS, THE
GREAT WINEPRESS, OF THE WRATH OF GOD.

"I have trodden the winepress alone; and of the people there
was no man with me: yea, I trod them in mine anger, and trampled them in my wrath; and their lifeblood is sprinkled upon my
garments, and I have stained all my raiment. For the day of vengeance was in my heart, and the year of my redeemed is come"
Isaiah 63:3,4.

THE WINEPRESS is identified with THE WRATH OF GOD
making the picture clearly that of judgment upon the wicked.
Men used their feet to tread upon the grapes for the purpose of
removing the juice, which then flowed through a channel from a
higher level to a lower level trough.

14:20 AND THE WINEPRESS WAS TRODDEN WITHOUT
THE CITY, AND THERE CAME OUT BLOOD FROM
THE WINEPRESS, EVEN UNTO THE BRIDLES OF
THE HORSES, AS FAR AS A THOUSAND AND SIX

149

HUNDRED FURLONGS.

WITHOUT THE CITY symbolically designates those who are not in the family of God. The flowing of BLOOD symbolizes the defeat of the wicked. UNTO THE BRIDLES is about four feet. HORSES were used in warfare in John's day. A THOUSAND AND SIX HUNDRED FURLONGS was about the distance from the northern border of Palestine to the southern border, about two hundred miles. The greatness of the sea of blood portrays vividly the awfulness of judgment upon the lost. A FURLONG is about 606 feet.

The picture of these verses serves as a strong warning for man to submit his life to the will of God. The fate of the unbeliever is both serious and severe. The entire earth will give an account to God. No man will escape the judgement of God. "It is appointed unto men once to die, and after this cometh judgment" Hebrews 9:27. "No man can serve two masters: for either he will hate the one, and love the other; or else he will hold to one, and despise the other. Ye cannot serve God and mammon" Matthew 6:24.

Blessed assurance is for those who heed the warning of these verses by receiving Jesus Christ as Saviour and Lord.

JUDGMENT

CHAPTERS FIFTEEN AND SIXTEEN

15:1   AND I SAW ANOTHER SIGN IN HEAVEN, GREAT AND MARVELOUS, SEVEN ANGELS HAVING SEVEN PLAGUES, WHICH ARE THE LAST, FOR IN THEM IS FINISHED THE WRATH OF GOD.

Having received both warning and assurance in chapter fourteen, which served a similar purpose as that of chapters seven, ten and eleven, we are now introduced to the LAST cycle of judgment contained in this book. You will observe a similarity in the cycles. There are also some striking differences. In addition to the progression that is indicated with each new cycle is also the note of increasing intensity of God's warning to sinful man.

The fact that what we read is said to be a SIGN must not be overlooked. A sign points to truth. So do not confuse the sign with the truth signified. In this instance God signifies truth with a word picture as He has done throughout this book. This SIGN IN HEAVEN is the third SIGN in the second portion of this book — the first two being of the woman and the dragon in chapter twelve. This SIGN is regarded as GREAT AND MARVELOUS, that is, it is both impressive and important. It will cause you to stand in awe and wonder. It will certainly get your attention.

God's purpose is accomplished with the SEVEN PLAGUES. His purpose is accomplished, realized — IS FINISHED. Before the flood, "Jehovah said, My Spirit shall not strive with man for ever" Genesis 6:3a. What was true then is true again. God has been patient. He has warned man. But the time comes when man will have no more opportunities to repent. Such a time is here indicated.

15:2   AND I SAW AS IT WERE A SEA OF GLASS MINGLED WITH FIRE; AND THEM THAT COME OFF VICTORIOUS FROM THE BEAST AND FROM HIS IMAGE AND

FROM THE NUMBER OF HIS NAME, STANDING BY THE SEA OF GLASS, HAVING HARPS OF GOD.

The SEA is probably intended to focus our attention upon the Red Sea of the Old Testament and that which happened there in the days of Moses. The following verses make this clear. GLASS suggests transparency. Perhaps it is intended to magnify the clarity of God's holiness and the administration of His justice. The same sea that brought deliverance for the Israelites brought destruction to the Egyptians. MINGLED WITH FIRE may denote the suffering and martyrdom of the saints or the judgment of God on the godless, or both. AS IT WERE reminds us that this is illustrative language.

Those who COME OFF VICTORIOUS are the Christians. The enemies of the church have been described earlier in this book and are simply listed here as THE BEAST, HIS IMAGE and THE NUMBER OF HIS NAME. "For whatsoever is begotten of God overcometh the world: and this is the victory that hath overcome the world, even our faith" 1 John 5:4. BY THE SEA may also be understood as ON THE SEA, the latter expressing the thought of above the area where destruction was taking place.

It was not uncommon for the people of God to use instruments in worship. "Sing aloud unto God our strength: Make a joyful noise unto the God of Jacob. Raise a song, and bring hither the timbrel, The pleasant harp with the psaltery" Psalm 81:1,2.

15:3 AND THEY SING THE SONG OF MOSES, THE SERVANT OF GOD, AND THE SONG OF THE LAMB, SAYING, GREAT AND MARVELOUS ARE THY WORKS, O LORD GOD, THE ALMIGHTY; RIGHTEOUS AND TRUE ARE THY WAYS, THOU KING OF THE AGES.

15:4 WHO SHALL NOT FEAR, O LORD, AND GLORIFY THY NAME? FOR THOU ONLY ART HOLY; FOR ALL THE NATIONS SHALL COME AND WORSHIP BEFORE THEE; FOR THY RIGHTEOUS ACTS HAVE BEEN MADE MANIFEST.

The SONG OF MOSES is recorded in Exodus 15:1-18. When the Jews sang this song every Sabbath evening, as was their custom in the synagogue service, they were reminded of their deliverance from Egyptian bondage, a great event in their history.

It became a fit symbol of our deliverance from sin through Christ.

Observe carefully the contents of the SONG OF THE LAMB. There is a conscpicuous absence of any reference to man. GOD and HIS WORKS and His WAYS provide the theme and content for the SONG OF THE LAMB. The more we learn about God and the closer we get to God the less we think about ourselves and our own accomplishments. To really know God personally is to be overwhelmed with His grace and holiness.

Observe further the use that is made of the scriptures in praising God. Nearly every word and phrase of this SONG is borrowed from the Old Testament. "How great are thy works, O Jehovah" Psalm 92:5a! "Oh sing unto Jehovah a new song; For he hath done marvelous things" Psalm 98:1a. "Jehovah is righteous in all his ways. And gracious in all his works" Psalm 145:17. "All nations whom thou hast made shall come and worship before thee, O Lord; And they shall glorify thy name" Psalm 86:9. "Holy and reverend is his name" Psalm 111:9b. "Jehovah hath made known his salvation: His righteousness hath he openly showed in the sight of the nations" Psalm 98:2. To be a careful student of God's Word is to prepare yourself for true expression of praise and thanksgiving to God.

Paul said, "Yea verily, and I count all things to be loss for the excellency of the knowledge of Christ Jesus my Lord:" Philippians 3:8a. the more we think of God the less we think of self. This victory is God's. "But we have this treasure in earthen vessels, that the exceeding greatness of the power may be of God, and not from ourselves" 2 Corinthians 4:7. "Now unto the King eternal, immortal, invisible, the only God, be honor and glory for ever and ever. Amen" 1 Timothy 1:17.

15:5 AND AFTER THESE THINGS I SAW, AND THE TEMPLE OF THE TABERNACLE OF THE TESTIMONY IN HEAVEN WAS OPENED:

TEMPLE refers to the Holy Place and the Holy of Holies. The addition of TABERNACLE takes us beyond Solomon's temple to the tabernacle in the wilderness in the days of Moses. The TABERNACLE was a TESTIMONY of God's presence throughout their sojourn to the promised land. It is here a fitting symbol of God's presence.

15:6 AND THERE CAME OUT FROM THE TEMPLE THE SEVEN ANGELS THAT HAD THE SEVEN PLAGUES, ARRAYED WITH PRECIOUS STONE, PURE AND BRIGHT, AND GIRT ABOUT THEIR BREASTS WITH GOLDEN GIRDLES.

The very manner in which THE SEVEN ANGELS are clothed identifies them as messengers of God. Their garments suggest royalty, purity and dignity as you would expect from those who come from the presence of God to do His will.

15:7 AND ONE OF THE FOUR LIVING CREATURES GAVE UNTO THE SEVEN ANGELS SEVEN BOWLS FULL OF THE WRATH OF GOD, WHO LIVETH FOR EVER AND EVER.

The imagery of the FOUR LIVING CREATURES is borrowed from Ezekiel one and ten. If these living ones, whom Ezekiel identifies as cherubim, are to be considered as representatives of nature, it is interesting to see that nature submits herself to God's will in the giving of the SEVEN BOWLS OF THE WRATH OF GOD, for God uses nature to adminster justice upon mankind, as will be noted in the study of the contents of the SEVEN BOWLS.

The BOWLS were containers out of which the contents could be emptied very quickly. God's judgment will not be delayed. Its execution will take place very rapidly.

THE WRATH OF GOD is to be understood as His inward, intense anger, occasioned by the sinfulness of man. Sin ought also to anger the Christian to the point that he intensifies his battle against it. It is a sad day when one can confront sin and not be moved by inner anger to positive action against it.

15:8 AND THE TEMPLE WAS FILLED WITH SMOKE FROM THE GLORY OF GOD, AND FROM HIS POWER; AND NONE WAS ABLE TO ENTER INTO THE TEMPLE, TILL THE SEVEN PLAGUES OF THE SEVEN ANGELS SHOULD BE FINISHED.

SMOKE is explained here as a picture of THE GLORY OF GOD as is also true in Exodus 40:34,35. When Isaiah "saw the Lord sitting upon a throne" he noted that "the house was filled with smoke" Isaiah 6:1,4. Man is powerless in the presence of all

154

power. On one occasion men were sent to seize Jesus and were unable to do so. When asked for a reason for their returning empty handed, they replied, "Never man so spake" John 7:46. There was great power in the words of Jesus. Here there is great power in THE TEMPLE and NONE WAS ABLE TO ENTER INTO IT at this time. When the SEVEN ANGELS complete their work, entrance will be open, but then it will be too late for man to repent. Remember, there is a finality in the SEVEN PLAGUES.

The SEVEN SEALS were broken to provide man with information. The SEVEN TRUMPETS were sounded to furnish man with warning. The SEVEN BOWLS are poured out in execution of judgment upon those who ignore the information and fail to heed the warning.

16:1　AND I HEARD A GREAT VOICE OUT OF THE TEMPLE, SAYING TO THE SEVEN ANGELS, GO YE AND POUR OUT THE SEVEN BOWLS OF THE WRATH OF GOD INTO THE EARTH.

The instructions come from God, OUT OF THE TEMPLE. GO YE is not for the purpose of world evangelism now. Men have rejected God's invitation, and have become the objects of His wrath. The GO YE is for the execution of divine judgment. This is not to say that the SEVEN BOWLS are to be equated with the final judgment, but are plagues which immediately precede the final judgment.

"Pour out thy wrath upon the nations that know thee not, And upon the kingdoms that call not upon thy name" Psalm 79:6. "Therefore wait ye for me, saith Jehovah, until the day that I rise up to the prey; for my determination is to gather the nations, that I may assemble the kingdoms, to pour upon them mine indignation, even all my fierce anger; for all the earth shall be devoured with the fire of my jealousy" Zephaniah 3:8.

16:2　AND THE FIRST WENT, AND POURED OUT HIS BOWL INTO THE EARTH; AND IT BECAME A NOISOME AND GRIEVOUS SORE UPON THE MEN THAT HAD THE MARK OF THE BEAST, AND THAT WORSHIPPED HIS IMAGE.

NOISOME means bad or evil. It suggests something that is morally wicked. GRIEVOUS also means bad, but carried with its meaning the idea of being painful. SORE is a wound, ulcer, boil, scab or leprosy or something akin to these. The words that describe the effects of the pouring out of the first bowl are intended to show that the persecution suffered by the Christians does not begin to compare with the punishment inflicted upon THE MEN THAT HAD THE MARK OF THE BEAST. Obviously, serving the BEAST and worshipping HIS IMAGE has serious consequences. Of course this is always the story of sin. As attractive as the allurement of sin may be the consequences are ultimately severe to the extent that a rational man has to acknowledge that the choice of sin is a bad choice. The sixth Egyptian plague had a similar effect on men. See Exodus 9:8-12.

Keep in mind that the language of Revelation is figurative to a great degree. When you remember this you are not disturbed in trying to explain how a bowl could be poured out that would only affect the non-Christian. When we seek a spiritual application of this truth it is easily understood. See 1 Samuel 5.

16:3   AND THE SECOND POURED OUT HIS BOWL INTO THE SEA; AND IT BECAME BLOOD AS OF A DEAD MAN; AND EVERY LIVING SOUL DIED, EVEN THE THINGS THAT WERE IN THE SEA.

In contrast with the seals and trumpets which partially affected nature we are here informed that EVERY LIVING SOUL DIED. See Exodus 7:20,21 for the counterpart of this BOWL in the first Egyptian plague. Man is surrounded with the stench of death. Another aspect of nature is affected and thus affects man.

16:4   AND THE THIRD POURED OUT HIS BOWL INTO THE RIVERS AND THE FOUNTAINS OF THE WATERS; AND IT BECAME BLOOD.

THE WATERS that can usually be counted upon to provide satisfaction and comfort no longer meet man's need and he finds himself in a state of desperation without any relief for his suffering. Man's vital resources become an instrument of judgment. See Exodus 7:19-25 and Revelation 8:10,11.

16:5   AND I HEARD THE ANGEL OF THE WATERS SAYING, RIGHTEOUS ART THOU, WHO ART AND WHO WAST, THOU HOLY ONE, BECAUSE THOU DIDST THUS JUDGE:

16:6   FOR THEY POURED OUT THE BLOOD OF SAINTS
       AND PROPHETS, AND BLOOD HAST THOU GIVEN
       THEM TO DRINK, THEY ARE WORTHY.

THE ANGEL OF THE WATERS is to be understood simi-
larly to the angels of the four winds. Apparently, an angel was as-
signed to control the WATERS in some way. At least, that is the
thought presented in this picture. This ANGEL speaks to affirm
the justice of God in pouring out the third BOWL. What God does
is right. God is eternal and, thus, is in a position to exercise sound
judgment. God is the HOLY ONE, totally untainted by sin.
THEY, referring to those who suffer from this plague, POURED
OUT THE BLOOD OF SAINTS AND PROPHETS. What, then,
should they expect from God? God of old spoke clearly. "Whoso
shedeth man's blood, by man shall his blood be shed: for in the
image of God made he man" Genesis 9:6. "And I will feed them
that oppress thee with their own flesh; and they shall be drunken
with their own blood, as with sweet wine: and all flesh shall know
that I, Jehovah, am thy Saviour, and thy Redeemer, the Mighty
One of Jacob" Isaiah 49:26. "Be not deceived; God is not mocked:
for whatsoever a man soweth, that shall he also reap. For he that
soweth unto his own flesh shall of the flesh reap corruption; but
he that soweth unto the Spirit shall of the Spirit reap eternal life"
Galatians 6:7,8.

THEY ARE WORTHY. They deserve it. The righteousness
and justice of God prevailed in the payment of the wages of sin.

16:7   AND I HEARD THE ALTAR SAYING, YEA, O LORD
       GOD, THE ALMIGHTY, TRUE AND RIGHTEOUS ARE
       THY JUDGMENTS.

Altars don't speak, but this is not a problem in apocalyptic
literature where language is used to paint pictures for the purpose of illustrating truth. The voice from THE ALTAR confirms
what THE ANGEL OF THE WATERS had just said. GOD is AL-
MIGHTY. His JUDGMENTS are TRUE AND RIGHTEOUS. God
has exercised His power and authority correctly. It is important
that every Christian grow in knowledge and understanding to the
point of recognizing and approving the righteous acts of God.

16:8   AND THE FOURTH POURED OUT HIS BOWL UPON
       THE SUN; AND IT WAS GIVEN UNTO IT TO SCORCH

MEN WITH FIRE.

God has used THE SUN in two ways. He darkened the SUN in one instance. This did not bring men to repentance. Now God intensifies the SUN to the point that it scorches MEN WITH FIRE. This picture is one of fearful torment. This illustrates the severity of God's wrath poured out upon sinful man.

16:9 AND MEN WERE SCORCHED WITH GREAT HEAT: AND THEY BLASPHEMED THE NAME OF GOD WHO HATH THE POWER OVER THESE PLAGUES; AND THEY REPENTED NOT TO GIVE HIM GLORY.

The same sun will harden clay and melt wax. The same boiling water will harden an egg and soften a potatoe. The difference is not explained by the sun or the boiling water; it is explained by the substance being affected. God intends that men should repent and GIVE HIM GLORY. When men's hearts are hardened it is not the fault of God but the fault of rebellious men.

To blaspheme is to speak hurt, to speak injury. NAME OF GOD is to be understood as incorporating all the attributes of GOD and is not simply a word designation. Much meaning is involved in the word NAME used in scripture with reverence to God. We speak of giving someone a bad name in the sense of giving someone a bad reputation. Or, we may state that one has a good name, meaning that he has a good reputation. In this broad sense we understand the NAME OF GOD.

GOD, WHO HATH THE POWER OVER THESE PLAGUES, manifests Himself to man in and through these PLAGUES. But, THEY, sinful men, REPENTED NOT. They did not change their minds and their lives. THEY refused to GIVE HIM, God, GLORY. There is no genuine repentance apart from giving God GLORY. Recall the sin of Achan that resulted in the defeat of Ai and the death of thirty-six men. "Joshua said to Achan, My son, give, I pray thee, glory to Jehovah, the God of Israel, and make confession unto him; and tell me now what thou hast done; hide it not from me. And Achan answered Joshua, and said, Of a truth I have sinned against Jehovah, the God of Israel, and thus and thus have I done" Joshua 7:19,20. Achan went on to state just exactly the manner in which he had sinned. There is no true confession of sin until this is done. When this is done, God is glorified, for the confession of our own wrong is the acknowledgement of God's righteousness. GLORY is given to God only when God is recognized and accepted and witnessed for Who He really is.

"The Lord is not slack concerning his promise, as some count slackness; but is longsuffering to you-ward, not wishing that any should perish, but that all should come to repentance" 2 Peter 3:9. The truth of this verse is emphasized again and again in the book of Revelation.

16:10 AND THE FIFTH POURED OUT HIS BOWL UPON THE THRONE OF THE BEAST; AND HIS KINGDOM WAS DARKENED; AND THEY GNAWED THEIR TONGUES FOR PAIN.

In John's day this would have been understood as a reference to the seat of government in Rome. THE BEAST symbolizes world power exercising the will of Satan. Thus, the application of this truth, as is the case with all other truths in this book, differs with the progression of history. When the Roman empire fell, Revelation did not cease to be a relevant book, for in each generation there have been those people and systems and philosophies that have served the devil's purpose in oppostion to Christ and His church. When considering THE BEAST AND HIS KINGDOM we must not lose sight of the fact that Christians are members of a kingdom "not of this world" as stated by Jesus in John 18:36. THE KINGDOM of the BEAST is to be understood as the Satanic counterpart of Christ's church.

The darkening of Satan's KINGDOM is illustrated in the second chapter of Daniel, where the kingdoms of this world "became like the chaff of the summer threshing-floors; and the wind carried them away, so that no place was found for them" Daniel 2:35b. "Shall the throne of wickedness have fellowship with thee, Which frameth mischief by statute" Psalm 94:20?

Darkness pictures great disruption and defeat in the kingdom. The greatness of the pain caused them to bite their tongues. FOR PAIN means out of pain or because of pain.

16:11 AND THEY BLASPHEMED THE GOD OF HEAVEN BECAUSE OF THEIR PAINS AND THEIR SORES; AND THEY REPENTED NOT OF THEIR WORKS.

The result of the fifth BOWL is like that of the fourth BOWL.

159

The picture is ugly, nevertheless, easy to understand in light of the many people today whose first words in the moment of injury are words of blasphemy. God's name is taken in vain because of physical hurt. The truth of verse eleven gives additional weight to the desire of God that all men should repent, though they don't. Thus, they are without excuse. "Knowing God, they glorified him not as God, neither gave thanks; but became vain in their reasonings, and their senseless heart was darkened" Romans 1:21.

WORKS are an outward expression of the heart, a revelation of the real person. "By their fruits ye shall know them. Do men gather grapes of thorns, or figs of thistles? Even so every good tree bringeth forth good fruit; but the corrupt tree bringeth forth evil fruit" Matthew 7:16,17.

16:12 AND THE SIXTH POURED OUT HIS BOWL UPON THE GREAT RIVER EUPHRATES; AND THE WATER THEREOF WAS DRIED UP, THAT THE WAY MIGHT BE MADE READY FOR THE KINGS THAT COME FROM THE SUNRISING.

The EUPHRATES RIVER was a natural boundary between nations. During the days of the Old Testament the Assyrians, to the east, were the enemies of the northern kingdom and the Babylonians,to the east, were the enemies of the southern kingdom. The EUPHRATES flowed through the ancient city of Babylon. The drying up of this river enabled the enemy to attack and ultimately bring the downfall of this once, great city and powerful world force. The drying up of WATER might bring many different pictures to the mind of the reader. One might think of the Red Sea in the days of Moses or the Jordan river in the days of Joshua.

The people of John's day would understand the EUPHRATES as the eastern boundary of the Roman empire, beyond which were the dreaded Parthians. In this picture all barriers to enemy power are gone and the way is cleared for the coming of destructive forces. It is an appropriate way to show the means by which the gathering takes place for the ultimate battle.

16:13 AND I SAW COMING OUT OF THE MOUTH OF THE DRAGON, AND OUT OF THE MOUTH OF THE BEAST, AND OUT OF THE MOUTH OF THE FALSE PROPHET,

160

THREE UNCLEAN SPIRITS, AS IT WERE FROGS:

Here is the Satanic trinity. THE FALSE PROPHET was designated as THE BEAST COMING UP OUT OF THE EARTH in chapter thirteen. THE DRAGON is Satan. THE BEAST represents Satanic world power of a political nature. THE FALSE PROPHET depicts false religion in all its many phases. The THREE UNCLEAN SPIRITS, though not FROGS, were filthy and dirty like FROGS pictured to their minds. Thus, the word UNCLEAN is amplified with the phrase AS IT WERE FROGS. The fact that these UNCLEAN SPIRITS come out of their mouths suggests lies, false propaganda. God is winning and will ultimately claim total victory against Satan with the skilful use of the "sword of the Spirit, which is the word of God" Ephesians 6:17b. Jesus was pictured in such a way as to show that "out of his mouth proceeded a sharp two-edged sword" Revelation 1:16b. The Lord identified Himself to the church in Pergamum as "he that hath the sharp two-edged sword" Revelation 2:12b. In the body of this same letter. He warned those who subscribed to the teaching of Balaam and the teaching of the Nicolaitans that unless they repented He should "make war against them with the sword of my mouth" Revelation 2:16b. We must never forget that "our wrestling is not against flesh and blood, but against the principalities, against the powers, against the world-rulers of this darkness, against the spiritual hosts of wickedness in the heavenly places" Ephesians 6:12. The battle will be won with truth. Satan, however, will wage war as long as possible with lies, deception and all things false and untrue.

16:14 FOR THEY ARE SPIRITS OF DEMONS, WORKING SIGNS; WHICH GO FORTH UNTO THE KINGS OF THE WHOLE WORLD, TO GATHER THEM TOGETHER UNTO THE WAR OF THE GREAT DAY OF GOD, THE ALMIGHTY.

SPIRITS OF DEMONS work SIGNS in an effort to deceive and to win people by this means to their cause. Satan gathers his forces together in an effort to defeat God. His ability to gain the aid of so many makes it appear that victory for him is assured, but this appearance does not prove to be reality. Satan is defeated!

161

THE WAR will, indeed, be THE GREAT DAY OF GOD, for His victory over Satan will prove Him to be THE ALMIGHTY. 16:15 (BEHOLD, I COME AS A THIEF. BLESSED IS HE THAT WATCHETH, AND KEEPETH HIS GARMENTS, LEST HE WALK NAKED, AND THEY SEE HIS SHAME.)

"But the day of the Lord will come as a thief; in the which the heavens shall pass away with a great noise, and the elements shall be dissolved with fervent heat, and the earth and the works that are therein shall be burned up" 2 Peter 3:10. Coming AS A THIEF emphasizes the fact that no man knows when Jesus will return and at the same time warns us to be alert and ready for it, whenever it may be. One who watches is prepared. One who KEEPETH HIS GARMENTS is clothed with Christ's righteousness and therefore will not be ashamed in the presence of the Lord. "And now, my little children, abide in him; that, if he shall be manifested, we may have boldness, and not be ashamed before him at his coming" 1 John 2:28.

NAKED pictures that absence of Christ's righteousness due to the rejection of Christ as Lord and Saviour. SHAME has been associated with sin from the beginning. "And Jehovah God called unto the man, and said unto him, Where art thou? And he said, I heard thy voice in the garden, and I was afraid, because I was naked; and I hid myself" Genesis 3:9,10.

16:16 AND THEY GATHERED THEM TOGETHER INTO THE PLACE WHICH IS CALLED IN HEBREW HAR-MAGEDDON.

HAR is the Hebrew word for mountain. Megiddo was a city overlooking the valley of Esdraelon in northern Palestine. Many battles were fought in this valley. It has been suggested that the word HAR-MAGEDDON would bring to mind a bloody battlefield.

In the instances of Gideon's defeat of the Midianites and Deborah's victory over Jabin and the Canaanites it is abundantly clear that God fought for them and enabled them to triumph. This adds significance to the picture of verse sixteen, for our victory over sin will never be explained by man's abilities and efforts but by God's power, the power of the gospel of Jesus Christ.

The HAR-MAGEDDON of Revelation has no geographical

location. This is another sign in this book pointing to important truth. The battle between God and Satan will involve all men and will be a severe conflict to the very end. God will win though it may not appear so during the battle. Why should Gideon let the thousands go and fight with only three hundred men? Not only because this was God's will but because it would make clear the fact that the victory was God's. Repeatedly our attention is focused upon the omnipotence of God.

HAR-MAGEDDON is symbolic of the conflict of the ages and because of its setting in this chapter our minds are drawn particularly to the final stage of this battle. Remember this is a spiritual conflict. It is not a war fought with swords and guns, tanks and airplanes, bombs and poison, but it is a war between righteousness and wickedness, between God and Satan which is not and will not be confined to a small area in the northern part of Palestine. We will learn the details of this battle in chapter nineteen.

16:17 AND THE SEVENTH POURED OUT HIS BOWL UPON THE AIR; AND THERE CAME FORTH A GREAT VOICE OUT OF THE TEMPLE, FROM THE THRONE, SAYING, IT IS DONE:

The war against sin comes to an end with the pouring out of this final BOWL. IT IS DONE applies to God's defeat of Satan just as certainly as "It is finished" applied to the redemptive work of Christ at Calvary. The GREAT VOICE OUT OF THE TEMPLE, FROM THE THRONE is an announcement that comes from God.

AIR is an absolute essential for the sustenance of life. Without it there is no life. Certainly the life of the ungodly is snuffed out in the final act of God's judgment. Paul identified Satan as "the prince of the powers of the air" Ephesians 2:2b. Satan and the demonic forces are being attacked in their own sphere — THE AIR.

16:18 AND THERE WERE LIGHTNINGS, AND VOICES, AND THUNDERS; AND THERE WAS A GREAT EARTHQUAKE, SUCH AS WAS NOT SINCE THERE WERE MEN UPON THE EARTH, SO GREAT AN EARTHQUAKE, SO MIGHTY.

The words of this verse have been used several times in this book to picture the judgments of God which manifest His power and majesty. Only God can move the earth in this GREAT and MIGHTY way. Security is not to be found in earthly things, only within the will of God. When we remember that the first century experienced many earthquakes it had to make a strong impression upon the early readers of Revelation to see this EARTH-QUAKE being the greatest one of all SINCE THERE WERE MEN UPON THE EARTH. There is finality in this judgment.

16:19 AND THE GREAT CITY WAS DIVIDED INTO THREE PARTS, AND THE CITIES OF THE NATIONS FELL: AND BABYLON THE GREAT WAS REMEMBERED IN THE SIGHT OF GOD, TO GIVE UNTO HER THE CUP OF THE WINE OF THE FIERCENESS OF HIS WRATH.

God's people are pictured both as a WOMAN and as a CITY. This is also true of Satan's people. BABYLON THE GREAT symbolically refers to the followers of Satan and may have had a partial application to the city of Rome in John's day because of the embodiment of evil in this place. The danger in suggesting this comes when we allow ourselves to think of this conflict in material terms. It is a spiritual war. Thus THE GREAT CITY can never be limited to a specific location. It is lost mankind.

THREE PARTS may indicate that the downfall of THE GREAT CITY was the work of God, THREE being the numerical signature of God. The contents of the CUP in this verse are in contrast with the contents she had been used to during the days of persecuting the church. This is explained in the next chapter. FIERCENESS adds vividness to HIS WRATH and is expressive of God's attitude toward all sin. BABYLON was GREAT in a worldly sense of the term. The inclusions of THE CITIES OF THE NATIONS along with BABYLON may have suggested the entirety of the great Roman empire, not just the city alone. Thus, it would symbolize the totality of the fall of sin—Satan's empire.

16:20 AND EVERY ISLAND FLED AWAY, AND THE MOUN-TAINS WERE NOT FOUND.

There was no place to escape. THE MOUNTAINS and EVERY ISLAND were gone. This further explains "it is done" of verse seventeen. There is no more hiding. Your sins have found

you out. At the time of this great catastrophe that brings history
and time to an end we are reminded of the answer Peter gave to
Jesus' question, "Would ye also go away? Simon Peter answered
him, Lord, to whom shall we go? thou hast the words of eternal
life" John 6:67. Those who have gone to Satan now learn that he
has no refuge for them. What had seemed secure and permanent
is now non-existent. No wonder Jesus taught us to place our in-
vestments "in heaven, where neither moth nor rust doth consume, and where thieves do not break through nor steal" Matthew 6:20.

16:21 AND GREAT HAIL, EVERY STONE ABOUT THE
WEIGHT OF A TALENT, COMETH DOWN OUT OF
HEAVEN UPON MEN: AND MEN BLASPHEMED GOD
BECAUSE OF THE PLAGUE OF THE HAIL; FOR THE
PLAGUE THEREOF IS EXCEEDING GREAT.

This GREAT HAIL made the destruction complete. To the
very end there is a refusal to repent. MEN BLASPHEMED GOD
as they had done many times before. The fact that their failure to
repent in this instance may suggest, as it probably does, that the
time for repentance is now past, even so, they continue to blaspheme.

A TALENT is approximately one hundred pounds.

It is not a new thought that hailstones should be used of God
to bring an end to the conflict. "And it came to pass, as they fled
from before Israel, while they were at the descent of Bethhoron,
that Jehovah cast down great stones from heaven upon them
unto Azekah, and they died: they were more who died with the
hailstones than they whom the children of Israel slew with the
sword" Joshua 10:11.

See Exodus 9:24.

Chapters fifteen and sixteen should be viewed as a unit, with
each verse being carefully understood in light of the other verses
in the context. The finality of the last bowl suggests that Revelation should not be considered chronologically. That which we
read in the next chapters fit into the time span already covered
several times in this book.

The judgment of God is inevitable.

THE CONSEQUENCES OF SIN

CHAPTERS SEVENTEEN AND EIGHTEEN

17:1 AND THERE CAME ONE OF THE SEVEN ANGELS THAT HAD THE SEVEN BOWLS, AND SPAKE WITH ME, SAYING, COME HITHER, I WILL SHOW THEE THE JUDGMENT OF THE GREAT HARLOT THAT SITTETH UPON MANY WATERS:

The JUDGMENT OF THE GREAT HARLOT had already been pronounced in chapter fourteen, verse eight. It will now be visualized. The MANY WATERS will be explained in verse fifteen. THE GREAT HARLOT is Babylon, according to verse eighteen. In Isaiah 23:16 the city of Tyre is called a harlot. In the third chapter of Nahum Nineveh is identified as a harlot.

"O thou that dwellest upon many waters" is Jeremiah's description of Historic Babylon in Jeremiah 51:13. This is a reference to the Euphrates river and the irrigation ditches fed by this river in Babylon.

17:2 WITH WHOM THE KINGS OF THE EARTH COMMITTED FORNICATION, AND THEY THAT DWELL IN THE EARTH WERE MADE DRUNKEN WITH THE WINE OF HER FORNICATION.

THEY THAT DWELL IN THE EARTH are all those who do not have the mind of Christ and whose affections are not set on those things which are above. The words HARLOT and FORNICATION come from the same root word—the word, when transliterated into the English language, is pornography. Immorality and drunkenness go together in the sinful world. Having said this we must be reminded again that we are dealing with symbolism so that the words FORNICATION and DRUNKEN go beyond their literal meaning to portray that estranged state of man who refuses to live in harmony with God's will and degrades himself with Satanic living. It is suggested that apostasy is signified in this picture.

In John's day the city of Rome, called by one, "a filthy

sewer," involved others in her sins.

17:3 AND HE CARRIED ME AWAY IN THE SPIRIT INTO A WILDERNESS: AND I SAW A WOMAN SITTING UPON A SCARLET-COLORED BEAST, FULL OF NAMES OF BLASPHEMY, HAVING SEVEN HEADS AND TEN HORNS.

This SCARLET-COLORED BEAST is identified with the "beast coming up out of the sea" 13:1. See comments on that verse.

IN THE SPIRIT is a phrase repeated in this book as a reminder that John did not actually have this experience in the flesh, but a vision. The WILDERNESS, where John received this vision, symbolizes the desolation of evil. It also indicates that there was some distance between John and what he saw, for he would have maintained his separation from sin as a man of God.

17:4 AND THE WOMAN WAS ARRAYED IN PURPLE AND SCARLET, AND DECKED WITH GOLD AND PRE-CIOUS STONE AND PEARLS, HAVING IN HER HAND A GOLDEN CUP FULL OF ABOMINATIONS, EVEN THE UNCLEAN THINGS OF HER FORNICATION.

The garments of THE WOMAN indicate great wealth. The contents of the GOLDEN CUP suggest great wickedness. Christians sometime find the prosperity of the wicked difficult to understand, but this is nothing new. Long ago the Psalmist said, "I was envious at the arrogant, When I saw the prosperity of the wicked" Psalm 73:3. Each descriptive word and phrase underscores the contrast of this WOMAN with the "woman" in chapter twelve. On the surface this WOMAN is attractive to the world around her, but the real person is known by the contents of the CUP IN HER HAND.

PURPLE is the color of royalty and has caused some to refer ;to her as a queen.

When the Christian is tempted by THE WOMAN because of her adornments the words of Peter should be called: "Whose adorning let it not be the outward adorning of braiding the hair, and of wearing jewels of gold, or of putting on apparel; but let it be the hidden man of the heart, in the incorruptible apparel of a meek and quiet spirit, which is in the sight of God of great price"

167

1 Peter 3:3,4.

Spiritual FORNICATION is committed when one turns away from God to idols. All idolatry is considered as abominable unto God. Idolatry continues to be a strong temptation to man.   Thus John admonished, "Love not the world, neither the things that are in the world. If any man love the world, the love of the Father is not in him. For all that is in the world, the lust of the flesh and the lust of the eyes and the vain-glory of life, is not of the Father, but is of the world. And the world passeth away, and the lust thereof: but he that doeth the will of God abideth for ever" 1 John 2:15-17. James reinforces the seriousness of idolatry with his statement, "Ye adulteresses, know ye not that the friendship of the world is enmity with God? Whosoever therefore would be a friend of the world maketh himself an enemy of God" James 4:4.

17:5   AND UPON HER FOREHEAD A NAME WRITTEN, MYSTERY, BABYLON THE GREAT, THE MOTHER OF HARLOTS AND OF THE ABOMINATIONS OF THE EARTH.

The identity of the WOMAN is made clear UPON HER FOREHEAD. It was a practice during the days of the Roman empire for prostitutes to identify themselves with names written on headbands and worn. That which is placed upon the FORE-HEAD is very obvious to others and that is the thought suggested here and elsewhere in this book where the term is used.

MYSTERY denotes that which is unknown by the uninitiated. It is a secret until someone reveals it. This MYSTERY is made known unto John, and thus, unto us. The NAME of this WO-MAN is understood in light of the description John has already given and will continue to give with greater elaboration. As a MOTHER we are convinced of her character by her offspring. THE ABOMINATIONS OF THE EARTH include everything that takes the place of God in the human heart. This is disgusting to God.

17:6   AND I SAW THE WOMAN DRUNKEN WITH THE BLOOD OF THE SAINTS, AND WITH THE BLOOD OF THE MARTYRS OF JESUS. AND WHEN I SAW HER, I WONDERED WITH A GREAT WONDER.

THE WOMAN persecuted the church, even with death, and

168

was thus DRUNKEN WITH THE BLOOD OF THE SAINTS AND MARTYRS. The persecutions under Nero and Domitian illustrate what is here described. THE SAINTS may be more inclusive than THE MARTYRS OF JESUS by including the people of God who suffered prior to the time of Christ's earthly ministry.

John's wonder is amazement, not admiration. This GREAT WONDER gave the angel an opportunity to explain further to John what he was seeing.

17:7 AND THE ANGEL SAID UNTO ME, WHEREFORE DIDST THOU WONDER? I WILL TELL THEE THE MYSTERY OF THE WOMAN, AND OF THE BEAST THAT CARRIETH HER, WHICH HATH THE SEVEN HEADS AND THE TEN HORNS.

I WILL TELL THEE THE MYSTERY. Once THE MYSTERY is explained it will no longer be knowledge concealed but truth revealed. MYSTERY refers to that which is known by means of revelation. THE BEAST is identified with the first picture of chapter thirteen. Additional information is now to be supplied relating to this BEAST.

17:8 THE BEAST THAT THOU SAWEST WAS, AND IS NOT; AND IS ABOUT TO COME UP OUT OF THE ABYSS, AND TO GO INTO PERDITION. AND THEY THAT DWELL ON THE EARTH SHALL WONDER, THEY WHOSE NAME HATH NOT BEEN WRITTEN IN THE BOOK OF LIFE FROM THE FOUNDATION OF THE WORLD, WHEN THEY BEHOLD THE BEAST, HOW THAT HE WAS, AND IS NOT, AND SHALL COME.

THEY THAT DWELL ON THE EARTH refer to the non-Christians, for their names do not appear IN THE BOOK OF LIFE, God's record book. THE BOOK OF LIFE contains the names of all God's people. Both designations, THEY THAT DWELL ON THE EARTH and THE BOOK OF LIFE, appear several times in this book, each time with the same meaning.

THE BEAST is Satanic world power. Some explain that the similarity of Domitian to Nero as a person and as an emperor is indicated in the phrase WAS, AND IS NOT, AND IS ABOUT TO COME UP. Others see it simply as a revival of Satanic world power. There were those in John's day that expected that Nero would live again. TO GO INTO PERDITION forecasts the final destiny of this BEAST. "And the beast was taken, and with him the false prophet that wrought the signs in his sight, wherewith he deceived them that had received the mark of the beast and them that worshipped his image: they two were cast alive into the lake of fire that burneth with brimstone" 19:20. "And the devil that deceived them was cast into the lake of fire and brimstone, where are also the beast and the false prophet; and they shall be tormented day and night for ever and ever" 20:10. John never loses sight of the ultimate defeat of evil.

THE FOUNDATION OF THE WORLD expresses the foreknowledge of God, not the fact that God has predetermined man's will. God does not rob man of his freedom of choice. Remember that the book of Revelation does not teach anything that is out of harmony or in contradiction with that which is taught elsewhere in scripture. This book must be understood in light of all scripture.

17:9 HERE IS THE MIND THAT HATH WISDOM. THE SEVEN HEADS ARE SEVEN MOUNTAINS, ON WHICH THE WOMAN SITTETH:

Here is intelligence that can make the proper explanation and application. Jesus called a man a fool who had knowledge but didn't act upon it properly. He also called one wise who not only received the truth but obeyed it. See His conclusion to the sermon on the mount in Matthew seven. "Wisdom is the principal thing; therefore get wisdom; Yea, with all thy getting get understanding" Proverbs 4:7.

MOUNTAINS symbolize great elevation. THE WOMAN SITTETH exalted as a world power. Some see a resemblance to Rome, a city builded on seven hills. Perhaps so, but there is more to this picture. Rome simply offers a prime example of power in opposition to God.

17:10 AND THEY ARE SEVEN KINGS; THE FIVE ARE FALLEN, THE ONE IS, THE OTHER IS NOT YET COME; AND WHEN HE COMETH, HE MUST CONTINUE A LITTLE WHILE.

How can SEVEN HEADS be SEVEN MOUNTAINS and at the same time be SEVEN KINGS? That's like asking, how can a lamb look like he has been slain while he is standing? See 5:6. Such questions become warnings not to see the pictures as literal facts but as symbolic truth. When a person is described from the standpoint of size you will use language different from what you would use to describe his personality, yet you describe the same person. The SEVEN HEADS are equivalent to SEVEN MOUNTAINS and SEVEN KINGS, but the perspective is different in each instance. Through it all we are seeing Satanic world power visualized. Intelligence, power, elevation, strength, authority are a few words that come to mind when seeking an explanation for these symbolic terms.

Who are the FIVE, THE ONE, and THE OTHER? Some make them refer to the emperors of Rome, but it is a guess as to which emperor you should start with unless you are certain of the date of Revelation. Another suggestion is that Rome was the sixth of the great world powers, the first being Egypt, followed by Assyria, Babylon, Persia, and Greece. Commentators add other possible meanings. At any point in time there is oppostion to God but the continuance of this oppostion is limited—HE MUST CONTINUE A LITTLE WHILE.

The purpose of this entire picture is to show us the power and authority of the BEAST. Key words in understanding the picture are HEADS, HORNS, MOUNTAINS, AND KINGS.

17:11 AND THE BEAST THAT WAS, AND IS NOT, IS HIMSELF ALSO AN EIGHTH, AND IS OF THE SEVEN; AND HE GOETH INTO PERDITION.

IS ONE OF THE SEVEN means that the EIGHTH is like the SEVEN. This may be a reference to Domitian in the mind of John's first readers. However, the BEAST is not to be limited to one person. Truth has its application in every generation.

HE GOETH INTO PERDITION. This is a restatement of verse eight. As strong and intelligent as the BEAST may be his end will be in hell.

17:12 AND THE TEN HORNS THAT THOU SAWEST ARE TEN KINGS, WHO HAVE RECEIVED NO KINGDOM AS YET; BUT THEY RECEIVE AUTHORITY AS KINGS, WITH THE BEAST, FOR ONE HOUR.

HORNS symbolize power and strength. TEN symbolizes

completeness. KINGS symbolize authority in the political arena. The relationship of the KINGS with the BEAST indicates lesser powers subservient to the greater power of the BEAST. The TEN HORNS may signify all the various Satanic powers that combine to make the BEAST, the totality of all Satanic dominion. FOR ONE HOUR indicates a short, but definite period of time. There is a limitation of the AUTHORITY given to the KINGS.

17:13 THESE HAVE ONE MIND, AND THEY GIVE THEIR POWER AND AUTHORITY UNTO THE BEAST.

The devil's propaganda is effective in uniting evil powers for the accomplishment of his will. Every sin, no matter what form it may take, serves the ultimate purpose of evil. The ONE MIND is Satan's mind. Sinful men submit to Satanic rule.

17:14 THESE SHALL WAR AGAINST THE LAMB, AND THE LAMB SHALL OVERCOME THEM, FOR HE IS LORD OF LORDS, AND KING OF KINGS; AND THEY ALSO SHALL OVERCOME THAT ARE WITH HIM, CALLED AND CHOSEN AND FAITHFUL.

THESE refer to the Satanic hosts mentioned in the preceding verse. WAR is inevitable because of the incompatibility of sin and righteousness. "What fellowship have righteousness and iniquity? or what communion hath light with darkness? And what concord hath Christ with Belial? or what portion hath a believer with an unbeliever? And what agreement hath a temple of God with idols? for we are a temple of the living God; even as God said, I will dwell in them, and walk in them; and I will be their God, and they shall be my people. Wherefore come ye out from among them, and be ye separate, saith the Lord" 2 Corinthians 6:14b-17a.

HE IS THE LORD OF LORDS AND KING OF KINGS, a fact no Christian should ever forget. Because of this "we are more than conquerors through him" Romans 8:37. Christians OVERCOME with God's omnipotence.

Christians are CALLED—invited, CHOSEN—have accepted the invitation, and FAITHFUL—remained true to the invitation which they accepted. "For many are called, but few are chosen" Matthew 22:14.

Christ conquers! Christians share the victory. All God's

people are involved in the war against Satan.

17:15 AND HE SAITH UNTO ME, THE WATERS WHICH THOU SAWEST, WHERE THE HARLOT SITTETH, ARE PEOPLES, AND MULTITUDES, AND NATIONS, AND TONGUES.

AND HE SAITH UNTO ME introduces four verses which are given as explanation to what was written in the preceding verses. Historic Babylon was situated on the Euphrates river which was the source of many irrigation ditches. The Psalmist wrote of "the rivers of Babylon" Psalm 137:1. The symbolism of waters with NATIONS is not unique to this book. Isaiah wrote, "Ah, the uproar of many peoples, that roar like the roaring seas; and the rushing of nations, that rush like the rushing of mighty waters" Isaiah 17:12! The pagan peoples are given a four-fold designation in this verse. This verse pictures a great empire.

17:16 AND THE TEN HORNS WHICH THOU SAWEST, AND THE BEAST, THESE SHALL HATE THE HARLOT, AND SHALL MAKE HER DESOLATE AND NAKED, AND SHALL EAT HER FLESH, AND SHALL BURN HER UTTERLY WITH FIRE.

Similar language is recorded in Ezekiel 23:25-29. The story of Judas illustrates how one can be so attracted to that which he later hates. The money was appealing in the beginning but rejected in the end. A life that seemed to find fulfillment ended in suicide, for that which appeared to satisfy was only deceptive.

TEN HORNS may refer to lesser powers when compared to THE BEAST, which may have been understood in John's day as a reference to Rome. THESE SHALL HATE THE HARLOT, which is identified as "the great city" in verse eighteen. Sin contains the seed of destruction. The HARLOT loses her attraction and her former friends turn against her. The tragedy of her end is made vivid with four words: DESOLATE, NAKED, EAT, and BURN. NAKED is understood in light of the gorgeous apparel she wore as pictured in verse four. This word suggests poorly clothed. Disappointment is always the end of the story of sin which may have begun with apparent delight. Read 2 Kings 9:30-37 and note the similarity of this account of Jezebel with this portion of the book of Revelation.

Some see the initial fulfillment of this verse in the fall of Rome which took place in 476 A.D.

17:17 FOR GOD DID PUT IN THEIR HEARTS TO DO HIS MIND, AND TO COME TO ONE MIND, AND TO GIVE THEIR KINGDOM UNTO THE BEAST, UNTIL THE WORDS OF GOD SHOULD BE ACCOMPLISHED.

Undoubtedly, wicked people have no awareness that God may be fulfilling His plan through their works. God manifests His greatness by making the very works of Satan accomplish His own glory. Sin caused Christ's death, but God used this event to magnify the greater power of the resurrection which is the basis of the Christian's hope. Consider God's use of the decree from Caesar Augustus to bring Mary to Bethlehem at the precise time for the birth of Jesus to fulfill prophecy relating to the place of birth. God's purpose cannot be defeated by Satanic power. Isaiah expressed it beautifully in these words: "For my thoughts are not your thoughts, neither are your ways my ways, saith Jehovah. For as the heavens are higher than the earth, so are my ways higher than your ways, and my thoughts than your thoughts. For as the rain cometh down and the snow from heaven, and returneth not thither, but watereth the earth, and maketh it bring forth and bud, and giveth seed to the sower and bread to the eater; so shall my word be that goeth forth out of my mouth: it shall not return unto me void, but it shall accomplish that which I please, and it shall prosper in the thing whereto I sent it" Isaiah 55:8-11.

God is in control of all things! This does not destroy man's freedom of choice, nor does it force certain events to take place. God's omnipotence is magnified by the fact that He can and does maintain control all the time man is exercising his own free will. God's control does limit Satan as is indicated in chapter twenty, and will ultimately bring all evil to the "lake of fire," the consequences of sin.

17:18 AND THE WOMAN WHOM THOU SAWEST IS THE GREAT CITY WHICH REIGNETH OVER THE KINGS OF THE EARTH.

THE WOMAN IS equivalent to THE GREAT CITY. Both signify Satan's people from different perspectives which explains two identities of the same group. Satan, himself, may take the

174

form of a monster or an angel, which ever serves his purpose best. WHICH REIGNETH OVER THE KINGS OF THE EARTH would best be understood as a reference to Rome in John's day. This is not the limitation of this symbolism however. Throughout history Satanic world power has dominated THE KINGS OF THE EARTH.

18:1   AFTER THESE THINGS I SAW ANOTHER ANGEL COMING DOWN OUT OF HEAVEN, HAVING GREAT AUTHORITY; AND THE EARTH WAS LIGHTENED WITH HIS GLORY.

AFTER THESE THINGS introduces a new scene but does not necessitate chronology. I SAW reminds us of one of the main characteristics of apocalyptic literature—visions. COMING DOWN OUT OF HEAVEN indicates that God is behind this action. The GREAT AUTHORITY makes this mission very important and further manifests the control God has in the universe. The GLORY of God's presence is manifested through the light that comes upon the EARTH. "And it came to pass, when Moses came down from mount Sinai with the two tables of the testimony in Moses' hand, when he came down from the mount, that Moses knew not that the skin of his face shone by reason of his speaking with him" Exodus 34:29. Verse one clearly indicates that something of great consequence is about to take place.

18:2   AND HE CRIED WITH A MIGHTY VOICE, SAYING, FALLEN, FALLEN IS BABYLON THE GREAT, AND IS BECOME A HABITATION OF DEMONS, AND A HOLD OF EVERY UNCLEAN SPIRIT, AND A HOLD OF EVERY UNCLEAN AND HATEFUL BIRD.

The fifth chapter of Daniel describes Belshazzar's feast and the handwriting on the wall which was explained by Daniel. "And this is the writing, that was inscribed: MENE, MENE, TEKEL, UPHARSIN. This is the interpretation of the thing: MENE; God hath numbered thy kingdom, and brought it to an end. TEKEL; thou art weighed in the balances, and art found wanting, PERES; thy kingdom is divided, and given to the Medes and Persians" Daniel 5:25-28. Concerning this time of total destruction for the historic city of Babylon, Isaiah wrote, "And Babylon, the glory of kingdoms, the beauty of the Chaldeans' pride, shall be as when

175

God overthrew Sodom and Gomorrah. It shall never be inhabited, neither shall it be dwelt in from generation to generation: neither shall the Arabian pitch tent there; neither shall shepherds make their flocks to lie down there. But wild beasts of the desert shall lie there; and their houses shall be full of doleful creatures; and ostriches shall dwell there, and wild goats shall dance there. And wolves shall cry in their castles, and jackals in the pleasant palaces: and her time is near to come, and her days shall not be prolonged" Isaiah 13:19-22.

Verse two is a repetition of verse eight in chapter fourteen. The fall of BABYLON is viewed as an accomplished fact before the time of the fall to serve as a warning from God to all those who are fascinated by THE GREAT CITY. The fulfillment of Isaiah's prophecy regarding historic Babylon is an impressive reminder of the judgment of God against all those who turn away from Him. The city of Rome provides a striking illustration for the truths of chapter eighteen in John's day.

18:3 FOR BY THE WINE OF THE WRATH OF HER FORNI-CATION ALL THE NATIONS ARE FALLEN; AND THE KINGS OF THE EARTH COMMITTED FORNICATION WITH HER, AND THE MERCHANTS OF THE EARTH WAXED RICH BY THE POWER OF HER WANTON-NESS.

Immorality and selfish luxury have serious consequences. Jeremiah wrote, "Babylon hath been a golden cup in Jehovah's hand, that made all the earth drunken: the nations have drunk of her wine; therefore the nations are mad. Babylon is suddenly fallen and destroyed" Jeremiah 51:7,8a.

Babylon is portrayed as a corrupting power over ALL THE NATIONS. The causes of Babylon's downfall are expressed in the words FORNICATION and WANTONNESS. WANTONNESS is arrogant and extravagant luxury. Anything wanton is unrestrained and undisciplined. Moral laxity is the picture John sees with its tragic affect upon the world. That all of this had its influence on the church is evidenced in the letter to the church in Laodicea. "Because thou sayest, I am rich, and have gotten riches, and have need of nothing; and knowest not that thou art the wretched one and miserable and poor and blind and naked" 3:17.

18:4 AND I HEARD ANOTHER VOICE FROM HEAVEN, SAYING, COME FORTH, MY PEOPLE, OUT OF HER, THAT YE HAVE NO FELLOWSHIP WITH HER SINS, AND THAT YE RECEIVE NOT OF HER PLAGUES:

Christians are urged to avoid participating in the sinful activities of Babylon. The Greek word *hagios* is frequently used in the New Testament to describe the Christian. The basic meaning of this word is separate or different. This thought is expressed repeatedly. "And be not fashioned according to this world: but be ye transformed by the renewing of your mind, that ye may prove what is the good and acceptable and perfect will of God" Romans 12:2. "Be not unequally yoked with unbelievers: for what fellowship have righteousness and iniquity? or what communion hath light with darkness? And what concern hath Christ with Belial? or what portion hath a believer with an unbeliever" 2 Corinthians 6:14,15? "...neither be partaker of other men's sins: keep thyself pure" 1 Timothy 5:22. The relation the Christian has with the world is expressed in Christ's prayer: "I pray not that thou shouldest take them from the world, but that thou shouldest keep them from the evil one. They are not of the world, even as I am not of the world. Sanctify them in the truth: thy word is truth" John 17:15-17. On another occasion Jesus said, "If ye were of the world, the world would love its own: but because ye are not of the world, therefore the world hateth you" John 15:19.

The cry to COME FORTH does not happen one time in history. It is the continual cry to all Christians. Day by day each Christian needs to be reminded to HAVE NO FELLOWSHIP WITH HER SINS. To share in HER SINS is to share also in HER PLAGUES. "Be not deceived; God is not mocked: for whatsoever a man soweth, that shall he also reap" Galatians 6:7.

The VOICE that calls for this separation is not identified except as FROM HEAVEN indicating that the message is sent by God. The temptation to compromise with the sinful world is an ever present temptation the Christian is warned to avoid. The church is in the world as a witness. The world must not be allowed in the church as a curse.

18:5 FOR HER SINS HAVE REACHED EVEN UNTO HEAVEN, AND GOD HATH REMEMBERED HER INI-

QUITIES.

"We would have healed Babylon, but she is not healed: forsake her, and let us go every one into his own country; for her judgment reacheth unto heaven, and is lifted up even to the skies" Jeremiah 51:9. When we begin to think that God allows evil to go on unhindered as if He were not even aware of it we need to read this verse to be reminded that nothing misses the attention of God. GOD HATH REMEMBERED HER INIQUITIES. There is nothing wrong with the memory of God. A day of accounting ultimately comes for all men. Woe to those who stand before God garbed with iniquity. "Be sure your sin will find you out" Numbers 32:23b.

18:6　RENDER UNTO HER EVEN AS SHE RENDERED, AND DOUBLE UNTO HER THE DOUBLE ACCORDING TO HER WORKS: IN THE CUP WHICH SHE MINGLED, MINGLE UNTO HER DOUBLE.

"Call together the archers against Babylon, all them that bend the bow; encamp against her round about; let none thereof escape: recompense her according to her work; according to all that she hath done, do unto her; for she hath been proud against Jehovah, against the Holy One of Israel" Jeremiah 50:29. The agents of divine justice are called upon to deliver the "wages of sin." DOUBLE is the counterpart. Picture the old scales with a weight on one side and that which is to be weighed on the other side. The true weight is determined when the two sides balance. Sin is on one side of the scales and punishment is on the other side. In this sense we are to understand the word DOUBLE as picturing the judgment which balances with HER WORKS. This is in harmony with the justice of God and clear teaching elsewhere in scripture. Read Galatians 6:7,8. DOUBLE pictures punishment as extreme but only because her sin is great. Her great sin was pictured in 17:4b as "a golden cup full of abominations, even the unclean things of her fornication" which explains the symbolic use of the word CUP in this verse.

18:7　HOW MUCH SOEVER SHE GLORIFIED HERSELF, AND WAXED WANTON, SO MUCH GIVE HER OF TORMENT AND MOURNING: FOR SHE SAITH IN HER HEART, I SIT A QUEEN, AND AM NO WIDOW, AND

178

SHALL IN NO WISE SEE MOURNING.

"A man's pride shall bring him low" Proverbs 29:23a. "For every one that exalteth himself shall be humbled; and he that humbleth himself shall be exalted" Luke 14:11. There is no security in worldly riches. All the wealth and power that contributed to a false sense of safety for the HARLOT will prove to be vain in the end. SHE GLORIFIED HERSELF by putting HERSELF on public display for the world to see her position and possessions. She WAXED WANTON, continually intensified her show of luxury and lewdness. The sin of pride has its serious consequences. This verse calls to mind the fifth chapter of Daniel and the record of Belshazzar's feast. Belshazzar was so certain that he was safe inside the luxurious city of Babylon until informed differently by the writing on the wall. Moses was right in assessing the "pleasures of sin for a season" Hebrews 11:25. The season for sin is so very short when compared to eternity. To SIT A QUEEN is a momentary experience when compared to an eternity of MOURNING. To think that health and happiness can be purchased with money and sustained with power is an illusion. It is an illusion that continues to serve the devil's purpose very well. Beware!

18:8   THEREFORE IN ONE DAY SHALL HER PLAGUES COME, DEATH, AND MOURNING, AND FAMINE; AND SHE SHALL BE UTTERLY BURNED WITH FIRE; FOR STRONG IS THE LORD GOD WHO JUDGED HER.

"Vengeance belongeth unto me; I will recompense, saith the Lord" Romans 12:19b. IN ONE DAY indicates suddenness. There will be no warning other than the warning that God gives on a day by day basis through His creation and through the proclamation of His divine revelation. Read the first three chapters of Romans to learn that no man is without excuse. The PLAGUES mentioned in the fourth verse are identified here as DEATH, MOURNING, FAMINE AND FIRE. These words speak for themselves with regard to the severity of punishment inflicted upon the wicked. DEATH is eternal separation from God. MOURNING pictures a continual state of sadness and grief. FAMINE implies a state of desperate need. UTTERLY BURNED WITH FIRE emphasizes the totality and completeness of the judgment. Once

179

again John reminds us of the omnipotence of God, FOR STRONG IS THE LORD GOD WHO JUDGED HER. To avoid the judgment of God Paul admonishes us to "be strong in the Lord, and in the strength of his might" Ephesians 6:10.

This verse shows a complete reversal of that which was pictured in chapter seventeen. God intends that the consequences of sin shall be clearly understood as ample warning for all to repent and get right with God.

18:9   AND THE KINGS OF THE EARTH, WHO COMMITTED FORNICATION AND LIVED WANTONLY WITH HER, SHALL WEEP AND WAIL OVER HER, WHEN THEY LOOK UPON THE SMOKE OF HER BURNING,

This verse begins the first of three dirges, songs of mourning sung by the KINGS, the MERCHANTS, and the MARINERS. All are concerned about the fall of BABYLON for selfish reasons. A relationship with BABYLON had sustained them, in other words, they had "fellowship with her sins" which Christians were admonished not to do in verse four.

FORNICATION and wanton living are used several times to describe the ugliness and extent of sin. When Paul listed the "works of the flesh" to the Galatians he began his list with "fornication" Galatians 6:19. This was a prevalent sin then and now and one that needs to be seen in the light of the consequences that follow. Sexual fornication is used here to denote spiritual unfaithfulness to God. It is a forsaking of the Lord to respond to the allurements of a wicked world. Living WANTONLY is living arrogantly in self-indulgence and undue material abundance. The KINGS WEEP AND WAIL OVER HER, WHEN THEY LOOK UPON THE SMOKE OF HER BURNING because the destruction of the city affects their own power. All of this is a picture intended to make vivid the terrible consequences of all those who align themselves with Satan against God.

18:10   STANDING AFAR OFF FOR FEAR OF HER TORMENT, SAYING, WOE, WOE, THE GREAT CITY, BABYLON, THE STRONG CITY! FOR IN ONE HOUR IS THY JUDGMENT COME.

There is a feeling of amazement that complete destruction could come so quickly to such a STRONG CITY! WOE is an expression of grief. Anyone who shares in the wickedness of the wicked has just cause to FEAR TORMENT. GREAT and STRONG are words used to describe the forces of evil but greater and stronger is the power of God manifested in the suddenness of JUDGMENT.

18:11 AND THE MERCHANTS OF THE EARTH WEEP AND MOURN OVER HER, FOR NO MAN BUYETH THEIR MERCHANDISE ANY MORE;

Where will the MERCHANTS sell THEIR MERCHANDISE? Their market is gone with the doom of the city. Recall how the preaching of the gospel by Paul at Ephesus affected the business of Demetrius and those involved in the craft of making silver shrines of Diana. Read Acts 19:23-41. Read the last half of Ezekiel 27 for the background of this verse in the Old Testament. Business is severely hurt, thus the MERCHANTS WEEP, cry aloud and MOURN. Selfishness is obviously involved in the reaction of the MERCHANTS. There is no expression of concern for the city apart from their profiteering.

18:12 MERCHANDISE OF GOLD, AND SILVER, AND PRECIOUS STONE, AND PEARLS, AND FINE LINEN, AND PURPLE, AND SILK, AND SCARLET: AND ALL THYINE WOOD, AND EVERY VESSEL OF IVORY, AND EVERY VESSEL MADE OF MOST PRECIOUS WOOD, AND OF BRASS, AND IRON, AND MARBLE;

This verse begins an extensive list of twenty-nine articles of trade possibly listed according to their value. There is a striking similarity of these verses to Ezekiel 26 and 27. Apparently the long list is intended to be impressive and underscore that which can draw man's attention away from God. This list helps us understand the luxury of the city portrayed in chapter seventeen and also the extensiveness of the merchants MERCHANDISE.

This marks the end of materialism along with greed and lust. Peter said to Simon, "Thy silver perish with thee, because thou hast thought to obtain the gift of God with money" Acts 8:20. Earlier Peter said to the lame beggar, "Silver and gold have I none; but what I have, that give I thee. In the name of Jesus Christ of Nazareth, walk" Acts 3:6. Later Peter wrote, "knowing that ye were redeemed, not with corruptible things, with silver or gold, from your vain manner of life handed down from your fathers; but with precious blood, as of a lamb without blemish and without spot, even the blood of Christ" 1 Peter 1:18,19.

PRECIOUS STONES AND PEARLS were regarded as having great value then as now. Paul compared the relative value of building materials with similar language. "But if any man buildeth on the foundation gold, silver, costly stone, wood, hay, stubble" 1 Corinthians 3:12. You have to appreciate the value of pearls to gain the full benefit of Jesus' parable of the kingdom. "Again, the kingdom of heaven is like unto a man that is a merchant seeking goodly pearls: and having found one pearl of great price, he went and sold all that he had, and bought it" Matthew 13:45,16.

Only the wealthy could afford garments made of FINE LINEN and PURPLE. "Now there was a certain rich man, and he was clothed in purple and fine linen, faring sumptuously every day" Luke 16:19. The shellfish provided the purple dye used on material identified as PURPLE. SILK was very expensive. SCARLET was a costly dye desired by the rich along with PURPLE.

THYINE WOOD was used in the making of furniture and valued highly for its grain and coloring and because it was fragrant. IVORY was used also in the making of furniture and was a status symbol for the rich.

The other items mentioned in this verse would not differ much from our present understanding of their worth and use.

18:13 AND CINNAMON, AND SPICE, AND INCENSE, AND OINTMENT, AND FRANKINCENSE, AND WINE, AND OIL, AND FINE FLOUR, AND WHEAT, AND CATTLE, AND SHEEP: AND MERCHANDISE OF HORSES AND CHARIOTS AND SLAVES: AND THE SOULS OF MEN.

SPICE was used for hair dressing. OINTMENT was used as a perfume or as a medicine. FRANKINCENSE was used as a perfume and as oil for lamps. WINE in Bible days was diluted with several parts of water. The word WINE does not define whether it is fermented or unfermented.

The striking commodity of this verse is the last one listed which does not differ from the next to last in the list. THE

SOULS OF MEN adds emphasis to SLAVES, thus the word "even" might be a better choice to join the two together. The slave market robbed man of his dignity and showed complete lack of respect. It has been estimated that there were sixty million slaves in the Roman empire. The rich would brag of their riches by counting the number of slaves they owned. Ultimately materialism of this nature leads to callousness of the heart. It is a sad day when men look upon a man as another piece of merchandise. Godless materialism is just as Satanic as atheistic communism.

18:14 AND THE FRUITS WHICH THY SOUL LUSTED AFTER ARE GONE FROM THEE, AND ALL THINGS THAT WERE DAINTY AND SUMPTUOUS ARE PERISHED FROM THEE, AND MEN SHALL FIND THEM NO MORE AT ALL.

That which made the city attractive to so many now ceases to exist. There are no more outlandish foods, THINGS THAT WERE DAINTY, and extravagant garments, that which is regarded as SUMPTUOUS. John often stresses the terminality of sin with repeated emphasis. ARE PERISHED FROM THIS is intensified with MEN SHALL FIND THEM NO MORE AT ALL.

18:15 THE MERCHANTS OF THESE THINGS, WHO WERE MADE RICH BY HER, SHALL STAND AFAR OFF FOR THE FEAR OF HER TORMENT, WEEPING AND MOURNING;

The reaction of the MERCHANTS is the same as that of the KINGS noted in verses nine and ten. The same selfish element is here along with the FEAR, WEEPING AND MOURNING.

18:16 SAYING, WOE, WOE, THE GREAT CITY, SHE THAT WAS ARRAYED IN FINE LINEN AND PURPLE AND SCARLET, AND DECKED WITH GOLD AND PRECIOUS STONE AND PEARL!

As might be expected the MERCHANTS manifest a concern for the passing of wealth from THE GREAT CITY whereas the KINGS showed their concern for the passing of strength.

18:17 FOR IN ONE HOUR SO GREAT RICHES IS MADE DESOLATE. AND EVERY SHIPMASTER, AND EVERY ONE THAT SAILETH ANY WHITHER, AND MARIN-

ERS, AND AS MANY AS GAIN THEIR LIVING BY SEA, STOOD AFAR OFF,

The first part of this verse is a continuation of the preceding verse expressing the end of that which "moth and rust consume and thieves break through and steal" Matthew 6:19b. ONE HOUR is an expression of brevity. DESOLATE is a picturesque term for the ultimate end of all godlessness.

EVERY ONE THAT SAILETH ANY WHITHER is a broad enough expression to include both the KINGS and the MERCHANTS. The final song of mourning is sung by all those who travel by sea. They maintained their distance, STOOD AFAR OFF, like the KINGS in verse ten. There is no attempt at any rescue operation.

18:18 AND CRIED OUT AS THEY LOOKED UPON THE SMOKE OF HER BURNING, SAYING, WHAT CITY IS LIKE THE GREAT CITY?

"And in their wailing they shall take up a lamentation for thee, and lament over thee, saying, Who is there like Tyre, like her that is brought to silence in the midst of the sea" Ezekiel 27:32? John makes frequent use of the Old Testament to make clear his meaning. Just as people lamented the destruction of Tyre so will men lament God's judgment upon the wicked world. "Heaven and earth shall pass away,..." (Matthew 24:35) but this does not enter into the thinking of those who set their affection upon the earth rather than upon those things which are above. What is the sign of true greatness? The wicked attach the word GREAT to the CITY which abounds in wealth, luxury and power. Only God is great! "Wherefore thou art great, O Jehovah God: for there is none like thee, neither is there any God besides thee, according to all that we have heard with our ears" 2 Samuel 7:22.

18:19 AND THEY CAST DUST ON THEIR HEADS, AND CRIED, WEEPING AND MOURNING, SAYING, WOE, WOE, THE GREAT CITY, WHEREIN ALL THAT HAD THEIR SHIPS IN THE SEA WERE MADE RICH BY REASON OF HER COSTLINESS! FOR IN ONE HOUR IS SHE MADE DESOLATE.

It was not uncommon for Orientals to CAST DUST ON THEIR HEADS as a sign of mourning. This chapter has presented a triple emphasis upon the destruction of BABYLON, the city of sin, Satan's kingdom. Do not allow yourself to become so preoccupied with the details of the picture that you fail to see the primary point John is making. Satan and all those who align themselves with him will be defeated once and for all. God's judgment upon historic Babylon supply important background material for understanding these words of John. "For thou hast trusted in thy wickedness; thou hast said, None seeth me; thy wisdom and thy knowledge, it hath perverted thee, and thou hast said in thy heart, I am, and there is none else besides me. Therefore shall evil come upon thee; thou shalt not know the dawning thereof: and mischief shall fall upon thee; thou shalt not be able to put it away: and desolation shall come upon thee suddenly, which thou knowest not" Isaiah 47:10,11.

18:20 REJOICE OVER HER, THOU HEAVEN, AND YE SAINTS, AND YE APOSTLES, AND YE PROPHETS; FOR GOD HATH JUDGED YOUR JUDGMENT ON HER.

How shall we reconcile this with the words of Ezekiel: "Say unto them, As I live, saith the Lord Jehovah, I have no pleasure in the death of the wicked; but that the wicked turn from his way and live: turn ye, turn ye from your evil ways; for why will ye die, O house of Israel" Ezekiel 33:11?

REJOICE is in contrast with the MOURNING in the preceding verses. The rejoicing is not over the destruction of the city but because God has proved Himself omnipotent and just. God hates sin and loves the sinner. Because the sinner has made his choice of sin in preference to God, God is left with no alternative but to bring judgment upon disobedience. John has painted a vivid picture in Revelation to warn mankind against the ultimate consequences of sin. John assures his readers often that God reigns and that justice will prevail. Christians rejoice in the evidence of God's sovereignty! The rejoicing of them that "dwell on the earth" (11:10) was but for a moment. The rejoicing of the church — SAINTS, APOSTLES AND PROPHETS — will be for eternity.

18:21 AND A STRONG ANGEL TOOK UP A STONE AS IT WERE A GREAT MILLSTONE AND CAST IT INTO THE SEA, SAYING, THUS WITH A MIGHTY FALL

185

SHALL BABYLON, THE GREAT CITY, BE CAST
DOWN, AND SHALL BE FOUND NO MORE AT ALL.

In verse ten the KINGS regarded BABYLON as THE
STRONG CITY! How appropriate for A STRONG ANGEL
(strong indeed) to announce once again the MIGHTY FALL OF
BABYLON. The heavenly messenger has true strength.

AS IT WERE reminds us to regard the language symbolically. The great size and weight of the boulder, MILLSTONE,
assure that which is attached to it will remain at the bottom of
the SEA. There is nothing casual or doubtful about the FALL OF
BABYLON. There is certainty in the words SHALL BE FOUND
NO MORE AT ALL. These words are repeated six times in the
final verses of this chapter. The number six symbolizes lost men,
men who have alienated themselves from God. The MILLSTONE
used to depict the MIGHTY FALL is likened unto the stone of
such size that only the donkey could turn it.

18:22 AND THE VOICE OF HARPERS AND MINSTRELS
AND FLUTE-PLAYERS AND TRUMPETERS SHALL
BE HEARD NO MORE AT ALL IN THEE; AND NO
CRAFTSMAN, OF WHATSOEVER CRAFT, SHALL BE
FOUND ANY MORE AT ALL IN THEE; AND THE
VOICE OF THE MILL SHALL BE HEARD NO MORE AT
ALL IN THEE;

Every aspect of life in the city shall come to an end. Nothing
will survive. The repetition in this verse and the next one makes
the picture of total destruction impressive. The music and sounds
of domestic activity are gone forever as far as sin city is concerned. What has been taken for granted is no longer around to be
taken for granted.

18:23 AND THE LIGHT OF A LAMP SHALL SHINE NO
MORE AT ALL IN THEE; AND THE VOICE OF THE
BRIDEGROOM AND OF THE BRIDE SHALL BE
HEARD NO MORE AT ALL IN THEE: FOR THY MER-
CHANTS WERE THE PRINCES OF THE EARTH; FOR
WITH THY SORCERY WERE ALL THE NATIONS
DECEIVED.

The absence of LIGHT is suitable for those who preferred
the darkness of sin as a lifestyle. Happiness, such as was ex-

perienced on the occasion of a wedding is no longer.

It is not easy to explain FOR which introduces THY MER-CHANTS WERE THE PRINCES OF THE EARTH. FOR indicates a reason for what precedes it, but the connection of this phrase with the wedding is not clear. Perhaps FOR should be understood to connect this phrase with the entire sentence. There was a time when all who lived outside the great city were attracted to the city by her allurements. The great city was a city of influence on others, but that time has come to an end. At one time her SORCERY was used to deceive the NATIONS, but this is no more. Judgment has come. SORCERY implies the deceptive tools of the devil. Satan is clever and has led the world into a false sense of security. Do not forget that deception is the devil's instrument. The Christian must have nothing to do with it. Truth conquers. Deception is defeated.

18:24 AND IN HER WAS FOUND THE BLOOD OF PROPHETS AND OF SAINTS, AND OF ALL THAT HAVE BEEN SLAIN UPON THE EARTH.

Christian martyrs are not and have not been limited to any one location. BABYLON, therefore, stands for the godless everywhere who wage war against God and in doing so kill the SAINTS. In the fifth seal, chapter six, verses nine and ten, the martyrs ask how long it would be until God would avenge their blood. The answer has now been given. Know this "the wages of sin is death" Romans 6:23a. Can anyone question the judgment of God upon seeing THE BLOOD OF PROPHETS AND OF SAINTS, AND OF ALL THAT HAVE BEEN SLAIN UPON THE EARTH flowing in BABYLON?

THE DEFEAT OF SATAN

CHAPTERS NINETEEN AND TWENTY

19:1 AFTER THESE THINGS I HEARD AS IT WERE A GREAT VOICE OF A GREAT MULTITUDE IN HEAVEN, SAYING, HALLELUJAH; SALVATION, AND GLORY, AND POWER, BELONG TO OUR GOD:

AFTER THESE THINGS points to the previous judgment upon BABYLON and calls for the praise of God by the heavenly host. The MULTITUDE IN HEAVEN is not identified. Some suggest angels and some suggest departed saints. It could be either or both. What is important is that God is praised for His righteous judgment. The word HALLELUJAH occurs four times in this chapter and is found no other place in the New Testament. It means "praise God." The redemption of God is described with three terms: SALVATION, AND GLORY, AND POWER. The number three is the signature of God. SALVATION is in contrast with the defeat and desolation of sin. GLORY is the beauty of victory in Christ as contrasted with the ugliness of sin and its collapse. POWER, all of it, belongs to GOD. What has appeared to be power in Satan's camp is proved to be a mere pretence.

19:2 FOR TRUE AND RIGHTEOUS ARE HIS JUDGMENTS; FOR HE HATH JUDGED THE GREAT HARLOT, HER THAT CORRUPTED THE EARTH WITH HER FORNICATION, AND HE HATH AVENGED THE BLOOD OF HIS SERVANTS AT HER HAND.

Once again we are reminded of the vision of the fifth seal. Read Revelation 6:9,10. TRUE AND RIGHTEOUS are the same attributes we read in Revelation 15:3 and 16:7. See comments on these verses. THE GREAT HARLOT is BABYLON. HER THAT CORRUPTED THE EARTH correctly describes Satan's host. The destroyer is destroyed.

19:3 AND A SECOND TIME THEY SAY, HALLELUJAH. AND HER SMOKE GOETH UP FOR EVER AND EVER.

A one time expression of praise is not adequate for such a

great victory. A SECOND TIME of saying HALLELUJAH expresses continuing adoration. Just as the evidence of the Harlot's judgment continues, HER SMOKE GOETH UP FOR EVER AND EVER, so the great multitude continues praising God.

19:4 AND THE FOUR AND TWENTY ELDERS AND THE FOUR LIVING CREATURES FELL DOWN AND WORSHIPPED GOD THAT SITTETH ON THE THRONE, SAYING, AMEN; HALLELUJAH.

THE FOUR AND TWENTY ELDERS are the representatives of God's people. THE FOUR LIVING CREATURES are cherubim representing nature. Some suggest they are cherubim and others suggest that they are both in a sense. See comments on chapter four, verse six.

FELL DOWN depicts a posture of humility and submission before holiness and sovereignty. GOD occupies the THRONE. Those surrounding the THRONE acknowledge the truth and righteousness of God's judgment in the word AMEN, so be it! HALLELUJAH; the praise of God continues in a great Hallelujah chorus.

19:5 AND A VOICE CAME FORTH FROM THE THRONE, SAYING, GIVE PRAISE TO OUR GOD, ALL YE HIS SERVANTS, YE THAT FEAR HIM, THE SMALL AND THE GREAT.

The VOICE FROM THE THRONE addresses God as OUR GOD. This may mean that the VOICE is that of one of the angelic beings that surround the THRONE. All of God's people are included in the phrase ALL YE HIS SERVANTS. God's SERVANTS FEAR, respect and reverence, HIM. God's SERVANTS include people from all walks of life, the rich and poor, bond and free, young and old, THE SMALL AND THE GREAT.

19:6 AND I HEARD AS IT WERE THE VOICE OF A GREAT MULTITUDE, AND AS THE VOICE OF MANY WATERS, AND AS THE VOICE OF MIGHTY THUNDERS, SAYING, HALLELUJAH: FOR THE LORD OUR GOD, THE ALMIGHTY, REIGNETH.

The theme of the entire book of Revelation could be summed up well in the words, HALLELUJAH: FOR THE LORD OUR GOD, THE ALMIGHTY, REIGNETH. This is what Revelation is all about. This is the truth towering throughout Revelation. GOD is ALMIGHTY. GOD REIGNETH. HALLELUJAH!

AS IT WERE describes the voice without identifying it. A GREAT MULTITUDE, MANY WATERS, AND MIGHTY THUNDERS combine to explain the VOICE John heard praising God. It was indeed an impressive and powerful VOICE speaking an impressive and powerful truth.

19:7 LET US REJOICE AND BE EXCEEDING GLAD, AND LET US GIVE THE GLORY UNTO HIM: FOR THE MARRIAGE OF THE LAMB IS COME, AND HIS WIFE HATH MADE HERSELF READY.

These words are similar to those of Jesus in His public ministry. "Rejoice, and be exceeding glad: for great is your reward in heaven: for so persecuted they the prophets that were before you" Matthew 5:12. The reason for rejoicing is not the same as that indicated in verse twenty of the preceding chapter. THE MARRIAGE OF THE LAMB is the occasion for rejoicing now. Our attention is now pointed to the future, IS COME. HIS WIFE, the church, HATH MADE HERSELF READY. WIFE means bride. In Bible days the bride and groom were called husband and wife during the one year of betrothal that preceded the consummation of the marriage. This one year period, somewhat like our engagement time, was regarded as a serious and important time for the bride and groom. The relationship of the bethrothal required divorce procedures to be dissolved. Because the term WIFE is applied to the bride after the marriage is consummated in present usage, this explanation is needed to understand the language of scripture.

The marriage metaphor is not unique to Revelation. Read Isaiah 54:6; Hosea 2:19; and Ephesians 5:25-32. Paul wrote, "For I am jealous over you with a godly jealousy: for I espoused you to one husband, that I might present you as a pure virgin to Christ" 2 Corinthians 11:2.

The relationship of the bride and groom is contrasted with the FORNICATION of the HARLOT. John employs the aspects of marriage that serve his purpose in conveying truth.

HIS WIFE HATH MADE HERSELF READY is explained in the next verse.

19:8 AND IT WAS GIVEN UNTO HER THAT SHE SHOULD ARRAY HERSELF IN FINE LINEN, BRIGHT AND PURE: FOR THE FINE LINEN IS THE RIGHTEOUS ACTS OF THE SAINTS.

John explains the symbolism of THE FINE LINEN which is in complete contrast with the "purple and scarlet" that garbed the HARLOT. It is important to note that THE RIGHTEOUS ACTS WAS GIVEN UNTO HER. "As it is written, There is none righteous, no, not one" Romans 3:10. "For we are all become as one that is unclean, and all our righteousness are as a polluted garment..." Isaiah 64:6. "Yea verily, and I count all things to be loss for the excellency of the knowledge of Christ Jesus my Lord: for whom I suffered the loss of all things, and do count them but refuse, that I may gain Christ, and be found in him, not having a righteousness of mine own, even that which is of the law, but that which is through faith in Christ, the righteousness which is from God by faith" Philippians 3:8,9. "Husbands, love your wives, even as Christ also loved the church, and gave himself for it; that he might sanctify it, having cleansed it by the washing of water with the word, that he might present the church to himself a glorious church, not having spot or wrinkle or any such thing; but that it should be holy and without blemish" Ephesians 5:25-27. "So then as through one trespass the judgment came unto all men to condemnation; even so through one act of righteousness the free gift came unto all men to justification of life. For as through the one man's disobedience the many were made sinners, even so through the obedience of the one shall the many be made righteous" Romans 5:18,19.

19:9 AND HE SAITH UNTO ME, WRITE, BLESSED ARE THEY THAT ARE BIDDEN TO THE MARRIAGE SUPPER OF THE LAMB. AND HE SAITH UNTO ME, THESE ARE TRUE WORDS OF GOD.

Emphasis is given to this beatitude with the command to WRITE. THOSE THAT ARE BIDDEN TO THE MARRIAGE SUPPER are identical with the bride. This freedom of expression is not uncommon in apocalyptic writing. It affords additional imagery to drive home the truth and to relate the truth from different perspectives.

The marriage feast was used by Jesus to explain the kingdom of heaven both in Matthew 22:1-14 and in Matthew 25:1-13. No detail of the MARRIAGE SUPPER is given by John. It is important, however, to observe that those attending the MARRIAGE SUPPER ARE BIDDEN. God takes the first step in the intimate relationship of love. The blessing should be easy to appreciate in light of the joy associated with a marriage.

Lest anyone should have doubts because of the prevalence of persecution and the seeming dominance of evil John assures his readers that THESE ARE TRUE WORDS OF GOD, you can count on them.

19:10 AND I FELL DOWN BEFORE HIS FEET TO WORSHIP HIM. AND HE SAITH UNTO ME, SEE THOU DO IT NOT: I AM A FELLOW-SERVANT WITH THEE AND WITH THY BRETHEN THAT HOLD THE TESTIMONY OF JESUS: WORSHIP GOD: FOR THE TESTIMONY OF JESUS IS THE SPIRIT OF PROPHECY.

Some have suggested that John momentarily mistakened the identity of the messenger for God but the text does not indicate this. Apparently John was overwhelmed with excitement at what he had heard and has the strong urge to respond with WORSHIP. Whatever the reason the truth is made very clear that GOD alone is to be the object of our WORSHIP. "Let no man rob you of your prize by a voluntary humility and worshipping of the angels,..." Colossians 2:8. The urge John felt here reminds us of the experience Peter had with Cornelius. "And when it came to pass that Peter entered, Cornelius met him, and fell down at his feet, and worshipped him. But Peter raised him up, saying, Stand up; I myself also am a man" Acts 10:25,26. Angels are fellow-servants with Christians and this is the basis given here for refusing WORSHIP.

The meaning of the last part of this verse is not clear. Is the TESTIMONY that which JESUS gives or is the TESTIMONY that which others give OF JESUS? Furthermore, are we to understand that he who has THE SPIRIT OF PROPHECY will testify of JESUS, or that he who has THE TESTIMONY OF JESUS will prophesy? The fact that more than one meaning is possible may or may not have been intentional. In either case we have truth. Certainly the Christian is to witness for Jesus. "But ye shall receive power, when the Holy Spirit is come upon you: and ye shall be my witnesses both in Jerusalem, and in all Judaea and Samaria, and unto the uttermost part of the earth" Acts 1:8. The Christian witnesses by his life and by his message. He is enabled to do so by the indwelling presence of the Spirit. However, he must first have received the message from Jesus. The Christian, IN THE SPIRIT OF PROPHECY, listens to Jesus and then shares what he has heard with others.

When messengers came from John the Baptist to inquire concerning Jesus' identity, "he answered and said unto them, Go and tell John the things which ye have seen and heard; the blind receive their sight, the lame walk, the lepers are cleansed, and the deaf hear, the dead are raised up, the poor have good tidings preached to them. And blessed is he, whosoever shall find no occasion of stumbling in me" Luke 7:22,23. When an effort was made to silence the testimony of Peter and John they responded, "we cannot but speak the things which we saw and heard" Acts 4:20.

The purpose of prophecy is to bear witness for Jesus. A prophet is a spokesman. THE SPIRIT OF PROPHECY describes the Christian, the FELLOW-SERVANT who is fulfilling his mission in life according to the instructions of the great commission.

19:11 AND I SAW THE HEAVEN OPENED; AND BEHOLD, A WHITE HORSE, AND HE THAT SAT THEREON CALLED FAITHFUL AND TRUE; AND IN RIGHTEOUSNESS HE DOTH JUDGE AND MAKE WAR.

In chapter five John was told to look at "the Lion" and when he looked he saw "a Lamb." In this present chapter John has presented us with the picture of the Bridegroom and all of a sudden we find ourselves looking at a Warrior. In each instance we have a unique picture of Jesus.

THE HEAVEN OPENED enabling John to see what could not be detected without the assistance of God. Divine truth is imparted as it had been in the past. "Now it came to pass in the thirtieth year, in the fourth month, in the fifth day of the month, as I was among the captives by the river Chebar, that the heavens were opened, and I saw visions of God" Ezekiel 1:1.

The rider of the WHITE HORSE is Christ. About this there can be no doubt in light of the several designations given Him in this and the following verses. The HORSE was used in waging war. The WHITE HORSE was ridden in a victory celebration by the conqueror.

The rider of the WHITE HORSE is described with important detail. He is CALLED FAITHFUL AND TRUE. He is FAITHFUL in that he can be trusted, depended upon at all times. If he said it, it is TRUE because He is truth, (John 14:6). He is TRUE in the sense of opposing all that is false. He is TRUE in the sense of being real and genuine as opposed to artificial and imitation. He makes His appearance both as JUDGE and warrior. IN RIGHTEOUSNESS HE DOTH JUDGE is a repetition of 16:5-7 and 19:2. See the comments on these verses. See Isaiah 11:3-5 for another reference to righteous judgment. The tense of the verbs indicate that the work of judging and warring is a continuing process. Christ leads the church in the battle against the forces of evil. The judgment upon the wicked and the war itself is according to RIGHTEOUSNESS. Read Ephesians 6:10-20 for a detailed picture of the Christian's involvement in this conflict. It is encouraging to know that our warfare against Satan will end in victory as illustrated with the WHITE HORSE upon which Christ is riding as our leader. "For though we walk in the flesh, we do not war according to the flesh (for the weapons of our warfare are not of the flesh, but mighty before God to the casting down of strongholds), casting down imaginations, and every high thing that is exalted against the knowledge of God, and bringing every thought into captivity to the obedience of Christ; and being in readiness to avenge all disobedience, when your obedience shall be made full" 2 Corinthians 10:3-6.

19:12 AND HIS EYES ARE A FLAME OF FIRE, AND UPON HIS HEAD ARE MANY DIADEMS; AND HE HATH A NAME WRITTEN WHICH NO ONE KNOWETH BUT HE HIMSELF.

The description of Christ in these verses is similar to that of chapter one. The EYES have a penetrating vision. Nothing escapes His attention. The FLAME OF FIRE may indicate a certain overpowering of the enemy. MANY DIADEMS were worn by conquering monarchs to demonstrate and display their victory and power. The greatness of Christ's dominion is symbolized in these words. All authority belongs to Him (Matthew 28:18). "The kingdom of the world is become the kingdom of our Lord, and of his Christ: and he shall reign for ever and ever" Revelation 11:15b.

HE HATH A NAME WRITTEN WHICH NO ONE KNOWETH BUT HE HIMSELF. "All things have been delivered unto me of my Father: and no one knoweth the Son, save the Father; neither doth any know the Father, save the Son, and he to whomsoever the Son willeth to reveal him" Matthew 11:27. Who among us can boast of complete comprehension of the character and person of Christ? We know much about Him and we may know Him, but there are depths of knowledge no one has yet attained, NO ONE KNOWETH BUT HE HIMSELF. Remember that the word NAME is more than a verbal designation of a person. It speaks concerning the character and reputation of that person.

19:13 AND HE IS ARRAYED IN A GARMENT SPRINKLED WITH BLOOD: AND HIS NAME IS CALLED THE WORD OF GOD.

Does the thought of BLOOD in this context draw your attention to Calvary or do you see the BLOOD of the enemy splashed on His GARMENT during the conflict? Either thought would fit this picture. However, preference should probably be given to the blood of Calvary in light of the several references to Jesus as the Lamb of God and the benefits derived from the blood of the Lamb that are mentioned throughout this book. Read Isaiah 63:1-6.

HIS NAME IS CALLED THE WORD OF GOD. This further identifies the rider of the WHITE HORSE. "In the beginning was the Word, and the Word was with God, and the Word was God...And the Word became flesh, and dwelt among us (and we beheld his glory, glory as of the only begotten from the Father), full of grace and truth" John 1:1,14. Thoughts are conveyed from one mind to another with the vehicle of words. Christ is the supreme revelation of the mind of God to man. God expresses Himself to His people through His Son. "God, having of old time

195

spoken unto the fathers in the prophets by divers portions and in divers manners, hath at the end of these days spoken unto us in his Son, whom he appointed heir of all things, through whom also he made the worlds" Hebrews 1:1.

19:14 AND THE ARMIES WHICH ARE IN HEAVEN FOLLOWED HIM UPON WHITE HORSES, CLOTHED IN FINE LINEN, WHITE AND PURE.

ARMIES WHICH ARE IN HEAVEN have been explained both as angels and as the redeemed who have passed from the earthly scene. "And there was war in heaven: Michael and his angels going forth to war with the dragon; and the dragon warred and his angels" Revelation 12:7. This verse adds weight to the suggestion of angels. It is interesting to observe that their garments are WHITE AND PURE, unstained by blood. The victory is the Lord's though shared with all who are on the Lord's side. It is because of His blood that we may be overcomers in the conflict. The garments worn by THE ARMIES are like those worn by Christians. See Revelation 19:8.

19:15 AND OUT OF HIS MOUTH PROCEEDETH A SHARP SWORD, THAT WITH IT HE SHOULD SMITE THE NATIONS: AND HE SHALL RULE THEM WITH A ROD OF IRON: AND HE TREADETH THE WINEPRESS OF THE FIERCENESS OF THE WRATH OF GOD, THE ALMIGHTY.

The battle between God and Satan is waged with the truth and the lie. It is a spiritual conflict. The SHARP SWORD is the word of God that is proclaimed and "is the power of God unto salvation to every one that believeth" Romans 1:16. See Hebrews 4:12 and Ephesians 6:17. THE NATIONS are smitten with the word of God so as to leave them either condemned or saved. They are condemned by the word through disobedience. They are saved by the word through obedience. "And if any man hear my sayings, and keep them not, I judge him not: for I came not to judge the world, but to save the world. He that rejecteth me, and receiveth not my sayings, hath one that judgeth him: the word that I spake, the same shall judge him in the last day" John 12:47,48.

The RULE WITH THE ROD OF IRON has previously been

explained as the firm, loving rule of a good shepherd. The firmness of the ROD makes clear that there is no place for compromise in the Christian faith. What the Lord had spoken stands. RULE emphasizes once again His authority as sovereign.

Treading THE WINEPRESS OF THE FIERCENESS OF THE WRATH OF GOD is clearly symbolic of the judgment upon the wicked. See Revelation 14:19,20. "Put ye in the sickle; for the harvest is ripe: come, tread ye; for the winepress is full, the vats overflow; for their wickedness is great" Joel 3:13. FIERCENESS and WRATH are telling of God's attitude toward sin. There is absolutely no toleration of that which is in opposition to truth and holiness. Such attitudes toward sin ought to characterize every child of God.

There is hope in the midst of the battle. God is ALMIGHTY!

19:16 AND HE HATH ON HIS GARMENT AND ON HIS THIGH A NAME WRITTEN, KING OF KINGS, AND LORD OF LORDS.

A NAME WRITTEN ON HIS THIGH would be about eye level for most adults while the KING OF KINGS rides the WHITE HORSE in triumph. In other words the absolute sovereignty of God is so obvious that there is no excuse for any man not recognizing it and submitting to it. "For the invisible things of him since the creation of the world are clearly seen, being perceived through the things that are made, even his everlasting power and divinity; that they may be without excuse" Romans 1:20. "And ye shall know the truth, and the truth shall make you free" John 8:32.

At no time in history has Christ been anything less than KING OF KINGS, AND LORD OF LORDS. This truth has not always been recognized but it has always been present, for those who have eyes to see and ears to hear. The return of the Lord will further demonstrate His sovereignty but the fact is a present reality. He is now Lord to those who obey Him. He is now King to those who are in His kingdom, that is, to those who obey Him. "Thy kingdom come. Thy will be done, as in heaven, so on earth" Matthew 6:10. This is a Hebrew parallelism. The same thought is expressed twice. The second expression helps explain the first expression or emphasize it as the case may be. Thus Jesus is

KING OF KINGS, AND LORD OF LORDS to all who do His will on earth as it is in heaven.

19:17 AND I SAW AN ANGEL STANDING IN THE SUN; AND HE CRIED WITH A LOUD VOICE, SAYING TO ALL THE BIRDS THAT FLY IN MID HEAVEN, COME AND BE GATHERED TOGETHER UNTO THE GREAT SUPPER OF GOD;

A striking picture adds emphasis to the total overthrow of the forces of evil. STANDING IN THE SUN where all can hear the LOUD cry calls for the BIRDS of prey to come and partake of a SUPPER provided by GOD. The menu for this supper is supplied in the next verse.

19:18 THAT YE MAY EAT THE FLESH OF KINGS, AND THE FLESH OF CAPTAINS, AND THE FLESH OF MIGHTY MEN, AND THE FLESH OF HORSES AND OF THEM THAT SIT THEREON, AND THE FLESH OF ALL MEN, BOTH FREE AND BOND, AND SMALL AND GREAT.

The position a man may have occupied in life means nothing to the scavangers. It has already been noted that judgment is no respecter of persons in 6:15. The power and wealth of the HARLOT did not prevent her destruction. Men of all walks of life will share in the final destruction if they have taken their places in the ranks of Satan's army. God has already determined the outcome of the conflict. This verse pictures completeness in the ultimate defeat. There will be no survivors on the devil's side.

19:19 AND I SAW THE BEAST, AND THE KINGS OF THE EARTH, AND THEIR ARMIES, GATHERED TOGETHER TO MAKE WAR AGAINST HIM THAT SAT UPON THE HORSE, AND AGAINST HIS ARMY.

In a final vain effort the Satanic forces are seen GATHERED TOGETHER TO MAKE WAR AGAINST Christ and all who follow Christ, HIS ARMY. See Revelation 16:13-16. The warring against Christ must not be limited to the final stages of the battle for it takes place throughout history. The end is seen in the midst of the conflict to serve as an encouragement to God's people. HIM THAT SAT UPON THE HORSE is Christ. HIS ARMY is the redeemed.

19:20 AND THE BEAST WAS TAKEN, AND WITH HIM THE

FALSE PROPHET THAT WROUGHT THE SIGNS IN HIS SIGHT, WHEREWITH HE DECEIVED THEM THAT HAD RECEIVED THE MARK OF THE BEAST AND THEM THAT WORSHIPPED HIS IMAGE: THEY TWO WERE CAST ALIVE INTO THE LAKE OF FIRE THAT BURNETH WITH BRIMSTONE:

This verse takes us back to chapter thirteen where two beasts are presented. The second beast is here designated THE FALSE PROPHET. The first beast symbolizes Satanic world power. The second beast, THE FALSE PROPHET, symbolizes Satanic religion, false doctrine, Caesar worship, idolatry, etc. See comments on 13:17 concerning THE MARK OF THE BEAST. Deception is again noted as Satan's weapon.

THEY TWO, the BEAST and THE FALSE PROPHET, WERE CAST ALIVE INTO THE LAKE OF FIRE. This marks their end once and for all. More is stated about THE LAKE OF FIRE in the next chapter. BRIMSTONE suggests a fire that has an offensive odor and is extremely hot.

19:21 AND THE REST WERE KILLED WITH THE SWORD OF HIM THAT SAT UPON THE HORSE, EVEN THE SWORD WHICH CAME FORTH OUT OF HIS MOUTH: AND ALL THE BIRDS WERE FILLED WITH THEIR FLESH.

THE REST includes all those who followed the BEAST and the FALSE PROPHET. ALL THE BIRDS WERE FILLED WITH THEIR FLESH intensifies the imagery of the ultimate and complete defeat of all wickedness.

20:1 AND I SAW AN ANGEL COMING DOWN OUT OF HEAVEN, HAVING THE KEY OF THE ABYSS AND A GREAT CHAIN IN HIS HAND.

The ANGEL is a messenger sent from God. The only importance attached to this ANGEL is seen in what he has and what he does. He has THE KEY, authority, and A GREAT CHAIN, the gospel. He has that which is necessary and adequate for the binding of Satan, limiting his power.

Two-thirds of the Satanic trinity have been destroyed—the BEAST and the FALSE PROPHET. It remains for Satan to be cast into THE LAKE OF FIRE. There is no need to see any time difference between chapters nineteen and twenty. the chronology of events is not the point of what John has written. The overriding truth is the triumph of God and the total defeat of Satan.

20:2   AND HE LAID HOLD ON THE DRAGON, THE OLD SERPENT, WHICH IS THE DEVIL AND SATAN AND BOUND HIM FOR A THOUSAND YEARS,

The four designations for the evil one are the same as previously noted in 12:9. See comments on 12:9. The DRAGON represents evil at work in world power. The SERPENT describes the cunning deception of evil. The DEVIL is a slanderer and false accuser. SATAN is the adversary of God and man.

How do you lay HOLD on that which is not matter? The answer to this question explains why the CHAIN in verse one cannot be made of material substance. Symbolic language is employed to explain the limitation that is placed upon Satan.

Other scriptures aid us in our understanding of the binding of Satan. Consider the words of Jesus on the occasion of healing a man possessed with a demon who was both blind and dumb. He was accused of doing this by Beelzebub. Jesus answered this charge by stating, "But if I by the Spirit of God cast out demons, then is the kingdom of God come upon you. Or how can one enter into the house of the strong man, and spoil his goods, except he first bind the strong man? and then he will spoil his house" Matthew 12:28,29. The strong man is an obvious reference to Satan. Satan's goods is a reference to the demons. Jesus, therefore, exerted a superior strength in the binding of Satan to enable Him to cast out the demon. This draws our attention to what happened to Satan with the coming of Christ.

Something very significant took place with the first advent of Christ with regard to Satan's power. Jesus said, "Now is the judgment of this world: now shall the prince of this world be cast out" John 12:31. Note the emphasis upon "now." The instrument used to bring judgment upon Satan was the cross as He indicates in the next verse. "And I, if I be lifted up from the earth, will draw all men unto myself" John 12:32. Not only was Christ lifted up on the cross but He is lifted up also in the preaching of Christ crucified. It is the gospel that is the CHAIN which restricts

Satan.

When the seventy returned from their preaching tour they reported "with joy, saying, Lord, even the demons are subject unto us in thy name. And he said unto them, I beheld Satan fallen as lightning from heaven" Luke 10:17,18. Jesus used the term "fallen" in the same way John did in Revelation 14:8 when he spoke of Babylon as "fallen" before the fact. In both instances an assured event is spoken of as having already taken place prior to the happening to emphasize the certainty of the event. The fall of Satan took place at Calvary and Jesus has this in mind when responding to the seventy. Revelation 12:10-12 sheds further light upon this truth. The "blood of the Lamb" enabled "our brethren" to overcome Satan. No wonder Paul wrote, "I determined not to know anything among you, save Jesus Christ, and him crucified" 1 Corinthians 2:2. "For the word of the cross is to them that perish foolishness; but unto us who are saved it is the power of God" 1 Corinthians 1:18.

"Be subject therefore unto God; but resist the devil, and he will flee from you" James 4:7.

A THOUSAND YEARS is a complete period of time. It is wise to know how this term is used elsewhere in scripture before reaching a conclusion regarding its meaning here. "Jehovah your God hath multiplied you, and, behold, ye are this day as the stars of heaven for multitude. Jehovah, the God of your fathers, make you a thousand times as many as ye are, and bless you, as he hath promised you" Deuteronomy 1:10,11! "For every beast of the forest is mine, And the cattle upon a thousand hills" Psalm 50:10. "But forget not this one thing, beloved, that one day is with the Lord as a thousand years, and a thousand years as one day" 2 Peter 3:8. The number ten is symbolic for completeness. A THOUSAND YEARS adds emphasis to the thought of completeness. When we see that this term is used metaphorically in scripture we ought to consider a similar use in a book that employs numerous metaphors. The following verses will help define the time indicated by A THOUSAND YEARS.

20:3 AND CAST HIM INTO THE ABYSS, AND SHUT IT, AND SEALED IT OVER HIM, THAT HE SHOULD DECEIVE THE NATIONS NO MORE, UNTIL THE THOU-

SAND YEARS SHOULD BE FINISHED: AFTER THIS
HE MUST BE LOOSED FOR A LITTLE TIME.

THE ABYSS is a place of intense depth which is sometimes
described as bottomless to accent the depth. It is the same place
as that noted in chapter nine when the fifth angel sounded the
trumpet. THE ABYSS is the symbolism used for the imprison-
ment of Satan, for it was SHUT AND SEALED to limit his activity.

Satan was limited only in THAT HE SHOULD DECEIVE
THE NATIONS NO MORE. Apart from this limitation Satan was
free to carry on and he has exercised his freedom in other areas
to the fullest. Picture a lion on fifty acres of fenced-in land. The
lion has complete freedom on the fifty acres but is unable to do
anything beyond the fence. Anyone who steps on the fifty acres is
subject to the lion's attack. So it is with Satan. Satan has freedom
in every area but one—he cannot DECEIVE THE NATIONS.
The continuing increase of Satanic activity should not surprise
anyone and does not contradict what is written here. Satan's
limitation has been suggested other places in this book with the
expression "is given."

That which limits Satan and prevents him from deceiving
THE NATIONS is the gospel. From the time of the incarnation
Satan has lost his control. With the dawn of the church age nations have had the gospel preached to them and those who have
obeyed the gospel have been liberated from the bonds of sin and
have been given a new life in Christ.

Long ago God promised Abraham that the nations of the
earth would be blessed through his seed. Genesis 12:1-3. "Now to
Abraham were the promises spoken, and to his seed. He saith not,
And to seeds, as of many; but as of one, And to thy seed, which is
Christ...And if ye are Christ's, then are ye Abraham's seed, heirs
according to promise" Galatians 3:16,29. The deliverance from Satan's deceptive power is beautifully stated by Peter in 1 Peter
2:9,10: "But ye are an elect race, a royal priesthood, a holy nation,
a people for God's own possession, that ye may show forth the excellencies of him who called you out of darkness into his marvelous light: who in time past were not a people, but now are the
people of God: who had not obtained mercy, but now have obtain-

ed mercy." It should be noted that many have chosen to reject Christ and remain in the darkness of sin.

Satan's limitation is further illustrated with the experience of Job against whom Satan was permitted to do many terrible things but he was not allowed to take his life. Satan's limitation is experienced in the life of the Christian. "There hath no temptation taken you but such as man can bear: but God is faithful, who will not suffer you to be tempted above that ye are able; but will with the temptation make also the way of escape, that ye may be able to endure it" 1 Corinthians 10:13.

The seal placed upon the ABYSS is God's way of showing there will be no escape for Satan. God's binding is secure. Satan's limitation is certain.

UNTIL THE THOUSAND YEARS SHOULD BE FINISHED indicates the duration of Satan's being bound and thus limited in his activity. Since "it was God's good pleasure through the foolishness of the preaching to save them that believe" 1 Corinthians 1:18, we may understand THE THOUSAND YEARS to be a reference to the gospel age—the age of the church—the time between Christ's first and second comings.

AFTER THIS HE MUST BE LOOSED FOR A LITTLE TIME. It has been suggested earlier in this study that the expression AFTER THIS does not necessarily denote chronology. If it does not denote chronology here the thought may be that the loosing and binding take place at the same time and thus A LITTLE TIME would be equated with THE THOUSAND YEARS. This view sees the binding of Satan explained in the Christian and the loosing of Satan demonstrated in the unredeemed. Since the Lord regards "a thousand years as one day" 2 Peter 3:8, it is not difficult to regard this A LITTLE TIME. Others, however, see God's plan showing a brief release of Satan before his final destruction. But even in this LITTLE TIME Satan will not be successful in his attempts for the omnipotence of God prevails all the way to the day of final victory. The "gates of Hades shall not prevail" against the church. "Heaven and earth shall pass away, but my words shall not pass away" Matthew 24:35.

20:4   AND I SAW THRONES, AND THEY SAT UPON THEM,
       AND JUDGMENT WAS GIVEN UNTO THEM: AND I

SAW THE SOULS OF THEM THAT HAD BEEN BE-
HEADED FOR THE TESTIMONY OF JESUS, AND FOR
THE WORD OF GOD, AND SUCH AS WORSHIPPED
NOT THE BEAST, NEITHER HIS IMAGE, AND RE-
CEIVED NOT THE MARK UPON THEIR FOREHEAD
AND UPON THEIR HAND; AND THEY LIVED, AND
REIGNED WITH CHRIST A THOUSAND YEARS.

Jesus' disciples were slow to learn the real nature of God's
kingdom. Jesus had said, "My kingdom is not of this world" John
18:36. Earlier He said, "Ye know that they who are accounted to
rule over the Gentiles lord it over them; and their great ones
exercise authority over them. but it is not so among you: but whosoever would become great among you, shall be servant of all"
Mark 3:42-44. At the time of His ascension the disciples' question
indicates they have still not understood His kingdom. "Lord, dost
thou at this time restore the kingdom to Israel" Acts 1:6? A correct understanding and proper concept of Christ's kingdom is essential to know the meaning of THRONES.

THRONES are occupied by those who LIVED AND REIGN-
ED WITH CHRIST A THOUSAND YEARS. Christians reign
with Christ now. "For if, by the trespass of the one, death reigned
through the one; much more shall they that receive the abundance of grace and of the gift of righteousness reign in life
through the one; even Jesus Christ" Romans 5:17. "Nay, in all
these things we are more than conquerors through him that loved
us" Romans 8:37. Read 2 Timothy 2:12.

JUDGMENT WAS GIVEN UNTO THEM that occupy the
THRONES, those who LIVED AND REIGNED WITH CHRIST
A THOUSAND YEARS. "or know ye not that the saints shall
judge the world?..." 1 Corinthians 6:2. The Christian life is a judgment upon the wicked. The proclamation of the gospel is a judgment upon those who reject it. Christians judge and reign as they
occupy thrones. This is symbolic language to describe the role of
the church throughout the Christian era. WAS GIVEN indicates
that the Christian judges through proclaiming and living the
message God has given him. This must not be seen as any individual Christian determining who is saved and who is lost.
Judgment comes through the individual's response to the word of

the Lord. Read John 12:47 and 48.

It is during the church age that Christians are martyred because of their allegiance to Christ and His word. It is during the church age that Christians do not worship the BEAST, NEITHER HIS IMAGE. It is during the church age that Christians RECEIVED NOT THE MARK UPON THEIR FOREHEAD AND UPON THEIR HAND identifying them with Satan. Each phrase in this verse describes that which takes place during the THOUSAND year period. The fact that every verb in this verse is in the same tense further underscores this truth. Verse four is to be understood in light of Christian activity in the conflict against Satan throughout the Christian dispensation. Even martyrdom is a judgment against sin and a reigning with Christ.

20:5　THE REST OF THE DEAD LIVED NOT UNTIL THE THOUSAND YEARS SHOULD BE FINISHED. THIS IS THE FIRST RESURRECTION.

20:6　BLESSED AND HOLY IS HE THAT HATH PART IN THE FIRST RESURRECTION: OVER THESE THE SECOND DEATH HATH NO POWER; BUT THEY SHALL BE PRIESTS OF GOD AND OF CHRIST, AND SHALL REIGN WITH HIM A THOUSAND YEARS.

"And you did he make alive, when ye were dead through your trespasses and sins,...that ye were at that time separate from Christ, alienated from the commonwealth of Israel, and strangers from the covenants of the promise, having no hope and without God in the world" Ephesians 2:1,12. THE REST OF THE DEAD are those who have not chosen to have life in Christ Jesus. Their existence upon the earth cannot be called real living. They are dead in sin. UNTIL does not mean that they will begin to live at the end of the THOUSAND YEARS. We are informed in 1 Samuel 15:35 that Samuel did not come to see Saul until he died. This does not mean that he came to see him at the time of his death or after his death. It means that he did not come to see Saul from that time forward to the time of his death. Those dead in sin do not live now or at any time in the future for life comes only in Christ.

THE FIRST RESURRECTION is a reference to the time of conversion. RESURRECTION is a rising from the dead and thus

205

a death is necessitated. The departure of the soul from the body is not a resurrection because the soul has not been in a dead state. Sin kills the soul. The resurrection of the soul comes at the time of the new birth. "Having been buried with him in baptism, wherein ye were also raised with him through faith in the working of God, who raised him from the dead. And you, being dead through your trespasses and the uncircumcision of your flesh, you, I say, did he make alive together with him, having forgiven us all our trespasses" Colossians 2:12,13. "We were buried therefore with him through baptism into death: that like as Christ was raised from the dead through the glory of the Father, so we also might walk in newness of life" Romans 6:4. "We know that we have passed out of death into life, because we love the brethren" 1 John 3:14. THE FIRST RESURRECTION implies a second without necessitating it. THE FIRST RESURRECTION distinguishes the time of conversion from the general resurrection spoken of in 1 Corinthians 15.

THE FIRST RESURRECTION is described by John in his gospel record. "Verily, verily, I say unto you, He that heareth my word, and believeth him that sent me, hath eternal life, and cometh not into judgment, but has passed out of death into life" John 5:24. Pay special attention to the tense of the verbs in this verse. The general resurrection is described in this same chapter. "Marvel not at this: for the hour cometh in which all that are in the tombs shall hear his voice, and shall come forth; they that have done good, unto the resurrection of life; and they that have done evil, unto the resurrection of judgment" John 5:28,29. The general resurrection is a bodily resurrection as Paul makes clear in his thorough treatment in 1 Corinthians 15. THE FIRST RESURRECTION is of the soul.

When we understand the meaning of THE FIRST RESURRECTION verse six is clear. It is because we are new in Christ that THE SECOND DEATH HAS NO POWER. As Christians we are PRIESTS OF GOD AND OF CHRIST. See 1 Peter 2:9. We do REIGN WITH HIM A THOUSAND YEARS. See comments on verse four above.

20:7   AND WHEN THE THOUSAND YEARS ARE FINISHED,
        SATAN SHALL BE LOOSED OUT OF HIS PRISON,

Before the end comes there will be a final strong effort made by Satan against God and the redeemed. The effort will be in vain.

20:8 AND SHALL COME FORTH TO DECEIVE THE NATIONS WHICH ARE IN THE FOUR CORNERS OF THE EARTH, GOG AND MAGOG, TO GATHER THEM TOGETHER TO THE WAR: THE NUMBER OF WHOM IS AS THE SAND OF THE SEA.

Deception continues to be the instrument of Satan to the end. FOUR CORNERS OF THE EARTH apocalyptically includes all the earth. FOUR is symbolism for the earth. GOG AND MAGOG symbolize the enemy of God. See Ezekiel 38 and 39. THE SAND OF THE SEA visualizes an extremely great NUMBER. It is important to note once again that things are not as they may appear. The appearance of this verse would suggest that there is no way the Christian can come out victorious in this conflict. He is outnumbered. But appearances may deceive. Could David defeat Goliath? God did through him. Could Gideon defeat the Midianites with only 300 when he might have had 32,000? God did through the 300. God is defeating and will ultimately defeat Satan and all evil forces. Christians must not be overwhelmed by disturbing appearances, but in Christ be "more than conquerors" through Christ.

20:9 AND THEY WENT UP OVER THE BREADTH OF THE EARTH, AND COMPASSED THE CAMP OF THE SAINTS ABOUT, AND THE BELOVED CITY: AND FIRE CAME DOWN OUT OF HEAVEN, AND DEVOURED THEM.

FIRE from HEAVEN pictures the destruction as the work of God. The experiences of Elijah illustrate God's use of FIRE. Christians, SAINTS, are presented as THE BELOVED CITY in contrast to BABYLON. God's people were presented with the imagery of a woman in chapter twelve and are here presented as THE BELOVED CITY. The fact that the CITY is COMPASSED ABOUT by the enemy indicates that earth is the scene, not heaven. The FIRE CAME DOWN OUT OF HEAVEN AND DEVOURED the enemy. This is God's judgment upon the foes of the church. Read 2 Thessalonians 1:7-9.

20:10 AND THE DEVIL THAT DECEIVED THEM WAS CAST INTO THE LAKE OF FIRE AND BRIMSTONE, WHERE ARE ALSO THE BEAST AND THE FALSE PROPHET; AND THEY SHALL BE TORMENTED DAY AND NIGHT FOR EVER AND EVER.

Note the repeated emphasis upon the deceptive character of the DEVIL. The LAKE OF FIRE is defined as the second death and pictures eternal destructon and torment. See verse fourteen. The unbearable odor and intensity of the fire are accented with BRIMSTONE, sulphur. THE BEAST AND THE FALSE PROPHET have always worked with THE DEVIL and now the three of them share in eternal TORMENT. All three are cast into the LAKE OF FIRE at the same time though the record of two of them occurs in the preceding chapter.

20:11 AND I SAW A GREAT WHITE THRONE, AND HIM THAT SAT UPON IT, FROM WHOSE FACE THE EARTH AND THE HEAVEN FLED AWAY; AND THERE WAS FOUND NO PLACE FOR THEM.

The GREAT WHITE THRONE is the one occupied by God whose judgments are pure and righteous. It is possible that THE EARTH AND THE HEAVEN FLED AWAY to make room for the new heaven and the new earth. "The heavens that now are, and the earth, by the same word have been stored up for fire, being reserved against the day of judgment and destruction of ungodly men" 2 Peter 3:7. "And I saw a new heaven and a new earth: for the first heaven and the first earth are passed away; and the sea is no more" Revelation 21:1. Apparently THE EARTH AND THE HEAVEN had served their purpose in the plan of God for THERE WAS FOUND NO PLACE FOR THEM now that the day of judgment has arrived.

20:12 AND I SAW THE DEAD, THE GREAT AND THE SMALL, STANDING BEFORE THE THRONE; AND BOOKS WERE OPENED: AND. ANOTHER BOOK WAS OPENED, WHICH IS THE BOOK OF LIFE: AND THE DEAD WERE JUDGED OUT OF THE THINGS WHICH WERE WRITTEN IN THE BOOKS, ACCORDING TO THEIR WORKS.

No one is exempt from judgment whether GREAT or

SMALL. The context suggests that the BOOKS contained the WORKS record. "For we must all be made manifest before the judgment-seat of Christ; that each one may receive the things done in the body, according to what he hath done, whether it be good or bad" 2 Corinthians 5:10. "And I say unto you, that every idle word that men shall speak, they shall give account thereof in the day of judgment. For by thy words thou shalt be justified, and by thy words thou shalt be condemned" Matthew 12:36,37. Judgment is to be feared indeed unless your sins have been removed by the blood of Jesus. THE BOOK OF LIFE contains the names of the redeemed. See Philippians 4:3. WORKS do not save. "For by grace have ye been saved through faith" Ephesians 2:8a. Man determines whether he is and will be saved now by whether he obeys or rejects the gospel of Christ. Keep this in mind in the study of this verse.

20:13 AND THE SEA GAVE UP THE DEAD THAT WERE IN IT; AND DEATH AND HADES GAVE UP THE DEAD THAT WERE IN THEM: AND THEY WERE JUDGED EVERY MAN ACCORDING TO THEIR WORKS.

More descriptive language is added to the preceding verse to stress the fact that all will face judgment. With this general truth clarified it is not important that arguments be settled concerning some of the specific meanings that may be attached to THE SEA AND DEATH AND HADES. HADES is the abode of dead. Is SEA to be understood literally or is it a figurative reference to the nations? Even DEATH cannot keep one from facing judgment. Judgment according to WORKS makes WORKS very important. When the Lord was asked by man what to do, He never questioned the use of "do." What man does is eternally important.

20:14 AND DEATH AND HADES WERE CAST INTO THE LAKE OF FIRE. THIS IS THE SECOND DEATH, EVEN THE LAKE OF FIRE.

"The last enemy that shall be abolished is death" 1 Corinthians 15:26. "He hath swallowed up death for ever; and the Lord Jehovah will wipe away tears from off all faces; and the reproach of his people will be taken away from off all the earth: for Jehovah hath spoken it" Isaiah 25:8. How can DEATH be thrown into THE LAKE OF FIRE? DEATH is the wages of sin. John pictures Satan and everything associated with sin as being totally destroyed. DEATH cannot survive when God conquers all.

20:15 AND IF ANY WAS NOT FOUND WRITTEN IN THE BOOK OF LIFE, HE WAS CAST INTO THE LAKE OF FIRE.

The unredeemed are those whose names are NOT FOUND WRITTEN IN THE BOOK OF LIFE. Jesus described judgment just prior to His own death with these words: "Then shall he say also unto them on the left hand, Depart from me, ye cursed, into the eternal fire which is prepared for the devil and his angels" Matthew 25:41. Observe that there is no indication that eternal fire was prepared for any man. God is "not wishing that any should perish, but that all should come to repentance" 2 Peter 3:9b. "But the heavens that now are, and the earth, by the same word have been stored up for fire, being reserved against the day of judgment and destruction of ungodly men" 2 Peter 3:7. God does not will that any man should perish but He is aware that many will chose the ungodly path to eternal condemnation. The awful truth of this fifteenth verse serves as a strong warning for all men everywhere to repent and get right with God. Sad indeed it will be to share in the defeat of Satan.

"Wherefore, brethren, give the more diligence to make your calling and election sure: for if ye do these things, ye shall never stumble: for thus shall be richly supplied unto you the entrance into the eternal kingdom of our Lord and Saviour Jesus Christ" 2 Peter 1:10,22.

Pay particular attention to the last part of verse twenty in light of its context in the following scripture. "And the seventy returned with joy, saying, Lord, even the demons are subject unto us in thy name. And he said unto them, I beheld Satan fallen as lightning from heaven. Behold, I have given you authority to tread upon serpents and scorpions, and over all the power of the enemy: and nothing shall in any wise hurt you. Nevertheless in this rejoice not, that the spirits are subject unto you; but rejoice that your names are written in heaven" Luke 10:17-20.

VICTORY IN CHRIST

CHAPTERS TWENTY-ONE AND TWENTY-TWO

21:1 AND I SAW A NEW HEAVEN AND A NEW EARTH: FOR THE FIRST HEAVEN AND THE FIRST EARTH ARE PASSED AWAY; AND THE SEA IS NO MORE.

It is refreshing to begin focusing upon good after so much attention has been given to evil, its activity and end. The present world order is gone. THE SEA IS NO MORE. Remember that the BEAST came from the SEA. "But the wicked are like the troubled sea; for it cannot rest, and its waters cast up mire and dirt" Isaiah 57:20. Some see the SEA as a symbol of barriers and thus view eternity where there will be nothing to separate one from another. The newness of the NEW HEAVEN AND NEW EARTH is explained by what is not there, possibly because this is all we are capable of comprehending in our earthly state.

21:2 AND I SAW THE HOLY CITY, NEW JERUSALEM, COMING DOWN OUT OF HEAVEN FROM GOD, MADE READY AS A BRIDE ADORNED FOR HER HUSBAND.

The NEW JERUSALEM pictures the redeemed as BABYLON pictured the unredeemed. The absence of sin makes it THE HOLY CITY. "Wherefore if any man is in Christ, he is a new creature: the old things are passed away; behold, they are become new" 2 Corinthians 5:17. Jesus said, "I will build my church" Matthew 16:18b. The church is not the work of man. It is the creation of God, thus the redeemed are pictured as coming FROM GOD. The picture of the church AS A BRIDE is enlarged in Ephesians 6:22-33

21:3 AND I HEARD A GREAT VOICE OUT OF THE THRONE SAYING, BEHOLD, THE TABERNACLE OF GOD IS WITH MEN, AND HE SHALL DWELL WITH THEM, AND THEY SHALL BE HIS PEOPLES, AND GOD HIMSELF SHALL BE WITH THEM, AND BE THEIR GOD:

TABERNACLE means tent and is here intended to draw our attention to the tabernacle of the Old Testament as the place of

211

God's presence with His people. The intimate communion of GOD WITH MEN is the dominant scene here. There is a triple emphasis in the verse on the union of God with man. In contrast with the temporary presence of God in the Old Testament tabernacle, God's dwelling here is permanent. Read Leviticus 26:11-13.

21:4 AND HE SHALL WIPE AWAY EVERY TEAR FROM THEIR EYES: AND DEATH SHALL BE NO MORE; NEITHER SHALL THERE BE MOURNING, NOR CRYING, NOR PAIN, ANY MORE: THE FIRST THINGS ARE PASSED AWAY.

This verse is very similar to Revelation 7:16. See comments there. Revelation is a book of contrasts. That which characterized life on the FIRST EARTH will be completely absent on the NEW EARTH, for THE FIRST THINGS ARE PASSED AWAY, cease to exist. All that has ceased was associated in some way with sin.

21:5 AND HE THAT SITTETH ON THE THRONE SAID, BEHOLD, I MAKE ALL THINGS NEW. AND HE SAITH, WRITE: FOR THESE WORDS ARE FAITHFUL AND TRUE.

God speaks. The emphasis is upon I. God says I MAKE ALL THINGS NEW. Long ago, Jeremiah wrote, "O Jehovah, I know that the way of man is not in himself; it is not in man that walketh to direct his steps" Jeremiah 10:23. Man has always been dependent upon God. These words are reliable. "Blessed be the God and Father of our Lord Jesus Christ, who according to his great mercy begat us again unto a living hope by the resurrection of Jesus Christ from the dead, unto an inheritance incorruptible, and undefiled, and that fadeth not away, reserved in heaven for you" 1 Peter 1:3,4.

21:6 AND HE SAID UNTO ME, THEY ARE COME TO PASS. I AM THE ALPHA AND THE OMEGA, THE BEGINNING AND THE END. I WILL GIVE UNTO HIM THAT IS ATHIRST OF THE FOUNTAIN OF THE WATER OF LIFE FREELY.

God declares that all things are done. He sees the end from the beginning. He offers this word of assurance as an encouragement to the Christian still involved in the current struggle against sin. ALPHA AND OMEGA are the first and last letters of

the Greek alphabet. BEGINNING means origin or source and
comes from the Greek word which gives us our word archeology.
This is not something which is a first of a series. This word emphasizes that God is the source. He is also the END, not the last of
a series but the consummation, the completion.

THIRST affirms man's need for God. God meets that need
FREELY. God never does anything halfway. WATER OF LIFE
symbolizes eternal life — life that is like God both in quality and in
quantity, that new life that begins with conversion. "Verily,
verily, I say unto you, He that heareth my word, and believeth
him that sent me, hath eternal life, and cometh not into judgment,
but hath passed out of death into life" John 5:24. Jesus said to the
Samaritan woman, "whosoever drinketh of the water that I shall
give him shall never thirst; but the water that I shall give him
shall become in him a well of water springing up into eternal life"
John 4:14. "As the heart panteth after the water brooks, So
panteth my soul after thee, O God. My soul thirsteth for God, for
the living God" Psalm 42:1,2a.

21:7   HE THAT OVERCOMETH SHALL INHERIT THESE
       THINGS; AND I WILL BE HIS GOD, AND HE SHALL
       BE MY SON.

Each time John uses the words OVERCOMETH we are reminded that our relationship with God is not something to take
for granted. Furthermore, life is a constant struggle and conflict.
We are engaged in war to the end and at no time dare we retreat.
We are admonished to be faithful to the end and such faithfulness
will make us overcomers. It will be worth it all to serve Jesus.
The overcomers SHALL INHERIT THESE THINGS. There will
be complete satisfaction. "For ye received not the spirit of bondage again unto fear; but ye received the spirit of adoption, where-
by we cry, Abba, Father. The Spirit himself beareth witness with
our spirit, that we are children of God: and if children, then heirs;
heirs of God, and jointheirs with Christ; if so be that we suffer
with him, that we may be also glorified with him" Romans 8:15-17.

21:8   BUT FOR THE FEARFUL, AND UNBELIEVING, AND
       ABOMINABLE, AND MURDERERS, AND FORNICA-
       TORS, AND SORCERERS, AND IDOLATORS, AND ALL
       LIARS, THEIR PART SHALL BE IN THE LAKE THAT

BURNETH WITH FIRE AND BRIMSTONE; WHICH IS
THE SECOND DEATH.

John would not have the reader get so caught up with the
benefits of being a Christian that he let down his guard against
Satan. He injects, as a sobering thought, this warning that identifies those who will not make it. This is John's way of saying what
Paul said to the Galatians. "Now the works of the flesh are manifest, which are these: fornication, uncleanness, lasciviousness,
idolatry, sorcery, enmities, strife, jealousies, wraths, factions,
division, parties, envyings, drunkenness, revelings, and such like;
of which I forewarn you, even as I did forewarn you, that they
who practise such things shall not inherit the kingdom of God"
Galatians 5:19-21.

THE FEARFUL are cowards. THE FEARFUL are those
who let being afraid keep them from doing God's will. Those who
experience fear in the line of Christian duty are not FEARFUL
unless they recant or cease serving. Those who are afraid and yet
fulfill their responsibilities to God find joy in serving Jesus who
provides the strength and guidance and removes the fear. To lack
courage as a Christian is to fail in trusting God who is almighty.
Beware of becoming cowardly.

The UNBELIEVING are those who don't trust God. They
have rejected Christ and refused to obey the gospel. Believing is
not just lip service; it is life service.

The ABOMINABLE are the defiled. The specific defilement is not named. The term may stand here for all defilements.
The ABOMINABLE engage in pagan ceremonies and partici-
pate in detestable activities which are both impure and unholy.
That which desecrates the temple of God is abominable. Our
bodies are temples of the Holy Spirit. Be careful what you take
into your body and what you do with your body.

MURDERERS include all who kill human life. It is a serious
thing to tamper with life to the extent that you put yourself or
someone else to death.

FORNICATORS are all those who live immorally. This is a
general term for sexual sin. "Ye have heard that it was said, Thou
shalt not commit adultery: but I say unto you, that every one that
looketh on a woman to lust after her hath committed adultery

with her already in his heart" Matthew 5:27,28.

SORCERERS use drugs, enchantments, witchcraft and the like. Read Deuteronomy 18:9-14 and then determine to never read a horoscope, or play with a Ouija board, or visit a fortune-teller. Christians must have nothing to do with that which so much displeases God.

IDOLATERS are those who give time and attention, money and effort, praise and glory to matter, to false ideologies, to anything that stands in the way of the one, true God. Your lawn, car, television, home, clothes can all become idols if you let them.

ALL LIARS leaves no liar out. Lies stand in direct opposition to Him who is truth. "Ye shall know the truth, and the truth shall make you free" John 8:32. The lie is the instrument of the devil used to deceive. Have nothing to do with half-truths, fibs, or any other expressions that are intended to deceive or mislead. ALL LIARS will BE IN THE LAKE OF FIRE.

THE LAKE OF FIRE is identified as the SECOND DEATH here as it was in the last two verses of the preceding chapter. Death is separation. Physical death is separation of the soul from the body. Spiritual death is the separation of the soul from God. The SECOND DEATH is the separation of man from God for eternity.

21:9   AND THERE CAME ONE OF THE SEVEN ANGELS WHO HAD THE SEVEN BOWLS, WHO WERE LADEN WITH THE SEVEN LAST PLAGUES; AND HE SPAKE WITH ME, SAYING, COME HITHER, I WILL SHOW THEE THE BRIDE, THE WIFE OF THE LAMB.

It is interesting that an angel who delivered a message of wrath is here called upon to bring this good news. Attention is now focused on the church, THE BRIDE, THE WIFE OF THE LAMB. See comments on 19:7. THE SEVEN LAST PLAGUES were presented in chapter sixteen. These were man's final warning to get right with God.

21:10 AND HE CARRIED ME AWAY IN THE SPIRIT TO A MOUNTAIN GREAT AND HIGH, AND SHOWED ME THE HOLY CITY JERUSALEM, COMING DOWN OUT OF HEAVEN FROM GOD,

John reminds us again that his is a spiritual experience. See

215

comments on 1:10. Whereas BABYLON was seen from the wilderness (17:3) THE HOLY CITY is seen from A MOUNTAIN GREAT AND HIGH, symbolizing his elevation in spirit. Some important truths are not understood because there has not been an adequate preparation of the mind and heart. John is prepared to see THE HOLY CITY with understanding by being CARRIED AWAY to the MOUNTAIN.

THE HOLY CITY is pictured as COMING DOWN OUT OF HEAVEN FROM GOD as in verse two. This repetition may be intended to impress upon the reader the important truth that the church is the work of God not man. The redeemed are saved by the grace of God. Paul wrote, "by the grace of God I am what I am" 1 Corinthians 15:10a.

21:11 HAVING THE GLORY OF GOD: HER LIGHT WAS LIKE UNTO A STONE MOST PRECIOUS, AS IT WERE A JASPER STONE, CLEAR AS CRYSTAL:

God's presence in the church is pictured in this verse as a glittering STONE and defined as THE GLORY OF GOD. The beauty and splendor of the church is presented in God's LIGHT as "holy and without blemish" Ephesians 5:27b.

21:12 HAVING A WALL GREAT AND HIGH; HAVING TWELVE GATES, AND AT THE GATES TWELVE ANGELS; AND NAMES WRITTEN THEREON, WHICH ARE THE NAMES OF THE TWELVE TRIBES OF THE CHILDREN OF ISRAEL:

Walls were placed around cities to protect the people. The GREAT AND HIGH WALL symbolizes God's protection and security for the church. Keep in mind that Christians do not live in THE HOLY CITY, Christians are THE HOLY CITY. THE NEW JERUSALEM, THE HOLY CITY, THE BRIDE and the church are all identical in the symbolism of Revelation. TWELVE is the signature of God's people. The GATES symbolize the entrance into the church. All of God's people are in the church. Passing through a gate that is attended, as this one is by an angel, suggests that entrance through the gate will require proper credentials or identification. Not just anyone may enter the church; only those who obey the gospel. "Jesus saith unto him, I am the way, and the truth, and the life: no one cometh unto the Father, but by me" John 14:6. The TWELVE ANGELS are at the TWELVE GATES to assure that only those whom the Lord adds enter in, Acts 2:47.

THE TWELVE TRIBES OF THE CHILDREN OF ISRAEL were used symbolically in chapter seven to represent the church on earth. John depends upon his readers' knowledge of the Old Testament to appreciate the wonderful truths he is expressing. Under the Old Testament THE CHILDREN OF ISRAEL were Jews by physical birth. Under the New Testament THE CHILDREN OF ISRAEL are Christians by spiritual birth. See Romans 2:28,29 and Galatians 3:26-29.

21:13 ON THE EAST WERE THREE GATES; AND ON THE NORTH THREE GATES; AND ON THE SOUTH THREE GATES; AND ON THE WEST THREE GATES.

From every direction on the compass people respond to the gospel and are added to the church. "This is good and acceptable in the sight of God our Saviour; who would have all men to be saved, and come to the knowledge of the truth" 1 Timothy 2:3,4. "They shall come from the east and west, and from the north and south, and shall sit down in the kingdom of God" Luke 13:29.

21:14 AND THE WALL OF THE CITY HAD TWELVE FOUNDATIONS, AND ON THEM TWELVE NAMES OF THE TWELVE APOSTLES OF THE LAMB.

"So then ye are no more strangers and sojourners, but ye are fellow-citizens with the saints and of the household of God, being built upon the foundation of the apostles and prophets, Christ Jesus himself being the chief corner stone; in whom each several building, fitly framed together, groweth into a holy temple in the Lord; in whom ye also are builded together for a habitation of God in the Spirit" Ephesians 2:19-22.

The TWELVE FOUNDATIONS bore the TWELVE NAMES OF THE TWELVE ̤APOSTLES. John does not say that the APOSTLES were the FOUNDATIONS. The reference to both the TWELVE TRIBES and the TWELVE APOSTLES is evidently to show the union of all of God's people in the ultimate fulfillment of His plan. This is not unique to this chapter. In chapter twelve the WOMAN was first presented as a representation of God's people under the first covenant and later God's people

217

under the new covenant. Imagery is borrowed from the Old Testament and the New Testament when speaking of God's people. The TWELVE APOSTLES are probably to be regarded corporately rather than individually. All the symbols associated with the number TWELVE stress the fact that God's people are being pictured. The number TWELVE in some form is used seven times in this chapter to enhance the picture of sacredness, completeness and perfection of THE HOLY CITY.

21:15 AND HE THAT SPAKE WITH ME HAD FOR A MEASURE A GOLDEN REED TO MEASURE THE CITY, AND THE GATES THEREOF, AND THE WALL THEREOF.

Measuring THE CITY has the same significance here as it had in the first two verses of chapter eleven when instructions were given to "measure the temple of God." In both instances measuring underscores the knowledge God has of those who are His own who are thus protected by Him. GOLDEN is a fitting way to describe the divine measuring instrument. The measurements will add further detail to the truth being pictured.

21:16 AND THE CITY LIETH FOURSQUARE, AND THE LENGTH THEREOF IS AS GREAT AS THE BREADTH: AND HE MEASURED THE CITY WITH THE REED, TWELVE THOUSAND FURLONGS: THE LENGTH AND THE BREADTH AND THE HEIGHT THEREOF ARE EQUAL.

THE CITY is not only FOURSQUARE, it is a cube. The cube symbolized perfection and reminds us of the Holy of Holies in the tabernacle and temple which was a cube. See 1 Kings 6:20. When the high priest entered the Holy of Holies on the annual day of atonement each year he came into the presence of God as he stood before the ark of the covenant. The Jews referred to God's presence as Shekinah. This verse causes us to think of this Old Testament history and thus see the present picture of the perfect fellowship God shared with all his people, His people described as THE HOLY CITY which is a cube by measurement. When TWELVE, the signature of God's people, is joined with THOUSAND, a multiple of ten which signifies completeness, the result is a figurative expression stressing all of God's people. Eight fur-

218

longs are equivalent to a mile.

21:17 AND HE MEASURED THE WALL THEREOF, A HUN-
DRED AND FORTY AND FOUR CUBITS, ACCORDING
TO THE MEASURE OF A MAN, THAT IS, OF AN AN-
GEL.

A cubit was the distance from the elbow to the tip of the fing-
er which was about eighteen inches. A HUNDRED AND FORTY
AND FOUR, as in chapter seven, is a numeric representation for
all the people of God. The last part of this verse may be suggesting that the ANGEL uses language that communicates to man,
THE MEASURE OF A MAN. Throughout this book divine truth
has been communicated through language which man can understand and which is the best language can do. Man's comprehension of things spiritual and eternal is limited. John is suggesting
here that the full picture is beyond human comprehension. Are
we not left feeling with the Psalmist "Such knowledge is too wonderful for me; It is high, I cannot attain unto it" Psalm 139:6?

21:18 AND THE WALL THEREOF WAS JASPER: AND THE
CITY WAS PURE GOLD, LIKE UNTO PURE GLASS.

The reader is impressed with the radiance and splendor of
the CITY. THE WALL is constituted of the same stone,
JASPER, used to describe God in chapter four, verse three. Even
the WALL speaks of God's presence. Only expensive materials
are used in the CITY. GOLD expresses precious value. "Wherein
ye greatly rejoice, though now for a little while, if need be, ye
have been put to grief in manifold trials, that the proof of your
faith, being more precious than gold that perisheth though it is
proved by fire, may be found unto praise and glory and honor at
the revelation of Jesus Christ" 1 Peter 1:6,7. PURE GLASS was
not readily available in Bible days and was affordable only to the
rich.

21:19 THE FOUNDATIONS OF THE WALL OF THE CITY
WERE ADORNED WITH ALL MANNER OF PRECIOUS
STONES, THE FIRST FOUNDATION WAS JASPER;
THE SECOND, SAPPHIRE; THE THIRD, CHALCE-
DONY; THE FOURTH, EMERALD; THE

21:20 FIFTH, SARDONYX: THE SIXTH, SARDIUS; THE
SEVENTH, CHRYSOLITE; THE EIGHTH, BERYL; THE

219

NINTH, TOPAZ; THE TENTH, CHRYSOPRASE; THE
ELEVENTH, JACINTH; THE TWELFTH, AMETHYST.

"For other foundation can no man lay than that which is laid,
which is Jesus Christ" 1 Corinthians 3:11. It is through the Lord
Jesus Christ that the beauty of God's holiness and glory shine
forth in the church. PRECIOUS STONES portray this matchless
beauty. God deserves the best and only the best is used here to
show the blessings of God to His people, the church, THE HOLY
CITY.

Note the similarity of the adornment given the FOUNDA-
TIONS OF THE WALL OF THE CITY to the breastplate of the
high priest. "And thou shalt set in it settings of stones, four rows
of stones: a row of sardius, topaz, and carbuncle shall be the first
row; and the second row an emerald, a sapphire, and a diamond;
and the third row a jacinth, an agate, and an amethyst; and the
fourth row a beryl, and an onyx, and a jasper: they shall be inclosed in gold in their settings" Exodus 28:17-20.

Various shades of four colors are represented in these
STONES. Blue is the dominant color of the AMETHYST,
JACINTH and SAPPHIRE. Red is the principal color of the
SARDONYX and SARDIUS. Green is the recognized color of the
JASPER, EMERALD, TOPAZ, CHRYSOPRASE, BERYL and
CHALCEDONY. CHRYSOLITE is yellow. Some of these stones
might be placed in a different color category, but this represents
one option.

What more can be written to describe the exquisite beauty
of THE HOLY CITY, yet John writes more.

21:21 AND THE TWELVE GATES WERE TWELVE PEARLS;
EACH ONE OF THE SEVERAL GATES WAS OF ONE
PEARL: AND THE STREET OF THE CITY WAS PURE
GOLD, AS IT WERE TRANSPARENT GLASS.

The intended impression these words are to make upon the
mind of the reader could easily be destroyed with a preoccupation
to detail. We need only to understand the meaning and use of the
terms used to appreciate the brilliant distinction the HOLY CITY
enjoys. The value of God's kingdom was illustrated by Jesus with
a pearl. "Again, the kingdom of heaven is like unto a man that is a
merchant seeking goodly pearls: and having found one pearl of

great price, he went and sold all that he had, and bought it" Matthew 13:45,46. Is it possible to imagine one pearl large enough to be a gate and the STREET made of PURE GOLD? The truth far surpasses the symbolism. Is it possible that one could compare BABYLON with THE HOLY CITY and not be constrained to put forth every effort to be totally surrendered to God and His will and thus become a part of this HOLY CITY?

21:22 AND I SAW NO TEMPLE THEREIN; FOR THE LORD GOD THE ALMIGHTY, AND THE LAMB, ARE THE TEMPLE THEREOF.

The TEMPLE is where men met God. Why, then, NO TEMPLE THEREIN? Because God's presence fills the city. God and His people are never apart. Fellowship is perfect and complete. Once again John reminds his readers that THE LORD GOD is ALMIGHTY. THE LAMB refers to Jesus Christ.

21:23 AND THE CITY HATH NO NEED OF THE SUN, NEITHER OF THE MOON, TO SHINE UPON IT: FOR THE GLORY OF GOD DID LIGHTEN IT, AND THE LAMP THEREOF IS THE LAMB.

"And this is the message which we have heard from him and announce unto you, that God is light, and in him is no darkness at all" 1 John 1:5. "Again therefore Jesus spake unto them, saying, I am the light of the world: he that followeth me shall not walk in the darkness, but shall have the light of life" John 8:12. The oneness of GOD and the LAMB is obvious in this verse. Were THE SUN or THE MOON present they would not be noticed because of the overwhelming illuminating power of God's glory. LIGHT is used in scripture to symbolize truth and righteousness.

21:24 AND THE NATIONS SHALL WALK AMIDST THE LIGHT THEREOF: AND THE KINGS OF THE EARTH BRING THEIR GLORY INTO IT.

The occupants of THE HOLY CITY come from every nation and people. All earthly authority recognizes the supremacy of God's authority and thus THE KINGS OF THE EARTH BRING THEIR GLORY INTO THE HOLY CITY.

21:25 AND THE GATES THEREOF SHALL IN NO WISE BE SHUT BY DAY (FOR THERE SHALL BE NO NIGHT THERE):

GATES are securely locked at night to protect people in the city. NIGHT and darkness are terms used to illustrate evil activity. Since the enemy no longer presents a threat, having been cast into "the lake of fire" there is no need to SHUT the GATES. NO NIGHT means no sin with its awful consequences. It's always DAY in the light of God's presence.

21:26 AND THEY SHALL BRING THE GLORY AND THE HONOR OF THE NATIONS INTO IT:

This verse magnifies the thought of verse twenty-four.

21:27 AND THERE SHALL IN NO WISE ENTER INTO IT ANYTHING UNCLEAN, OR HE THAT MAKETH AN ABOMINATION AND A LIE: BUT ONLY THEY THAT ARE WRITTEN IN THE LAMB'S BOOK OF LIFE.

"I said therefore unto you, that ye shall die in your sins: for except ye believe that I am he, ye shall die in your sins" John 8:24. Sin keeps men out of the HOLY CITY. Those who ENTER are those whose names are recorded IN THE LAMB'S BOOK OF LIFE, that is, those who come through Christ, who alone can save.

Sin is given three descriptions for emphasis. ANYTHING UNCLEAN is a broad designation for sin, for that which corrupts and defiles. Only the pure in heart will see God. HE THAT MAKETH AN ABOMINATION AND A LIE is added stress to the thought of verse eight. Read comments on verse eight.

This verse does not bar sinners from the church. It does, however, make clear that nothing short of the blood of Christ will cleanse a man from his sin and purify him for citizenship with God both now and for ever.

22:1 AND HE SHOWED ME A RIVER OF WATER OF LIFE, BRIGHT AS CRYSTAL, PROCEEDING OUT OF THE THRONE OF GOD AND OF THE LAMB,

In the last two chapters of Revelation LIFE is symbolized with three words—BOOK (21:27; 22:19), WATER (22:1,17) and TREE (22:2,14). "There is a river, the streams whereof make glad the city of God" Psalm 46:4. "Blessed are they that hunger and thirst after righteousness: for they shall be filled" Matthew 5:6. "Now on the last day, the great day of the feast, Jesus stood and cried, saying, If any man thirst, let him come unto me and drink.

He that beleiveth on me, as the scripture hath said, from within him shall flow rivers of living water. But this spake he of the Spirit, which they that believed on him were to receive: for the Spirit was not yet given; because Jesus was not yet glorified" John 7:37-39. God is the source of all LIFE and thus the WATER OF LIFE, eternal life, proceeds OUT OF THE THRONE OF GOD AND OF THE LAMB. Again the oneness of God and Christ is shown.

22:2   IN THE MIDST OF THE STREET THEREOF. AND ON THIS SIDE OF THE RIVER AND ON THAT WAS THE TREE OF LIFE, BEARING TWELVE MANNER OF FRUITS, YIELDING ITS FRUIT EVERY MONTH: AND THE LEAVES OF THE TREE WERE FOR THE HEALING OF THE NATIONS.

"And by the river upon the bank thereof, on this side and on that side, shall grow every tree for food, whose leaf shall not wither, neither shall the fruit thereof fail: it shall bring forth new fruit every month, because the waters thereof issue out of the sanctuary; and the fruit thereof shall be for food and the leaf thereof for healing" Ezekiel 47:12.

"And Jehovah God said, Behold, the man is become as one of us, to know good and evil: and now, lest he put forth his hand, and take also of the tree of life, and eat, and live for ever — therefore Jehovah God sent him forth from the garden of Eden, to till the ground from whence he was taken. So he drove out the man; and he placed at the east of the garden of Eden the Cherubim, and the flame of a sword which turned every way, to keep the way of the tree of life" Genesis 3:22-24.

TWELVE symbolizes God's people who are provided with water, food and health. THE LEAVES OF THE TREE WERE FOR THE HEALING OF THE NATIONS. Life with God is abundant living. There is no thirst, no hunger and no sickness. How attractively life with God is presented in these verses. HEALING does not mean that sickness will be an occasion for healing. Rather it means that there will be no sickness at all.

22:3   AND THERE SHALL BE NO CURSE ANY MORE: AND THE THRONE OF GOD AND OF THE LAMB SHALL BE THEREIN: AND HIS SERVANTS SHALL SERVE HIM;

The reason for NO CURSE is no sin. The expression of God's wrath against sin may be called a CURSE. Again the presence of God with His people is enunciated in the words AND THE THRONE OF GOD AND OF THE LAMB SHALL BE THEREIN. The service of HIS SERVANTS is understood by some as worship. Ceaseless praise characterizes eternal life with God.

22:4 AND THEY SHALL SEE HIS FACE; AND HIS NAME SHALL BE ON THEIR FOREHEADS.

"Beloved, now are we children of God, and it is not yet made manifest what we shall be. We know that, if he shall be manifested, we shall be like him; for we shall see him even as he is" 1 John 3:2. "Follow after peace with all men, and the sanctification without which no man shall see the Lord" Hebrews 12:14.

The obvious identity of God's people is signified with HIS NAME ON THEIR FOREHEADS. See comments on 7:3 and 14:1.

22:5 AND THERE SHALL BE NO NIGHT NO MORE; AND THEY NEED NO LIGHT OF LAMP, NEITHER LIGHT OF SUN; FOR THE LORD GOD SHALL GIVE THEM LIGHT: AND THEY SHALL REIGN FOR EVER AND EVER.

The first part of this verse is a restatement of verse twenty-two in the preceding chapter. See comments on that verse. THEY SHALL REIGN FOR EVER AND EVER is a fitting climax to this great book. It is a climax in the sense that the verses that follow in this chapter are an epilogue to the book. The main story has been told. It ends with victory in Christ. This victory receives the finishing touch with the declaration THEY, Christians, SHALL REIGN FOR EVER AND EVER, time without end. John makes no explanation of the nature of this reign. Perhaps we shouldn't inquire. Let the statement stand as is.

22:6 AND HE SAID UNTO ME, THESE WORDS ARE FAITHFUL AND TRUE: AND THE LORD, THE GOD OF THE SPIRITS OF THE PROPHETS, SENT HIS ANGEL TO SHOW UNTO HIS SERVANTS THE THINGS WHICH MUST SHORTLY COME TO PASS.

This verse begins the conclusion of the book of Revelation. The conclusion confirms the message of the book. THESE WORDS ARE FAITHFUL AND TRUE. You can rely upon their accuracy and importance. THESE WORDS refer to the entire book. They are FAITHFUL AND TRUE becasue they are the WORDS of God. THE GOD OF THE SPIRITS OF THE PROPHETS is the God Who inspires the prophets and Who inspired the writing of Revelation. What has been recorded in the other portions of sacred scripture is completely in harmony with the contents of this book — the author is the same.

There is a marked similarity between the last part of this verse and the first verse of the book. SHOW is a key word in the study of this book. Truth has been presented with pictures, symbols, drama and visions. SERVANTS are Christians for whom this book was written to be an encouragement to remain faithful unto God throughout the entirety of the conflict against Satan and sin. MUST denotes necessity. SHORTLY is God's term and thus should be understood in light of His manner of reckoning time. Short is a relative term and we must be careful that we do not put a meaning with it that is not in harmony with God's use of the term. Indeed every thing in this book MUST SHORTLY COME TO PASS. God has spoken. It will happen. For the events described in this book to begin to take place soon after it was written would be a proper meaning for the word SHORTLY.

22:7 AND BEHOLD, I COME QUICKLY. BLESSED IS HE THAT KEEPETH THE WORDS OF THE PROPHECY OF THIS BOOK.

I COME QUICKLY may mean soon or suddenly. In light of what Jesus said with regard to His own coming the thought of suddenly is preferred. "Watch therefore: for ye know not on what day your Lord cometh. But know this, that if the master of the house had known in what watch the thief was coming, he would have watched, and would not have suffered his house to be broken through. Therefore be ye also ready; for in an hour that ye think not the Son of man cometh" Matthew 24:42-44.

BEHOLD is intended to get our attention for what is to be said. The way to be sure of being ready for the coming of the Lord is to claim the blessing promised to those who keep THE WORDS OF THE PROPHECY OF THIS BOOK. KEEPETH is an expression of obedience. John regards the contents of THIS BOOK as PROPHECY. Read the prophetic books of the Old Testament to be reminded that there is more to prophecy than prediction, though predicton is an important element. Warning plays a vital role in prophecy. A prophet is a spokesman. God's prophet proclaims God's message. John identifies Revelation as a message from God. God provides the blessing for all those who hear and heed this message. See comments on 1:3 for the meaning of BLESSED.

22:8 AND I JOHN AM HE THAT HEARD AND SAW THESE THINGS. AND WHEN I HEARD AND SAW, I FELL DOWN TO WORSHIP BEFORE THE FEET OF THE ANGEL THAT SHOWED ME THESE THINGS.

JOHN identifies himself as the human instrument used of God in the recording of this message. The contents of this book are not hearsay, they are the witness of one who both HEARD AND SAW THESE THINGS. What he HEARD AND SAW made such a profound influence on him that he FELL DOWN TO WORSHIP BEFORE THE FEET OF THE ANGEL THAT SHOWED him THESE THINGS.

22:9 AND HE SAITH UNTO ME, SEE THOU DO IT NOT: I AM A FELLOW-SERVANT WITH THEE AND WITH THY BRETHREN THE PROPHETS, AND WITH THEM THAT KEEP THE WORDS OF THIS BOOK. WORSHIP GOD.

This is a repeat performance of chapter nineteen and verse ten. See comments on that verse. This additional emphasis is not without good reason. Even today there is the temptation to worship the instrument God uses rather than worship God. Some instruments of God encourage this to their shame. John the Baptist was an instrument of God. When asked who he was, he replied, "I am the voice" John 2:23a. When he compared himself to Jesus, he said, "he that cometh after me, the latchet of whose shoe I am not worthy to unloose" John 1:27. In his later testimony John said, "He must increase, but I must decrease" John 3:30. The role of God's servant is never elevated high enough to receive worship. Only GOD is worthy of WORSHIP. Humility is the proper garment for all of God's servants.

22:10 AND HE SAITH UNTO ME, SEAL NOT UP THE WORDS OF THE PROPHECY OF THIS BOOK; FOR THE

TIME IS AT HAND.

To SEAL would be to conceal. The admonition here is to make known the PROPHECY OF THIS BOOK. People need to hear it and heed it now! This is opposite of the instructions John received concerning the voice of the seven thunders in chapter ten. The message of Revelation is to be proclaimed today. It is not our business to predict a date for the Lord's return, but it is our business to be ready for it today and to warn others to prepare for it today. THE WORDS OF THE PROPHECY OF THIS BOOK are God's warning to man to get right with God. Now is THE TIME.

22:11 HE THAT IS UNRIGHTEOUS, LET HIM DO UN-RIGHTEOUSNESS STILL: AND HE THAT IS FILTHY, LET HIM BE MADE FILTHY STILL: AND HE THAT IS RIGHTEOUS, LET HIM DO RIGHTEOUSNESS STILL: AND HE THAT IS HOLY, LET HIM BE MADE HOLY STILL.

This is a warning for each individual to consider carefully his course in life. If the path of unrighteousness is chosen then be prepared to accept the fact that this path leads to eternal unrighteousness with all its consequences. "Be not deceived; God is not mocked: for whatsoever a man soweth, that shall he also reap. For he that soweth unto his own flesh shall of the flesh reap corruption; but he that soweth unto the Spirit shall of the Spirit reap eternal life" Galatians 6:7,8.

Any one who believes that all people will ultimately be saved must reckon with this verse. Any one who thinks he will get a second chance needs to ponder this verse a little longer. Today man has a choice. The day comes quickly when he will live with the consequences of his choice. Decision determines destiny. This verse urges careful thought in making your decision in light of decision's results.

22:12 BEHOLD, I COME QUICKLY; AND MY REWARD IS WITH ME, TO RENDER TO EACH MAN ACCORDING AS HIS WORK IS.

The suddenness of the Lord's return and the judgment according to works adds to the warning of verse eleven. It is a serious thing to procrastinate when it comes to your relationship

227

with God. "For we must all be made manifest before the judgment-seat of Christ; that each one may receive the things done in the body, according to what he hath done, whether it be good or bad" 2 Corinthians 5:10. See comments on 20:12.

22:13 I AM THE ALPHA AND THE OMEGA, THE FIRST AND THE LAST, THE BEGINNING AND THE END.

The eternality of Christ is emphasized in this last chapter as it was in chapter one, verses eight and seventeen. See comments on 21:6.

22:14 BLESSED ARE THEY THAT WASH THEIR ROBES, THAT THEY MAY HAVE THE RIGHT TO COME TO THE TREE OF LIFE, AND MAY ENTER IN BY THE GATES INTO THE CITY.

See comments on 7:14. The blessing is given to those THAT WASH, literally, go on washing, THEIR ROBES. The continuing action of washing calls to mind the continual cleansing of the blood John wrote about in his first epistle. "If we walk in the light as he is in the light, we have fellowship one with another, and the blood of Jesus his Son cleanseth us from all sin" 1 John 1:7. ROBES refer to man's character. THE TREE OF LIFE is eternal life promised only to those whose sins have been forgiven. THE CITY refers to the fellowship of God's people. GATES symbolize God's plan of salvation. Read John 14:6. See verse two for additional comments on the TREE OF LIFE.

22:15 WITHOUT ARE THE DOGS, AND THE SORCERERS, AND THE FORNICATORS, AND THE MURDERERS, AND THE IDOLATORS, AND EVERY ONE THAT LOVETH AND MAKETH A LIE.

"Beware of the dogs, beware of the evil workers, beware of the concision" Philippians 3:2. "For dogs have compassed me: A company of evil-doers have inclosed me" Psalm 22:16a. This parallelism identifies THE DOGS as "evil-doers." Note the specific form of evil attributed to this term in Deuteronomy 23:17,18 "There shall be no prostitute of the daughters of Israel, neither shall there be a sodomite of the sons of Israel. Thou shalt not bring the hire of a harlot, or the wages of a dog, into the house of Jehovah thy God for any vow: for even both these are an abomination unto Jehovah thy God."

228

The other sins listed in this verse were included in verse eight of the preceding chapter. See comments on 21:8. To love and make a LIE is to love and serve Satan, "for he is a liar, and the father thereof" John 8:44b. Strong emphasis has been made against the LIE throughout this book. The LIE is the devil's weapon against the truth of God.

22:16 I JESUS HAVE SENT MINE ANGEL TO TESTIFY UNTO YOU THESE THINGS FOR THE CHURCHES. I AM THE ROOT AND THE OFFSPRING OF DAVID, THE BRIGHT, THE MORNING STAR.

JESUS authenticates the contents of the book with His authority. YOU is plural meaning that the message is for all Christians, not just John.

An interesting conversation in the experience of Jesus comes to mind when thinking of Jesus as THE ROOT AND THE OFFSPRING OF DAVID, both his ancestor and descendant. "Now while the Pharisees were gathered together, Jesus asked them a question, saying, What think ye of the Christ? whose son is he? They say unto him, The son of David. He saith unto them, How then doth David in the spirit call him Lord, saying, The Lord said unto my Lord, Sit thou on my right hand, Till I put thine enemies underneath thy feet? If David then calleth him Lord, how is he his son? And no one was able to answer him a word,..." Matthew 22:41-46.

The tree sprouts forth from the root. The tree receives its life and strength from and through the root. Jesus is not only THE OFFSPRING OF DAVID, He is THE ROOT. The fact that He was THE ROOT made it possible for Him to be his OFFSPRING. In the plan of God the Davidic kingdom was typical of the everlasting kingdom of Jesus Christ, both springing from the same root.

Jesus was the fulfillment of Old Testament prophecy. "And there shall come forth a shoot out of the stock of Jesse, and a branch out of his roots shall bear fruit...And it shall come to pass in that day, that the root of Jesse, that standeth for an ensign of the peoples, unto him shall the nations seek; and his resting-place shall be glorious" Isaiah 11:1,10.

THE MORNING STAR is an indication that the night is almost over. A new day dawns and a new life begins in Christ. Because of the hope man has in Christ He is indeed THE BRIGHT MORNING STAR! "Again therefore Jesus spake unto them, saying, I am the light of the world: he that followeth me shall not walk in the darkness, but shall have the light of life" John 8:12.

22:17 AND THE SPIRIT AND THE BRIDE SAY, COME. AND HE THAT HEARETH, LET HIM SAY, COME. AND HE THAT IS ATHIRST, LET HIM COME: HE THAT WILL, LET HIM TAKE THE WATER OF LIFE FREELY.

"Jesus said unto them, I am the bread of life: he that cometh to me shall not hunger, and he that believeth on me shall never thirst" John 6:35. Through the church, THE BRIDE, THE SPIRIT offers the invitation to all the unredeemed to come and have their thirst quenched with THE WATER OF LIFE, eternal life in Christ. There must be a willingness to accept this gracious invitation. THE WATER OF LIFE is not forced upon anyone. For the willing it is offered FREELY. Salvation is a gift. "For the wages of sin is death; but the free gift of God is eternal life in Christ Jesus our Lord" Romans 6:23. Note that the invitation is extended by the church as a body and by the individual members of the church, HE THAT HEARETH, LET HIM SAY, COME. God desires that all men be willing to TAKE THE WATER OF LIFE FREELY, for they must be willing before they can drink.

22:18 I TESTIFY UNTO EVERY MAN THAT HEARETH THE WORDS OF THE PROPHECY OF THIS BOOK, IF ANY MAN SHALL ADD UNTO THEM, GOD SHALL ADD UNTO HIM THE PLAGUES WHICH ARE WRITTEN IN THIS BOOK:

22:19 AND IF ANY MAN SHALL TAKE AWAY FROM THE WORDS OF THE BOOK OF THIS PROPHECY, GOD SHALL TAKE AWAY HIS PART FROM THE TREE OF LIFE, AND OUT OF THE HOLY CITY, WHICH ARE WRITTEN IN THIS BOOK.

This book and the New Testament ends with a solemn warning which has been given before. "Ye shall not add unto the word which I command you, neither shall ye diminish from it, that ye may keep the commandments of Jehovah your God which I command you" Deuteronomy 4:2. "Add thou not unto his words, Lest

230

he reprove thee, and thou be found a liar" Proverbs 30:6. But though we, or an angel from heaven, should preach unto you any gospel other than that which we preached unto you, let him be anathema. As we have said before, so say I now again, If any man preacheth unto you any gospel other than that which ye received, let him be anathema" Galatians 1:8,9.

In contrast to the blessing promised in chapter one, verse three to all who read, hear and keep this message is the present caution to those who might be tempted to tamper with the contents in any way. Nothing is to be added or subtracted. God has stated it according to His will. So serious is this forbiding that GOD SHALL ADD UNTO HIM THE PLAGUES WHICH ARE WRITTEN IN THIS BOOK if he does not heed. THE PLAGUES refer to the lot of unredeemed man that is pictured in many ways throughout the book. That which is WRITTEN IN THIS BOOK stands written. This is the last word on the subject. To add to any part of scripture or to exercise freedom in suggesting that any part of scripture is not important or essential is to pretend to know more than God or better than God. This is serious and God says so in these verses.

It is a serious thing to fall away from the faith. Apostasy is a possibility and a threat to the Christian. Christianity is not to be taken for granted. There is a repeated emphasis upon faithfulness throughout this book and the entire Bible. "Be thou faithful unto death" (2:10) is the instruction of God. GOD SHALL TAKE AWAY HIS PART FROM THE TREE OF LIFE, AND OUT OF THE HOLY CITY says more than just tampering with the word of God is serious; it may cost you your eternal life. Read Hebrews 6:4-6.

22:20 HE WHO TESTIFIETH THESE THINGS SAID, YEA: I COME QUICKLY. AMEN: COME, LORD JESUS.

HE WHO TESTIFIETH is "Jesus Christ, who is the faithful witness" Revelation 1:5. THESE THINGS refer to the contents of Revelation which the Lord transmitted to the churches through John using the assistance of angels. Verses seven and twelve contain the same words I COME QUICKLY. This is the promise upon which all Christians base their hope. AMEN, so be it. You can depend upon the Lord to keep this promise. With anticipation and

readiness let us pray COME, LORD JESUS.
22:21 THE GRACE OF THE LORD JESUS BE WITH THE
SAINTS. AMEN.

The benediction that brings this book and the New Testament to an end stands in sharp contrast with the "curse" that ends the last book of the Old Testament. Victory in Christ is possible only by His GRACE which gives us strength and assurance "while we are at home in the body" 2 Corinthians 5:6. "But by the grace of God I am what I am" II Corinthians 15:10a. AMEN. This is true!